# A Time of th ᴄtion

## A Covid-19 Diary

## March 2020 – April 2021

# David Vincent

Independently published.


ISBN 9798378795024

# Preface

This collection of Covid-19 diaries is a companion piece to *The Fatal Breath. Covid-19 and Society*, published by the Polity Press in September 2023.

In March 2020, as the scale of the global pandemic became apparent, I was invited by my friend and former vice chancellor Brenda Gourley, and her Australian collaborator Anne Chappel, to join an international body of witnesses recording their engagement with Covid-19. A website was created, Covid2020diary, to which a group of writers from around the world contributed their contrasting thoughts and experiences.

At the time I was busy with the *History of Solitude* which after a long gestation was published just as the coronavirus began to spread through Britain. The lockdown created an enhanced interest in the question of how people negotiated the boundaries between sociability and withdrawal. As with undertakers, Covid-19 was good for my business. It was my intention then to begin work on a successor volume on the history of sound and silence in the modern world. I began collecting material, and at the same time started writing, early each morning, 500-750 word pieces for the Covid2020diary project. Although I am by preference and practice a long-form writer, I found I enjoyed the task, and over the following twelve months I contributed nearly 150 entries amounting to almost 90,000 words.

By the end of 2020, I had given so much thought and attention to what was the greatest disruption to the way of life of British and other populations since at least the Second World War, that there seemed a case for embarking on a full-length academic study of British society during the pandemic. This would expand on the insights and incidents of the diary entries and engage more broadly with the many other diary collections launched during the crisis, as well as the host of reports published by official and academic bodies and the widespread commentary in the media. The first draft of the book, which had been researched almost entirely online, was completed in the autumn of 2022, and the copy-edited text was delivered to Polity at the beginning of the following Spring.

I had no intention of seeking a publisher for the diaries themselves. They were not written for that purpose, and amidst all the personal reflections brought forth by the pandemic seemed too far from the centre of the crisis. As a shielded emeritus professor, fortunate to escape the direct impact of Covid-19, I was one voice amongst many living through the strange events. I neither made a direct contribution to the battle against Covid-19, nor suffered unduly from its consequences.

Nonetheless there is a case for seeking a more permanent form for writings which at the time had a limited readership. They are distinctive in presenting a rural view of the crisis. Covid-19, especially during the lockdowns, made everyone's life local, in my case a small but ancient village on the edge of the Severn in Shropshire. As a scholar with more than four decades of writing about the social history of Britain and Europe, the pieces are informed by an extensive sense of the past. Indeed, in places they give up on the present altogether and include material and incidents from the long sequence of European pandemics. The relatively relaxed writing expands the much more tightly written, and heavily referenced, pages of the academic study. Like the Polity volume, *A Time of the Infection* takes its title from Defoe's *Journal of the Plague Year* which itself took the form of a fictional memoir. Whichever route the reader takes from the history to the diaries or vice versa, the whole will constitute an unusually full and diverse account of the pandemic.

My initial diary entry was written at the end of the first week of lockdown, and the last just over a year later (other than a valediction as the project finally closed in November 2021). As with many other collections, the early intensity of observation and writing by the Covid2020diary contributors slackened during the year. At the outset every aspect of living was suddenly new and requiring a response. Twelve months later, weariness had set in. The suffering had been charted, the multiple changes to everyday life had been described. The overriding desire was for some form of normality to be restored, and some kind of retribution to be visited on a government that had so mishandled its responsibilities. And then, on the very same day that Johnson declared the end of all Covid-19 restrictions on behaviour, Putin invaded Ukraine, and an entirely new narrative was created.

I have made only minimal changes to the entries. They are presented in this volume as they appeared in the online collection, subject to some basic copyediting. After a while, with the growing possibility of launching an academic study, I began adding references, which are now grouped at the end of this text. I also started illustrating my pieces with photographs and other images, some taken by me, most culled from a variety of internet sources. Because of the inconsistency of their employment and copyright issues they have been excluded from this version. Some of the pieces include responses to the diverse and illuminating contributions by other diarists in the group. These can be found in COVID2020diary. Personal stories from around the world during the year of COVID-19 (https://covid2020diary.wordpress.com).

David Vincent
Shrawardine. October 2023.

**Sunday, 29 March 2020. Going Local.**

I live not in the county town of Shrewsbury but in a village a few miles upstream on the edge of the recently and repeatedly flooded River Severn. It is a small but ancient settlement, fully recorded in the 1086 Domesday Book. Now it has no services beyond the church on Sunday. But it has always displayed a collective spirit, mostly for seasonal entertainments and the maintenance of a village green which contains the ruins of a castle built to keep the Welsh in Wales. Planning was taking place for a formal ball in a marquee on the green this autumn, and it may yet take place. In the meantime, the 'Neighbourhood Watch' group, in place to deal with very rare criminal activity, has delivered a card to all residents, offering help 'picking up shopping, posting mail, collecting newspapers, or with urgent supplies.' There is a 'WhatsApp' group 'where there are lots of people wanting to offer support.' By this means we will all survive.

The village clerk sends a notification that the planned 75th anniversary celebration of VE [Victory in Europe] Day has been cancelled. We were to have a sit-down tea in the parish hall. As many are now commenting, the Home Front in the Second World War is the nearest parallel to the current crisis. When will we be celebrating (as the Chinese are now doing) VC – Victory over Covid-19-Day?

The Eurovision Song Contest has been cancelled. Amidst the destruction, there is some gain.

And in the same vein, the Research Evaluation Framework for Higher Education is postponed *sine die*.

Although a national event, Coronavirus remains a patchwork of local incidents. The fourteenth-century plague was worse in the countryside, where most people lived and where disease-carrying fleas had plenty of livestock to feed on. The 1665 plague was, by contrast, a metropolitan event with those who could afford to do so fleeing to small towns or country estates. The same this time. A friend who lives on the East Anglian Coast tells me that the fashionable resort of Southwold, full of Londoners' second homes, has doubled its population in a week, much to the dismay of the local services. It is reported this weekend that the West Midlands, the region in which I live, is an unexpected and unexplained hotspot. On closer examination this refers to what is known as The Black Country, a decayed industrial centre north and west of Birmingham. The cause is unclear, though it may be at least partly to do with public and private deprivation. It's only about 40 miles from my home, but the current statistics for my rural area are much lower. Distance matters.

So far we have been fortunate in that no family or close friends have become infected. For us, the anxiety has been at one remove. I have two lifelong friends with near terminal illnesses which are made just about unmanageable and unbearable, especially for their families, by this event. You might think that in such a pandemic, normal disasters would be suspended, but they are not. In one case, what began as cancer has spread other conditions, whilst the sufferer's children and friends are increasingly unable to provide any support. Two daughters, long since moved away from home by marriage and careers, were unable to fly across the country because of the collapse of the Flybe airline, then were forbidden to make any contact at all with a father alone and possibly dying in an Edinburgh hospital.

In the second case, my oldest friend (we shared a desk on our first day at secondary school) broke his neck in a freak swimming accident. He and his wife had emigrated to France on retirement, and did it properly, taking out French citizenship and immersing themselves in the Occitan music scene. They had gone on holiday to the French possession of Guadeloupe and now are marooned there, unable to get back to France whose hospitals are overwhelmed by Covid-19 patients. In ordinary times we could respond to such a tragedy by visits, or by organising help. Now the wife is completely alone, (Guadeloupe shares the French lockdown), and all around her are wholly unable to help beyond supportive phone calls. I hope my friends will both survive, but their trauma, psychological as well as physiological, will not turn up in the statistics.

**Monday, 30 March 2020. Transports and their absence.**

One of the reasons why my wife and I chose to live in our village was its transport connections. Its position on the bank of the River Severn meant that there was little through traffic and wide-open views into Wales. But two miles to the East the A5 trunk road (built at the end of the eighteenth century, the first new road in England since Roman times) connected us to the major regional centres of Birmingham and Manchester. Fifteen minutes' drive took us to Shrewsbury railway station, with through trains to London, the North and everywhere in Wales. The town possessed its own theatre and two cinemas, one lodged in a seventeenth-century market hall. There were two major regional airports, with international flights, within an hour's drive.

In this we behaved as any modern country-dweller. Where once there were shops, a post office and a pub in the village, now there is nothing. We looked to urban centres for services, connections and entertainments, and were careful not to locate ourselves too far from them.

A consequence of the Covid-19 crisis is to make Britain local again. Where the A5 goes, no longer matters. The rail services are attenuated, the airports shut, as also entertainments and restaurants. Urban supermarkets are dangerous, understocked, and inaccessible to the vulnerable. Instead, several nearby farm shops, stocking only local produce and enterprising enough to offer a delivery service, have become our main supply of food. All we need now is for the river once more to become a source of transport, for the community to be carried back into the eighteenth century.

That said, the supply of edible and non-edible goods in Britain still depends on national and international networks. Britain grows only just over half its food and we have yet to institute a dig-for-victory programme. In early Spring, the only items that are truly local in the farm shops are meat from the diminishing number of livestock farmers, and items such as potatoes, carrots and apples retrieved from cold stores (plus rhubarb which we are eating out of our own garden). As specialists in food supply are beginning to warn us, the illusion of self-sufficiency will be exposed sooner than we would like it to be.

The news today is that Dominic Cummings, author of the strategic lies that propelled us out of the European Union, has been infected with the virus, possibly by the man he manoeuvred into Number 10. As Oscar Wilde said of the death of Little Nell, it would take a heart of stone not to laugh.

**Wednesday, 1 April 2020. 'The greatest misery of sickness is *solitude'* .**

I have spent the last three years preparing a history of solitude in the modern era. Its long-planned publication later this month has suddenly turned a niche subject into a topic of wide interest. I have been writing for various online publications on this subject, in some cases with my colleague Professor Barbara Taylor who runs a large Wellcome Trust-funded project on the 'Pathologies of Solitude' based at Queen Mary University in London. Barbara is an early-modernist, and has drawn my attention to the encounter with isolation experienced by the poet John Donne, at the time Dean of St Paul's Cathedral.

In 1623 Donne, was suddenly struck down by a mysterious illness which left him feverish and sweaty (historians are not sure what it was; the most likely culprit was a form of typhus). As he wrote in his Meditation V of *Devotions Upon Emergent Occasions*, published the following year, he found the experience terrible:

> [T]his minute. I am surpriz'd with a sodaine change, & alteration to worse, and can impute it to no other cause, nor call it by any name.

Weak and frightened, Donne was confined to the St Paul's deanery, where fear of infection kept everyone away from him, even his physicians.

> As *Sickness* is the greatest misery, so the greatest misery of sickness is *solitude*;
> when the infectiousness of the disease deters them who should assist, from
> coming...*Solitude* is a torment which is not threatened in *hell* itself.

The instinctive response of the healthy to the afflicted did nothing except increase his suffering:

> when I am but sick, and might infect, they have no remedy but their absence, and my solitude.

Donne's Almighty was a social being:

> there is a plurality of persons in God, though there be but one God; and all his external actions testify a love of society, and communion. In heaven there are orders of angels, and armies of martyrs, and in that house many mansions; in earth, families, cities, churches, colleges, all plural things; and lest either of these should not be company enough alone.

In this regard, Donne, stood against a Christian practice that stretched back to the fourth century and thence to Christ's sojourn in the Wilderness. The desert fathers, who rejected company and material comfort in search of an intense communion with a lonely God, had a profound influence on the early church. Their example was institutionalised in monasteries which sought to combine individual meditation with a structure of routine and authority that would protect practitioners from mental collapse or spiritual heterodoxy.

In Britain the monastic tradition had been almost obliterated by the Reformation. Instead there was growing emphasis on the natural and necessary sociability of mankind. Further on in the same publication, Donne wrote in Meditation 17 one of the most famous passages in the English language, yet more relevant in this moment:

> No man is an island, entire of itself; every man is a piece of the continent, a part of the main; if a clod be washed away by the sea, Europe is the less, as well as if a promontory were, as well

as if a manor of thy friend's or of thine own were; any man's death diminishes me, because I am involved in mankind, and therefore never send to know for whom the bell tolls; it tolls for thee.

**Thursday, 2 April 2020. The loss of public confidence.**

Trust and communication police the boundary of acceptable and unacceptable isolation. It is probable that the British population will accept any amount of inconvenience if the reasons for it are clearly stated, and if the government and its agencies are believed to be competent.

Over the last twenty-four hours there are worrying signs that these conditions no longer apply.

Hitherto, vocal criticism of public policy has been muted. There is a general sense that this is the moment to replace the divisive discourse of Brexit, which has dominated politics over the last three years, with a nurtured consensus. There is an acceptance that short-term hindsight is unreliable and unproductive. Whatever might have been done, Covid-19 could not have been fully anticipated. Better to leave the search for mistakes to historians in later years. There is also the contingent factor that the three leading figures who could be interrogated, the Prime Minister, the Minister of Health, and the Chief Medical Officer, are all self-isolating with the disease. And the Labour Party, which might have held ministers to account, is currently largely absent, conducting a leadership contest (which will be over on April 4$^{th}$).

But this morning's press, particularly and worryingly for the government, the right-wing newspapers such as the *Daily Telegraph*, the *Daily Mail* and *The Times*, have front-page headlines denouncing official policy.

There have been rumblings of discontent, particularly from front-line medical practitioners, about the shortages of ventilators and personal protection equipment (PPE). But what has translated complaints into focussed anger is the failure to provide testing facilities. These are fundamentally necessary, as the Director General of the World Health Organisation has stated from the outset, to track the incidence and transmission of the disease. They are also vital for health professionals, who need to know whether they are safe to go to work. As is now pointed out, however, the government deliberately stopped testing on 11 March, when the policy of containing the disease was abandoned. It would only be used for those seriously ill in hospital. This policy was amended after the lockdown was declared on March 23, and the number of infections threatened to overwhelm the health services.

But now the government seems unable to source an adequate number of testing kits, and is competing on a hostile open market for new supplies. At its daily press conferences it is setting out ambitions for testing which are contradicted by its own statistics. Today's headlines are driven by the report that of the half million or so front-line health workers, only 2,000 have been tested. The charges against officials embrace strategic mis-judgment, operational incompetence, and poor messaging.

This may be a blip. It is possible that the tests will ramp up, the PPEs will be delivered, the ventilators manufactured, and public trust restored. But on this day, none of this seems likely. That the criticism may harm Conservative prospects in some future election is irrelevant. Doctors and nurses are dying now who should live, or are isolating at home when they should be at work. Confidence in those policing the lockdown may not recover.

As a footnote, I was interviewed on Monday about my book on solitude by the London correspondent of *Die Welt*. When we finished, I asked her where she would rather now be living. She replied that although she had an English husband and loved the country, she would feel safer in Germany: 'better health service, better political leadership.'

**Friday, 3 April 2020. The Sounds of Covid-19.**

As with any place, my village has a recognisable soundscape. The church bell, the defining, encompassing call to the community, only rings before a Sunday service, and only on one note. There is little traffic, but tractors rumble through on their way to and from the farms. A cock some three hundred yards away starts crowing at around four every morning. My neighbour's chickens more softly cluck as they turn over leaves looking for food. Another neighbour is incapable of addressing his garden without a power tool in his hands. If the wind is in the west, we can hear the cattle munching in a field on the other side of the river. And of course there is birdsong, crowned by the mewling of a pair of buzzards high above the house and from time to time the rhythmic beating of a skein of geese commuting from lake to lake. It's a familiar mix of the natural and the mechanical age.

But then the suggestion was made that households come out onto the street at 8 p.m. on a Thursday to applaud the health workers risking their lives in the fight against Covid-19. I have to say that I did not regard this prospect with enthusiasm. Such acts of unspontaneous, collective enthusiasm do not appeal. I am a reserved, professorial Englishman. We are told that the Italians are singing arias to medical staff from balconies. No balcony here, and I can't carry a tune. However, Charlotte persuaded me out of doors and we duly clapped. Then we stopped, and to my amazement I could hear the sound of applause all across our dispersed village. It was an oddly impersonal noise, a little like rain drumming on a tin roof. Unlike the banging of saucepans and shouting out that has happened in towns, it was a quiet gesture, but it seemed boundless. A sound like no other this village has heard in its thousand-year history.

We have a couple of GPs, a hospital consultant, and several health workers in Shrawardine. If they were home, I hope they were cheered.

**Monday, 6 April 2020. Two Victories.**

Two long-term victories over the weekend.

Firstly, after several weeks trying to unlock the supermarket delivery system, we finally succeeded, thanks to a government scheme that actually seems to be working. The scheme goes like this:

1. The NHS circulates GP surgeries for information on patients who might be vulnerable not only to infection as such, but to developing severe conditions once infected.

2. It writes to a million and half patients, including my household, telling them that they are exceptionally vulnerable and instructing them to stay at home under all circumstances, except medical appointments that cannot be conducted remotely.

3. Those receiving the letter are urged to log in to the Gov UK site, and enter details of their residence and their circumstances.

4. Gov UK then contacts the nearest supermarket at which the vulnerable individual is registered, asking it to make delivery slots available.

5. The supermarket (in my case Tesco) writes to the customer informing them of their special status.

6. The customers, to their astonishment, discover that whereas the unavailable slots had stretched away to the edge of doom in all the major supermarkets, now there are delivery times open all next week.

Thanks to local farm shops, and friends adding our needs to their shopping lists, we weren't hungry nor were likely to be. But the prospect of regular deliveries takes away a significant degree of worry and effort. We have submitted our list. Due for delivery on Friday.

Secondly, Keir Starmer has been elected leader of the Labour Party. I had re-joined the Labour Party specifically to vote for this outcome (as had many others). It is the first time since 2005 that I have cast my vote on the winning side in a public election. In the words of Polly Toynbee in *The Guardian*, 'a trusted, tried and tested, big-brained grown-up arrives'. It is too soon to know how he will turn out.

During the election Starmer had to tread very carefully as he took on the Corbynistas who had spent the last four years trying to ensure that they would never again lose control of the party. He comes to the position not as a life-long politician, but as a professional who has run a complex, value-driven organisation. Those of us who have been involved in managing universities know that it requires a different skill set than being a political advisor or, for that matter, an academic historian. And unlike Corbyn, a failed Shropshire public schoolboy whose tertiary education lasted one week at North London Polytechnic, who, according to his recent biographer, thereafter never read a book in his life, Starmer has an applied intelligence. Helena Kennedy, who was a colleague in a human rights law chambers, said 'he was the smartest by far, and we need clever'. At this moment, we do indeed.

**Tuesday, 7 April 2020.  Learning about Learning.**

My daughters, as with most in their generation and mine, have always seen themselves as part-time teachers.  Virtually from birth, their children were read to.  Educational toys were purchased.  Early encounters with the meanings of print or the shape of numbers were assisted.  Trips to appropriate galleries and museums were organised.  Care was exercised in the choice of nursery and primary school.  Parents evenings were dutifully attended.  Yet there remained a basic division of labour.  At around nine every term-time morning, children were sent off to learn with trained teachers.  When they came home at three, they were not in the least interested in giving a blow-by-blow account of their lessons.  That part of the day was done; now they wanted to get to the next diversion.  At some later point they might talk of a discovery that had interested them, or a problem they had experienced with another child, but this was randomised, opaque information.

Suddenly the children were at home, with the teacher sending instructions to the parents about what kind of lessons they should engage in.  The consequence for my daughters has been labour, pleasure, and discovery.  In both cases they have undertaken a crash course of learning about learning.  The outcome has been a seriously enhanced respect for the pedagogy of the modern primary school.  They have discovered, for instance, how the phonic method of teaching literacy, which is now the dominant methodology, actually works.  They can see the logic, the order, and the effectiveness of the process, where before they could only note that their children were suddenly making rapid progress towards fluent reading. The professionalism, as well as the dedication and humanity, of the teachers, has been borne in on them.

A friend and contemporary of mine, a retired electronic engineer, has taken it upon himself to spend two hours a day in online teaching of various scientific subjects with his two secondary-school-age grandchildren. He has discovered odd gaps in their knowledge, but in the round he has been astonished by how much they already know. A good deal more, he thinks, than he did at their age. The unconsidered view, that schools lack the discipline, or the resources, or the methods, to teach as well as once they did, is for him shown to be a myth. Schooling is just better than in the days when he and others were setting out on their academic careers.

That said, one of my friend's grandchildren had quietly to intervene towards the end of last Friday's lessons. 'You do know, Grandpa, that next Monday we are supposed to be on Easter holiday. Perhaps we could stop the lessons for a while.'

**Wednesday, 8 April 2020. Prime Ministers, Loneliness and Solitude.**

We are all of us having to adjust to the shocking prospect that the Prime Minister might actually die of Covid-19. The historian in me struggles to find a previous case. There have been examples in modern times of more or less concealed incapacitating illnesses (see Boris Johnson's idol Winston Churchill, *passim*), and of sudden resignations following the diagnosis of a fatal disease - Henry Campbell Bannerman in 1908 and Andrew Bonar Law in 1923. Two leaders of the Labour Party, Hugh Gaitskell and John Smith, died in post, paving the way for the fortunate Harold Wilson and Tony Blair. But not the nation's leader at a time of absolute national crisis. The nearest equivalent of such an event would be Pitt the Younger, who died in 1806 in the midst of the Napoleonic Wars (see also Spencer Perceval in 1812, though he was assassinated, and George Canning who expired in more peaceful times in 1827 after just 119 days in office).

Amongst the immediate responses was a curious tweet from Andrew Neil (note for non-Brits: grizzled former editor of the *Sunday Times* and now the most feared BBC political interviewer. In the recent General Election, Boris Johnson, alone of the candidates, refused to submit himself to an extended interrogation by him, which diminished his reputation as it enhanced Neil's). A reason, he said, why Johnson has proved vulnerable to Covid-19 was his 'loneliness' in Number 10. It was not clear whether he meant social loneliness, given that Johnson has been living by himself in the flat above Number 11 while his pregnant partner self-isolates in the official country retreat of Chequers, or political loneliness in the Shakespearean sense of 'Uneasy lies the head that wears the crown.'

Whichever is the case, it raises the question of the balance between solitude and loneliness in the present crisis. The former, the tendency, as Johann Zimmermann wrote, 'for self-collection and freedom', has over the period since the eighteenth century become an increasingly valued and enjoyed condition. The latter, which can be seen as failed solitude, the condition, as Stephanie Dowrick writes, of being 'uncomfortably alone without someone' has been a growing cause for concern in recent decades.

Enforced isolation has an ambiguous effect on the two experiences. On the one hand it has made solitude a still more valued practice. In families where the adults are working at home, the children are about all day long, the garden is small or non-existent, periods of solitary escape have become as desirable and unattainable as supermarket delivery slots. The most basic form of solitude, taking a stroll out of doors, is limited to once a day. Walking the dog, for two centuries the most commonplace way of taking time out alone, is suddenly a basic luxury. A French friend tells me that Parisian dogs are exhausted, as neighbours borrow them from their owners to legitimise exercise in the fresh air.

On the other hand, it has made loneliness still more threatening. It becomes more difficult to make physical contact with such friends as the individual possesses. Intermittent escapes from an empty home to shops, cafes, local libraries, public entertainments, are now forbidden. Access to medical or social services is yet more of a problem. This outcome has been early recognised, and attempts are being made in functioning communities to identity those uncomfortably alone and provide them with necessary support. And there is, of course, the ever-increasing use of digital connections.

Where the balance will finally be struck in these contrasting effects of isolation remains to be seen. At least we should emerge with an enhanced awareness of both conditions.

**Thursday, 9 April 2020. Walnut Tree.**

In the early stages of the crisis, I bought a walnut tree for a new space I had cleared in my garden. It was a bet on the future, as is all planting. There was little chance that I would get any walnuts for four years, and it would not reach maturity for ten. But I liked the idea of picking my own nuts, and was prepared to wait. I ordered a tree from an online nursery. It arrived looking less like a living organism, and more like a walking stick with bare roots. No side-shoots, no leaves. Just a metre-high pole, perhaps 3cm in diameter at the base, with very dormant buds. I planted it with appropriate care, scattered the roots with mycorrhizal fungi to stimulate growth, watered it regularly. And after a month, I still have a walking stick in the middle of my lawn. Nothing has changed. If anyone out there knows about the cultivation of walnut trees, do let me know.

Amongst all the grief, I continually give thanks that I live in the northern hemisphere. What we would have done if this pandemic had broken out in Britain in, say, early November, is beyond imagining. As it is, while we cope with the worsening health situation, every day is longer, lighter and warmer. In my third of an acre of God's creation, the damson, plum and peach trees are now in full blossom. The tulips are coming out, as is the magnolia tree opposite the house. The vine is in leaf in the greenhouse. I begin each day walking the bounds of my plot, examining the changes since the day before, celebrating the alterations, occasionally mourning the setbacks (I planted two roses with the walnut tree. Within a week their abundant foliage had been stripped by a passing rabbit; now they recover surrounded by their own miniature fences).

The fundamental pleasure of gardening is that it is a time-infused event. Whilst we are in complete domestic lockdown, going nowhere, everything is in motion. Whenever I think about what to plant, how to tend what is growing, I am contemplating a future independent of the political and medical crisis. And because of that crisis I have more time this year than ever before to give to the necessary labours of early Spring.

But you will have to take my word for this. There is no-one to show it to. By the time we receive visitors in Shropshire again, much of the spring and summer will be over.

**Friday, 10 April 2020.  An Infection Foretold.**

Now it's personal.  I learnt last night that my niece, my sister's younger daughter, has Covid-19.  She is a twenty-eight-year-old, recently-qualified doctor, working in a city-centre hospital.  She was infected five days ago and is resting at home.

I am of course anxious about her, though her symptoms do not seem serious.  She is young and fit and the likelihood must be that she will make a full recovery.  I am also concerned for her parents' anxiety.  But most of all I am just infuriated by the event.  Many of the cases of coronavirus can be described as random misfortunes.  Not this one.  She was told three weeks ago that she was being posted to a Covid-19 ward.  I was in touch with her parents, who were very worried that she would not be given appropriate personal protection equipment (PPE).  The press was full of stories about shortages, and I could understand their fears.  But I did think that by the time she entered the ward, something would have been done.

It was not.  She lasted just a week before a coughing patient got through her inadequate protection.  This was a predictable and predicted outcome.  A monument, amongst many others, to the criminal lack of preparedness of the NHS, and the Government that funds and manages it.  We are now nearly three months beyond the point when the spread of the epidemic to Britain became a realistic likelihood. And still every part of the system is in arrears.

There is my niece's suffering – it started with a fierce headache, and she was tested and sent home when she complained she could not taste the chocolates a well-wisher had sent to the ward. Now she feels extremely tired. And there is the sheer misuse of resources. My niece was freshly trained and full of enthusiasm. She shared a flat with another young doctor who as a consequence has had to self-isolate as well. So that's two doctors who should be on the front line, shut up at home.

It is an utterly stupid, avoidable waste.

**Tuesday, 14 April 2020. Borders.**

Every morning, I draw back the curtains in my bedroom and look across the Severn into Wales. About six miles away, as the crow flies, there is a volcanic outcrop called The Breiddens in what was once Montgomeryshire and is now Powys. On the summit of the hill sits Rodney's Column, a forerunner of Nelson's monument in Trafalgar Square. It was erected in 1781-82, by the 'Gentlemen of Montgomeryshire' to commemorate the victorious battles of Admiral Rodney. The Admiral and I greet each other, and go about our day's business.

The Welsh Border weaves through the Marches, the outcome not of rational planning but the bloody skirmishes fought in the Middle Ages. If we drive north from our English home, we pass into Wales around

Wrexham and then back into England as we approach Chester, once a Roman defensive outpost. Shrewsbury is not only an English county town, but much the largest commercial centre between England and the Mid-Wales coast. In the streets you hear Welsh accents, and from time to time a different language spoken by those who have travelled in for a day's shopping. The town's railway station is the main hub for the otherwise fractured Welsh system.

People and cultures are irretrievably mixed. I was therefore astonished to hear in last Wednesday's government briefing a journalist ask the Minister whether the four nations of the United Kingdom would adopt different policies of social isolation when it came to relaxing the Covid-19 lockdown. This would mean adjacent and interleaved communities pursuing different contact regimes. The prospect seemed so insane that I expected an immediate denial. None came. This was presumably because earlier in the day the First Minister of Wales had been widely reported speculating on the policy he might adopt on this critical question, without any reference to what other devolved administrations might do. He has the power to go his own way, and at present does not seem to be consulting with the English Government. Today the Scottish First Minister, Nicola Sturgeon has announced that she may introduce her own scheme.

There is evidence that staff in the nations are now fighting each other for essential kit. Welsh and Scottish care home managers have complained that their usual suppliers have told them that all their PPE stock was now earmarked for England. Each administration has its own

Chief Medical Officer (or did so until the Scottish official was forced to resign because she had twice visited her holiday home in defiance of the lock-down policy she herself had promulgated) and is running its own systems. The NHS scheme for identifying the especially vulnerable that I discussed on April 6 I now discover applies only to England. Were I living a few miles to the west, I would not be affected by it.

Within England, Covid-19 has further exposed the incoherence of devolved power. To the south of my home the newly created Mayor of the West Midlands has authority over regional transport but little else. To the north the Mayor of Manchester actually has power over health provision, though it is too soon to know how well that is working. The adjacent Mayor of Liverpool, on the other hand, is responsible merely for 'leading the city, building investor confidence, and directing new resources to economic priorities.' The new Mayor of Leeds, like the West Midlands, just does trains and buses. There is little sense of local ownership of medical services. The Strategic Health Authorities might have pulled an integrated regional policy together, but they were abolished in 2013.

It is now recognised that a reason why Germany has been so much better than Britain at developing Covid-19 testing systems is that the Länder, whose identities in some cases pre-date Germany itself, had long built up effective networks linking public and private provision in their regions, which they were able to mobilise in ways in which Public Health England has conspicuously failed to do. The ritual that has now been established of daily, London-based briefings merely accentuates the sense that everything that matters in terms of decision-making and public spending is based in the capital.

This crisis is placing all our systems under an unforgiving spotlight, not least the incoherent mix of centralisation and regional initiative that has built up in Britain. This sense of impoverished local ownership and dislocated national devolution had much to do with Brexit, and is now being further exposed by the pandemic.

**Wednesday, 15 April 2020. England expects every driveller to do his Memorabilia.**

The ordinary people began to write and publish accounts of their daily lives at the beginning of the nineteenth century. The innovation was not universally welcomed. The editor of the Tory *Quarterly Review* denounced the new voice:

> The classics of the *papier mâché* age of our drama have taken up the salutary belief that England expects every driveller to do his Memorabilia. Modern primer-makers must needs leave *confessions* behind them, as if they were so many Rousseaus. Our weakest mob-orators think it a hard case if they cannot spout to posterity. Cabin-boys and drummers are busy with their commentaries *de bello Gallico*; the John Gilpins of 'the nineteenth century' are historians of their own *anabaseis;* and,

thanks to 'the march of intellect', we are already rich in the autobiography of pickpockets.[1]

Since then the literary marketplace has become accustomed to the diaries and memoirs of the common people. Their popularity has surged at moments of public crisis. Lockhart was protesting at accounts that were appearing of the Napoleonic Wars, the first conflict to foreground the role of ordinary soldiers and sailors. Subsequently the First and Second World Wars, and the Slump of the 1930s, stimulated the keeping of private accounts and the publication of more structured literary narratives.

There is ample evidence that the pandemic is another such moment. The Covid2020diary project is only one amongst a multitude of personal or collective ventures. It differs from others in its valuable international perspective. Diary-keeping is driven by three obvious conditions.

Firstly, it is evident that we are living through a global crisis on a scale that historians will be writing about for the rest of the twenty-first century.

Secondly everyone has a role in the drama. Whilst scientists, medical professionals and politicians have their particular responsibilities, the behavior and experience of every citizen of almost every country will be critical to the outcome.

Thirdly, those with something to say, now have the time to say it, in the old way in private diaries, or in the new media of semi-public blogs, which surely would have horrified Lockhart.

The problem for historians will be that of engaging with this mass of material in any kind of systematic form. In the Second World War, the pioneering social research body, Mass Observation, which had been founded in 1936, was used by the government to investigate the morale of the Home Front. It both undertook its own surveys and commissioned the keeping of 480 diaries. Its material, which has been digitised and archived by the University of Sussex, is an immensely useful resource for historians, including myself. In 2020 there are a host of opinion-poll organizations, campaigning organisations for at-risk groups, hurriedly commissioned academic inquiries, such as the project at Oxford looking at children's mental health in the crisis, together with all the memoirs which are more or less available.

I am tempted to see whether I can write a rapid sequel to my *History of Solitude* to which Brenda kindly drew attention yesterday. A project which began as something of a niche subject three years ago is by complete accident appearing at a moment of maximum relevance. The advantage is that many of the categories of inquiry in my book could be taken forward into the present crisis. I would have both the historical context necessary to measure change, and an outline structure of analysis. *Isolation. A Social History* might well find a market. The challenge, which I am still contemplating, is whether, even as an interim report, it would be possible to marshal the cornucopia of evidence into a coherent and representative narrative.

**Thursday, 16 April 2020. Postman Pat.**

Many of us still struggling to stay on the right side of the middle-age/old-age boundary have discovered that one of the least acceptable consequences of the Covid-19 crisis has been the enforced passivity.

It is not so much that there is nothing to do all day long. Even when teaching students or administering universities, I have always spent long periods in isolation, in libraries or at my desk. The garden is an infinite task; nothing is ever in order for more than a week, particularly as Spring takes hold. It is rather that I can do so little to respond to the crisis, other than going back to my desk to write more articles and blogs, and prepare to make the transition from the first to the second draft of history. Although it is obviously far less dangerous to be outside a care home than inside one, there is a general sense that those of my age are now fit only to be looked after.

In terms of friends and relations who are in trouble, either with Covid-19, or some parallel health problem made worse by the pandemic, I would expect to ease my anxiety by making a visit or undertaking some other intervention. When my old colleague fell seriously ill with cancer in his home near Edinburgh last autumn, my wife and I twice drove three hundred miles north to render such support as we could. Whatever good it did him, we somehow felt that the misfortune had been given a frame by our effort, a pattern that could be managed. Now we just keep in touch with an occasional email which my friend, understandably enough as he lies in his hospital bed, is not great at responding to.

As my household is one of the million or so forbidden by the NHS to go out for any purpose, there is almost nothing we can do for anyone else, other than redirect, through a neighbour, unwanted weekly Government provision boxes to the local food bank. Our world is now divided into helpers and helped, and perforce, we are in the latter group.

As others have discovered, being helped requires a mind-set which is not easy to acquire, particularly if, on a daily basis, you are generally fit. It's an old question, is it better to give or receive? The wise always reply the former, and there is truth in that. Gratitude without reciprocity can be a hard virtue to learn. In better times there is always the prospect, however distant, of returning the favour. When exchange declines into dependency, an effort has to be made not to let embarrassment become the dominant emotion. Everyone whose increasing age and declining health has forced them to abandon their own home knows about this. If only temporarily, we are getting an unwelcome preview of this circumstance.

At a more mundane level, it would be so good to get out of the house and undertake some practical assistance. There can be no surprise that the appeal for volunteers to help out the NHS was so heavily oversubscribed. How content I would be if I could spend my days driving about collecting and delivering. There is a Postman Pat hiding deep inside all of us.

## Friday, 17 April 2020. Back to the 1950s?

Commentators on the impact of the lockdown on the roads have been comparing traffic to the 1950s. The density is down to levels not seen since the post-war years when car ownership was still largely the preserve of the middle classes, and the railways carried a large, if declining, volume of freight.

Yesterday I had the opportunity to test this thesis. I had to break my house arrest for the one permitted purpose, a medical appointment (not related to Covid-19) in Manchester, which is a round trip of 150 miles. It was the first time I had started my car, or passed through my front gate, for almost a month. I was both curious and a little nervous as I set out on the journey.

What I found was a change, but less of a transformation than I had expected. The roads were quiet, but not deserted. They felt less like one o'clock in the morning than six. There was a good deal of heavy traffic and about as many cars. The lanes around my house still were obstructed by tractors, one carrying an immense harrow which threatened to decapitate any passing motorist. Despite all the closures in retail and manufacture, there were goods to be transported, and a fair few people who apparently had necessary journeys to make. Britain still seemed to be alive and, relatively speaking, busy. The roads felt not so much empty as carrying the traffic they were originally designed for. There were no queues at lights or roundabouts, no bottlenecks as the Manchester conurbation was reached. When Charlotte and I drive in for a play or a concert, we leave at least half an hour for delays. This time I swept in and out of the city without a moment's loss.

There is more to the experience of roads than the statistical density of traffic. I was a passenger in the 1950s and 1960s, buying my first car out of tutorial earnings as a Cambridge postgraduate in 1972. My parents owned a series of Morris Minor Travellers, the iconic half-timbered estate. They were for their time reliable and versatile. But against any modern car, they were slow, noisy and cramped. We three children were jammed together on a beltless back seat. My Volvo is incomparably more comfortable, more spacious, more pleasant to drive, and safer. The roads may have carried fewer cars, but they took them through rather than round the built-up areas. My route to Manchester would have had to negotiate the high streets of Welsh market towns and the city suburbs. My actual journey time yesterday, along the A5 and the M56, door-to-door, was 80 minutes in each direction for 75 miles, an inconceivable speed in the fabled fifties.

Whether we shall all get back into our cars once the lock-down is over remains to be seen. The only way to enjoy the benefits of the 1950s without the inconvenience, is to revive the post-war networks of public transport (but with better trains, trams and buses).

**Monday, 20 April 2020. 'I have measured out my life with coffee spoons'.**

My wife and I keep in touch with our London-based family through Zoom and Skype: a get-together of the entire tribe at 4 on Sundays, bi-laterals with each of our three children and the grandchildren at intervals during the week. In one of these, my second daughter, having gone through all the projects she had undertaken with her two young, now unschooled, children, and described her re-entry into home-based work after three weeks of inactivity, turned the conversation back to her parents:

'So, what have you two been doing?' We both of us realised that we really had no answer to that question.

Our days had not been empty. We had gardened, cooked, shopped online. I had sat at my desk writing odd pieces and collecting material for books which may never be written. Thanks to the discovery of sites such as Curzon Films, and, in particular, MUBI, we had watched an increasing range of art-house films late at night. Our physical art-house, The Old Market Hall, a seventeenth-century building in the town square, skilfully converted into a compact cinema, with an adjacent café to supply food and drink, is like all public entertainment, firmly closed.

But we had not really *done* anything worth reporting. Nothing to change our circumstances. Nothing to impact upon the world and its suffering.

It is of course otherwise with those, who include my children and their spouses, who are at home but still pursuing their careers. And with those who are using their enforced idleness to undertake useful voluntary work. But for those of us who are both retired and shielded, each day just follows another.

We no longer have plans with outcomes. There are occasional disjunctions, but for the most part action has been replaced by rituals and routines. In our household, as in much of British culture, these are largely secular and private. Unlike the celebrations so vividly described by Nike in Katerini, Easter has never passed so unremarked as it did with us. The upcoming May Bank Holidays have no meaning. Nor do the summer holidays beyond them. The Queen will have no guns firing for her birthday.

Now we focus attention on the weekly round of Zoom conversations. In the early evening we take a turn round the adjacent field, circling a flock of mildly curious sheep. Within each day my wife and I not only eat together but make a particular point of meeting at the coffee and tea breaks which punctuate our particular labours.

Two public rituals have been introduced. The first is the daily press conference given by some hapless minister. The second is the Thursday

8 p.m. public applause for the front-line workers, which is partly a genuine show of gratitude, and partly a demonstration that we remain connected members of a larger society.

'I have measured out my life with coffee spoons' wrote J Alfred Prufrock (as it happens in the middle of the national crisis of the First World War). So, for the time being, with us.

**Tuesday, 21 April 2020.  On National Pride.**

British readers will recall the carefully crafted address by the Queen on 5th April.  It studiously avoided saying anything about the Government whose leader had so embarrassed her over the proroguing of Parliament last Autumn.  Instead it concentrated on national character:

> I hope in the years to come everyone will be able to take pride in how they responded to this challenge.  And those who come after us will say the Britons of this generation were as strong as any.  That the attributes of self-discipline, of quiet good-humoured resolve and of fellow-feeling still characterise this country.  The pride in who we are is not a part of our past, it defines our present and our future.

The question of whether we still have any right to take a national pride in the response to coronavirus has been thrown into relief by the revelations in the press over the weekend, particularly the 5,000-word piece in the Sunday Times.

The generalised 'attributes of self-discipline, quiet good-humoured resolve and fellow-feeling' remain valid. Indeed they have proved stronger than the Government initially feared as it hesitated about imposing a lock-down. The street protests against restrictions on movement in the USA reported this week demonstrates what can happen in the absence of such resolve. That said there are also worrying reports about a sudden growth of domestic abuse inside closed-down families which may yet disfigure the celebration of fellow-feeling.

In terms of public policy, however, shame is the more appropriate sentiment. Just ask yourself this question, of all the countries fighting the pandemic, which are seen as a model to be followed? South Korea, New Zealand, Taiwan, Germany and some others. No-one is viewing the daily British news conferences for lessons about what they should be doing.

It is not as though we have no inherited strengths. We have an economy strong enough to withstand emergency bail-outs worth many billions of pounds. We have a sophisticated production and distribution system which has ensured, unlike many developing countries, that there is still food in the shops. We have a health service which, in contrast to Trump's America, covers the whole population. And once we led the world in the specific field of pandemic resolution. No longer. According to the Sunday Times:

Several emergency planners and scientists said that the plans to protect the UK in a pandemic had once been a priority and had been well funded for the decade following the 9/11 terrorist attacks in 2001. But then austerity cuts struck. 'We were the envy of the world,' the source said, 'but pandemic planning became a casualty of the austerity years, when there were more pressing needs.' [to judge from a TV interview I saw, that 'source' is Sir David King, a former Chief Scientific Officer]

The planning had atrophied. The funding had been cut. And once the crisis began, the wrong decisions were taken by a Cabinet whose members had been appointed solely on the basis of their attitude to Brexit. Its leader fulfilled all the expectations which his career had predicted:

'There's no way you're at war if your PM isn't there,' the adviser said. 'And what you learn about Boris was he didn't chair any meetings. He liked his country breaks. He didn't work weekends. It was like working for an old-fashioned chief executive in a local authority 20 years ago. There was a real sense that he didn't do urgent crisis planning. It was exactly like people feared he would be.'

What we still have is a world-class scientific community (though universities, including Imperial, are going to be very hard hit by a combination of the pandemic and Brexit). It may yet be that those working on a vaccine at Oxford and elsewhere will come up with the solution that will save the world. Then, and only then, will we have a cause for national pride in how we responded.

**Wednesday, 22 April 2020. Distance Learning in a siege.**

A few years ago I was sent by the British Council to give some lectures to the Al Quds Open University in Palestine on new developments in distance learning. At their site in Bethlehem I was introduced to the heads of the different sections, except the vice-rector for Gaza. It was explained that because of the siege, he only ever attended meetings online. Nonetheless the Gaza branch was flourishing. Of all the higher education offerings in the territory, it was much the best suited to a life of long-term shut-down interspersed with outbreaks of violence. There was no need for a permanent physical presence. When the bombing got too bad, the university could close for a few weeks and the recommence its online courses supplemented with small-scale face-to-face tuition.

Britain is not under that kind of siege, but there is a sense that the form of learning pioneered by the Open University half a century ago is ideally suited to the present circumstances. The University has had to make emergency changes to its examination and tutorial support systems, but is not faced with anything like the disruption forced upon conventional universities. Its Open Learn site, which delivers selections from validated courses free to any user, has seen a fourfold increase in traffic. It has no residential income at risk, no overseas student fee-income to lose.

In the short-term, the whole sector has embraced on-line learning. My son-in-law, a philosophy senior lecturer at a research-led university, is currently running tutorials from his spare bedroom, emerging from time to time to quieten his boisterous children. This kind of improvisation is necessary and inevitable towards the end of an academic year which when it started last autumn can have had no expectation of such a circumstance.

The critical question is whether higher education's enforced embrace of distance education continues once the crisis is over. Already there has been a dispute at Durham, where the UCU (the lecturers' union) claimed the university 'wants to slash face-to-face teaching by as much as 25%, and outsource its online learning to private providers.' Durham's management denies this, but there is no doubt that conventional institutions are paying much more attention to the potential of online learning to cut costs in a future when budgets are going to be under severe pressure.

The problem is that high-quality distance education cannot be done on the cheap. The Open University did not invent remote learning. Its innovation half a century ago was to create sophisticated multi-media courses supported by person-to-person tutorial support. This required technical imagination and pedagogic expertise, and could only pay its way at scale. Putting a camera in front of a lecturing academic and otherwise leaving small groups of students to their own devices guarantees a third-rate education.

For conventional universities, what may work to complete this academic year looks much more risky in the long term. The UCU is right to attack the threat to the role of its members. The Office for Students should be in pursuit of institutions which seek to embed the emergency devices as permanent practice. And in what is in the UK an open market, school-leavers are surely going to think twice about spending, or borrowing, £27,000, plus accommodation costs, for so remote a learning experience. Still more so, the overseas students whose enhanced fees are critical to many universities, including those at the forefront of the Covid-19 response, are hardly likely to travel to the UK just to look at lectures on computer screens.

**Thursday, 23 April 2020. The Newspaper Habit.**

The media is full of advice on how to survive the lockdown, which for my household is now projected to last the whole of this calendar year. The advice is generally of two kinds: those things that you might normally do but should do more, like take exercise or keep in touch with your family; and those things that you might normally do but should do less, particularly consume alcohol.

By and large we are following these injunctions. My one besetting sin, which is doing serious damage to my peace of mind to say nothing of the time available for more useful projects, is reading newspapers. Before the crisis, we bought hard copy print whenever we were out shopping. We live too far from a newsagent to get a daily delivery. These papers were the prime cause of untidiness in the house. In every room, on every coffee table, were copies not yet finished and not sufficiently out of date to be dispatched to the wastepaper basket. Even when the news was stale, there were crosswords and sudokus to complete. We have a log burner which needs lighting most evenings and for this purpose the large pink sheets of the *Financial Times* were invaluable. The shrunken tabloid pages of the *Guardian* and the *Times* not so much.

These days every surface is clear of print, except dog-eared pages of the *London Review of Books* which arrives by post. Instead, I am reading online. I always checked the free *Guardian* site when we had not bought a copy. Now I subscribe to the *Times* to get an alternative point of view. Also the *New York Times* to look at the world from outside the UK. And thanks to the OU virtual library, I can read the *Financial Times* each morning [an illuminating story yesterday about the plight of second-home owners in the crisis]. There is the potential to consume hours a day wandering about these electronic journals. And whereas hard copy papers have a back page as well as a front, the links in the stories mean that I can endlessly travel to yet further corners of the internet universe.

I can try to persuade myself that by this means I am collecting material for what one day might be a history of this crisis. But in truth it would probably be simpler, and much more restful, if I just turned off the media and tuned in again when it is all over, to find out what happened.

The one defence of this virtual habit is that the press is having a golden period, despite the loss of advertising revenue. Almost all the detailed analysis of the epidemic, and most of the stories exposing the shortcomings of the government, are starting life in the papers, which in turn are being fed material by informed academics, exasperated health workers, insubordinate public officials, and outraged members of the public. This is true not just of dissenting journals such as the *Guardian*, but of papers which traditionally support the Conservative Party. In recent weeks nothing has done more damage to the reputation of Johnson's Government than the lethal 5,000 word 'Thirty-Eight Days' article written by the *Sunday Times* insight team last week. Even the *Daily Telegraph*, which slavishly followed Johnson's line throughout the Brexit crisis, is running front-page stories critical of various shortages. The BBC is doing its best, but is constrained by the need to take a balanced view of the Administration. Little critical information, so far, has emanated from opposition politicians, although this may change now that Labour has a new leader and Parliament has reconvened. Yesterday's Prime Minister's Questions with Keir Starmer was a promising start.

What is so seductive, and so dangerous, about keeping abreast of events in this way is that every time I open my laptop and call up a paper, the news has changed. There is no fixed point, no moment when I can be assured that I am abreast of the day's developments. Is there a newspaper equivalent of alcoholics anonymous? If not, it may need inventing.

**Friday, 24 April 2020. Going backwards.**

Towards the end of *Wanderlust*, her fine history of walking, Rebecca Solnit passes by a glass-fronted gym, and looks in at the men and women relentlessly working on their exercise machines. 'The treadmill', she writes, 'is a corollary to the suburb and the autotropolis: a device with which to go nowhere in places where there is now nowhere to go. Or no desire to go.'[2]

The contrast was with more purposeful forms of exercise, the walk in the countryside, the bicycle ride from one place to another. This, of course, was in a time where it was possible to undertake such movement. Now it describes the fate of most citizens in most countries. In my case I have a private field adjacent to my house, but the Shropshire and Welsh hills basking in this morning's sunshine are out of reach and are likely to be so for the rest of the year.

Instead I keep fit on a rowing machine. It is a Concept 2, for those who take an interest in such matters. A professional-level device which has withstood heavy use over the years. British readers might know that it was on just such a machine that the broadcaster Andrew Marr gave himself a near fatal stroke seven years ago. It is said to be the most efficient of all the gym equipment, exercising muscles from the calves to the shoulders, and also, of course, heart and lungs. This morning I managed 2,924 metres in my standard fifteen minutes, which at my time of life is hard work.

I learnt to row at school in Kingston-upon-Thames. I loved the business, the walk to the riverside, the sleek fours and eights on their racks in the boathouse, lifting them out as a team and lowering them into the water, adjusting the foot straps, gripping the oars, and on command, a racing start, going up through the gears to a full stroke. The surge of power so close to the water is one of the great sensory experiences. Better still was the single scull that I learned how to use. Difficult to balance, but when you mastered it you could race like a motorbike across the surface. Then back to the boathouse, lifting the boat and turning it upside down to empty the river water, and onto the racks.

My Concept 2 has none of these pleasures. The machine is housed in what was once a medieval cellar below my house. The room has been tanked out, fitted with bookshelves, a light-well and bunks for the grandchildren. It is a pleasant enough space, but nonetheless underground. There is no view. No sound of the rest of the household, or indeed a rippling river. Just the seat running back and forth on its track while I listen to the news on the Today programme.

It is difficult not to view the rowing machine as a metaphor for our current circumstance. A disciplined activity which preserves my health and is going nowhere at all, day after day, backwards.

But there is another, more famous metaphor associated with movement on water, the last line of *The Great Gatsby*: 'So we beat on, boats against the current, borne back ceaselessly into the past.' I am by profession and practice an historian. This does not seem a problem to me.

### Monday, 27 April 2020. Following the Science.

When the time came to choose my A levels, I thought that as well as History and English, it would be useful to take Maths. This was immediately forbidden. The school timetable could only cope with science *or* humanities. No mixing. So my third subject became Latin. This may have helped my prose style over the years, but I have always regretted my lack of any engagement with the world on the other side of the fence.

In the course of time, I found employment as a history lecturer at Keele University. Keele had been founded in 1949, by A. D. Lindsay, a visionary Oxford philosopher. His premise was that the urgent task of post-war reconstruction would place scientists and engineers at the forefront of change. It was critical, therefore, that they knew how to engage with politics, society, history and ethics if they were to make an appropriate contribution. Conversely, those governing and administering the reconstructed country would need to be able to understand the work of the technicians.

The solution, therefore, was a higher education curriculum which required those undertaking specialist subjects to spend time studying, at least in outline, topics in other parts of the curriculum. A physicist would do a first year course in Western Civilisation and take minor subjects in the social sciences and humanities throughout the degree programme. A political scientist would spend quality time in a science laboratory. By the time I arrived, some quarter of a century later, the vision had been weakened by the ingrained conservatism of the schools and the professions, but it still existed as a model which, by and large, the rest of the sector was failing to follow. Its relevance to the forthcoming task of post-pandemic reconstruction can scarcely be understated.

The consequences of this failure are evident in the current crisis. Britain has tended to address the task of politicians communicating with scientists by ensuring that figures such as Chief Scientific and Medical Officers are capable of engaging with non-specialists, not the other way round. Thus it is that Johnson's cabinet contains just two people with scientific backgrounds, Alok Sharma who studied Physics, and Therese Coffey, who, alone of her colleagues, has a Ph.D., in Chemistry. She has been virtually invisible throughout the crisis. There are three farmers educated at agricultural colleges – perhaps they have transferable knowledge of rural epidemics such as BSE or Foot and Mouth.

Starmer's shadow cabinet is no better. In academic terms it is decidedly brighter than Johnson's, but again only two scientists – Valerie Vaz,

Biochemistry, and Thangam Debbonaire, Maths. All the rest are social scientists or historians (except three who left school at sixteen). The current debate over running the NHS is conducted by an Oxford PPE student for the Government and a Durham Philosophy and Politics graduate for Labour. Margaret Thatcher has been repeated as a female prime minister, not as a research-level scientist. Angela Merkel has demonstrated just how valuable such a background is in this crisis.

Then there is Dominic Cummings, by far the most powerful figure in Number 10. He is currently in trouble for taking part in meetings of SAGE (the Scientific Advisory Group for Emergencies), then running round to the other side of the table and receiving its 'independent' advice. Cummings is, I am sorry to say, an historian. He was taught at Oxford by Norman Stone, Professor of Modern History, right-wing newspaper columnist and possessor of other serious moral failings. Stone died last year. His obituary, written by the authoritative figure of Sir Richard Evans, recently retired Regius Professor of History at Cambridge, ended with the following paragraph:

> Journalists often described him as 'one of Britain's leading historians', but in truth he was nothing of the kind, as any serious member of the profession will tell you. The former prime minister, Heath, was wrong about many things, but he was surely right when he said of Stone during his time in Oxford: 'Many parents of Oxford students must be both horrified and disgusted that the higher education of our children should rest in the hands of such a man.'

Whether Cummings' parents came to regret their choice is not recorded. Its impact on their son seems to have been considerable.

Specialised knowledge still matters, never more so. The point for non-scientists is not to know what scientists know, but to know how they think. Yesterday, Brian Cox, the astronomer, was interviewed on the Andrew Marr show in his capacity as a contributor to the BBC 'Bite-Size' programmes which are providing curriculum for home-schooled children. He referred to the great populariser Richard Feynman and his argument that the chief characteristic of scientific activity was the embrace of doubt. There was no such thing as a monolithic, unchallengeable body of facts, particularly in the case of a virus that has only existed for a few months.

'The point is', concluded Cox, 'that we are facing the unknown … if you hear a politician saying that we're following the science, what that means is that they don't really understand what science is.'

**Tuesday, 28 April 2020. Follow the Tortoise.**

Casual walking out of a house, down the street, into a park or out to the countryside, has long-been the most practised and least studied form of recreation.

For most people in most times, it was the basic form of relaxation. Until the twentieth century, domestic over-crowding meant that it was often the only means of escaping the press of people and finding some privacy. Because it was essentially unstructured and unrecorded, it has rarely received the attention of historians. Rebecca Solnit's *Wanderlust*, to which I referred on April 24, is, like a handful of other such books, essentially an account of literary walkers, from Rousseau and Wordsworth onwards. The one exception is the now elderly account by Maurice Marples, *Shank's Pony* (1959).

In Britain, however, one of its most common forms, walking the dog, has long been counted. During the nineteenth century an increasingly firm distinction was drawn between walking with a dog, and dog-walking. Next to the immobile pedestrian, the greatest fear of polite town dwellers was the uncontrolled dog. It was at best a source of noise, pollution, and unwanted physical contact for other pedestrians, and at worst a threat to life through the widely-feared disease of hydrophobia, or rabies. Taxing dogs, which began in 1796, was a means of policing their mainly urban owners. Rural working dogs were exempt. Following reforms to the cost and efficiency of taxation in 1867, reliable records were kept. By 1877, there were nearly 1.4 million licensed dogs in Britain, mostly in towns and cities. At least as many owners again were believed to be avoiding the tax. By the second half of the twentieth century the figure had reached four million, doubling again before the licence fee was finally abolished in 1987.

In most countries in the Covid-19 lockdown, some kind of exemption has been allowed for exercising a pet. Last week a story went viral of an Italian woman who had been fined for exceeding the time limit for this activity. Her excuse was that the pet was not a dog, but a tortoise, and there was a photograph to prove it.

Initially I had much sympathy for the woman. In my adult life the only pet that I have owned myself, as distinct from the family cat, was a tortoise, named Herodotus, or Hod for short, after the first historian. It always seemed an appropriate companion for an historian, or indeed anyone engaged in the slow business of writing a full-length book. At this time of the year Hod would be trundling about the garden, eating buttercups and clover as he recovered his strength after the winter's hibernation.

But then again, a tortoise really does, in Kipling's terms, walk by itself. Cats are in fact always aware of human company and generally seek to be close to it. But a tortoise is entirely indifferent. That is what makes it so relaxing a pet. No complex emotional interactions. Our cat would walk surprisingly long distances with us when we were out on an expedition. Not Hod. It is not so much about mobility. On a hot day, especially if there is a tortoise maid in the offing, a tortoise can manage a turn of speed. Rather it is a matter of independence. There is just no way in the world you can get such an animal to follow you down the street.

I am afraid the Italian police had the right of it.

**Wednesday, 29 April 2020. Beetles and Universities.**

The future of universities is a microcosm of the larger debate about the aftermath of the pandemic. Will the outcome be a couple of years of readjustment, then a continuation of life as before, with a few tweaks to work and leisure and some fading memories of bad times? Or will there be a fundamental change in the way in which many organisations go about their activities, with new business models, new techniques, new roles for staff?

On April 22, I wrote about an attempt by the Durham Vice Chancellor to get ahead of change. It has since been rejected by the University senate, as the *Guardian* reported:

> The plans, which would also reduce the number of modules taught in person by a quarter in the next academic year, were condemned by the Department of English as 'dangerous and damaging to the short- and long-term viability of the university'. The department's submission to the senate, seen by the Guardian, criticised suggestions from a private education firm consulted on the plans that lecturers would only need six hours training in order to teach online. The document said Cambridge Education Digital's estimation of the work required to shift learning online displayed no realistic sense of the realities the staffing and technological support required to develop and

deliver it. 'Training staff to teach effectively online will take far, far more than the six hours indicated,' it added. The submission also warned the plans posed a potential conflict of interest because CEG Digital is owned by private equity group Bridgepoint Capital, whose chief investment officer is a member of Durham's 'chancellor's circle' of donors. The plans will now be returned to the university's council, where they will be redrawn before being returned to the senate.

A welcome dose of common sense by the English Department, and a reminder that universities still retain an element of democratic decision making.

But the problem has not gone away. In the past week more universities have been projecting imminent deficits as room rents collapse and overseas students disappear. The sector as a whole has been lobbying the Government for a subsidy, which has generated a hostile reaction in some quarters, not least because many of the most threatened institutions are also in possession of large reserves and extensive research income. An op. ed. in *The Times* welcomed the prospect of closures on the familiar grounds that Vice Chancellors were paid too much, the sector had over-extended, and Bath Spa University was running a degree in contemporary circus.[3]

In fact, where higher education is largely in the public sector, as in Britain and much of Europe, universities are like beetles (allegedly) in a nuclear war, very hard to destroy. It is said that three of Europe's 20 universities were closed by the Black Death, but as that pandemic killed between a third and a half of the population, it may be said that the sector got off lightly. Since then, outright closure has been almost unknown, despite the recent expansion. It is otherwise in the United States where a large, sometimes corrupt, private sector suffered bankruptcies during the Great Depression and will do so again.

It may be that a few more staff will in future investigate what happens to their teaching when a computer is turned on, and that a few more students will tolerate less face-to-face contact. Or it may be that the declining eighteen-year-old cohort, the lost overseas students, the accumulated deficits, will force universities to investigate radical change.

The fundamental things still apply. High quality distance education is very expensive. Academic staff like talking to students. And the students go to bricks and mortar universities for a rich social experience and are unlikely to pay £9,000 a year just to sit in their rooms and be taught on their laptops.

**Thursday, 30 April 2020. Screen Life.**

Like everyone else, the fixed points in my week are mostly through the medium of Skype, Zoom and Microsoft Teams.

Those connected with my work are relatively stress free. There is widespread use of microphone cancelling to preserve the signal in multi-participator events, so every sound in the house does not have to be quietened. The Open University History Department meetings, involving over twenty people, have adopted the etiquette of turning off the video. This means that colleagues cannot see that you have temporarily ceased to pay rapt attention to the matter in hand, or are sneaking a look at emails on your phone, or are briefly leaving the room to make a cup of coffee.

With calls to family and friends it is quite otherwise. There is no point at all in forbidding the sight of children and grandchildren you would give so much to see in person. Or in turning the sound on and off when small parties are prone to make unscripted interventions. This makes the whole experience both pleasurable and surprisingly tiring. After an hour's interaction, you feel drained of energy.

There are several reasons for this. The first is the technology. Smart though the competing sites are, the quality of the sound is often poor, and the picture of limited quality. In talking to each other we are all of us minutely attuned to tiny movements in facial expression. The video images, under stress with so much increased use, can be insufficiently sharp, or require intense concentration to decode. There is also the question of positioning the camera. My younger daughter, a BBC producer, is long used to this business. She strongly advises two techniques; always place the camera at head height so that the viewer is not focussing on the underside of your chin; and always sit back, so that your face does not dominate the screen.

The second is the intensity. In normal life we don't often talk to someone without a break for a whole hour, and when we do there are pauses, moments when we are looking elsewhere, or have briefly diverted attention to our own thoughts. In my *History of Solitude* I examine what I term 'abstracted solitude', the capacity to withdraw from pressing company. Daniel Defoe in his second sequel to *Robinson Crusoe*, caused his hero to write that, 'all the Parts of a compleat Solitude are to be as effectually enjoy'd, if we please, and sufficient Grace assisting, even in the most populous Cities, among the Hurries of Conversation, and Gallantry of a Court, or the Noise and Business of a Camp, as in the Desarts of *Arabia* and *Lybia*, or in the desolate Life of an uninhabited Island.'[4] It is very difficult to be there but not there, if you are constantly on camera.

The third, unique to this medium, is the accompanying presence of your own image, particularly on ZOOM. The one thing you never do in ordinary conversation is look at yourself. I am not fond of my own image at the best of times, and now, two months and counting since my last haircut, I am beginning to look like Al Pacino in his later manifestations. To be faced with such a sight for so long is deeply dispiriting.

These limitations have caused some of my friends to revert to the older technology of the telephone, where you are free to concentrate on the conversation, without the distracting video technology.

But then again. A video call yesterday was held up when my five-year grandson discovered, to his great satisfaction, that if he put his bare foot up against the camera on the laptop, it would appear five times larger than the rest of him. Can't do that on a telephone.

**Friday, 1 May 2020. Scavenging.**

Yesterday, the Zoom session was with my younger daughter and her two daughters aged two and five. It began badly. I asked the older child what she had been doing during the day. It was now four in the afternoon so plenty had happened. There was a long silence before she finally said, 'we had lunch'.

I should have known, I do know, that children of that age do not go through life narrativizing their activities. Any parent greeting a child back from school soon gives up trying to find out what went on that day. Interesting things do happen, and when the child is interested in talking about them, it will. Until then, the point is what it is doing now, and might do next.

So we quickly moved on. My wife read a story to the two girls which last she had read to their mother when she was at the same age (*Sally's*

*Secret* by Shirley Hughes). Mother and children were equally pleased. Then the five- year-old, who is rapidly mastering the skill, read us a school book, which featured a grandmother who bought blue shoes to see the Queen. A heel broke and she was in despair until a kindly palace official produced a bag of spare blue shoes, and all was well.

Last week we played the well-known game of scavenging. A list is sent of things to find in the house and garden, and the video session begins with a show-and-tell, which displays the energy and ingenuity of the finder. The five-year-old is now old enough to reverse the game. For the following session, the grandparents were sent a list of things to collect, and we were required to display them in front of two critical grandchildren. The list was as follows: we had to find something that was

- really bouncy
- has a strong smell
- prickly
- smooth
- sticky
- fluffy
- a cone shape
- multicoloured
- made of rubber
- very heavy
- very light
- has a switch

Good luck with this. You can show and tell on Monday. Enjoy the weekend.

**Monday, 4 May 2020. Before the lockdown.**

All of us, especially those in complete lockdown, spend quality time wondering what we might have done when we had the chance to do it.

In Britain we had perhaps six to eight weeks when we knew that Covid-19 was not something that just happened in faraway countries. We had a week to ten days when it was clear that an imposed lockdown was coming. What use did we make of this precious time?

Visiting the hairdresser is so obvious and so universal (except for those no longer burdened with a thatch) that it is barely worth mentioning. A friend sent us a cartoon. A sex worker is leaning through a car window. 'I'll do anything you want for £50.' A voice from inside the car: 'Do you cut hair?'

For us the major regret is not attending a family celebration of my wife's birthday in London. As it happened this was arranged for March 14, just over a week before the closure. My wife and I were still considering that we might travel when we received fierce instruction from each of our children. They addressed us much as we did them in the most irresponsible phase of their adolescence: 'What you are proposing to do represents an unnecessary threat to your health and wellbeing. We have a duty of care towards you, and you will do as we say.' Thus the tables were turned, perhaps for good.

Since then, the risk register has evolved. Dying has become one of the activities to get through before the shut-down. On Sunday we had a grocery delivery, and fell to talking (at a safe distance) to the man who had pushed the trolley up the drive. He said that he had lately lost his father. We sympathised with his Covid-19 suffering, but he explained that his father had died, much to his relief, just before the outbreak. He had been in and out of hospital for a year and would have hated to have his treatment side-lined by the pandemic. His family had been with him during his final hours. And they had a good funeral (he also explained the difficulty of arranging it in the midst of severe flooding in our area, but that is now a forgotten story).

The last funeral that I attended myself before the crisis was of a cousin. He too had been undergoing hospital treatment for a year. He too died in the company of his wife and children. He too had a great send-off, at which his grandchildren and a university colleague spoke movingly of his life.

The widespread stories of final hours being spent only in the company of medical staff, of tight restrictions on attendance at funerals, of cancer appointments falling by three quarters, of cancelled treatments for a host of serious conditions, reinforce the tale told by the delivery man.

For those who still have time ahead of us, better of course to stand and take our chance. But for those for whom the grim reaper was already at the door, better he entered before all this happened.

**Tuesday, 5 May 2020.  Unlocking.**

We are now into the beginning of the unlocking of Britain.  The prospect is raising the question of where the power lies in this crisis.

The *Guardian* reported at the weekend that 'Fewer than one in five of the British public believe the time is right to consider reopening schools, restaurants, pubs and stadiums. The findings, in a new poll for the *Observer*, suggest Boris Johnson will struggle to convince people to return their lives to normal if he tries to ease the lockdown soon.'[5]

You can be certain that Johnson and his advisers took this information very seriously.  It is a truism long known to politicians and political historians, that successful social reform follows rather than changes public opinion.  This was the case for instance with Roy Jenkins' epochal tenure of the Home Office in the mid-1960s when he radically reformed the law on homosexuality, abortion, race relations and censorship.  In each case popular sentiment was more than ready for such changes.  The same is true, more recently, of the liberalising reforms in the Republic of Ireland.

It is not just a matter of a government avoiding grief in polls and subsequent elections. If a society is not, with the exception of inevitable die-hards, largely in favour of reform, it will not observe the new legal framework, and no amount of punitive policing or judicial intervention will be effective.

In the speeded-up metabolism of successive social changes in the Covid-19 pandemic, the same rules apply. Johnson held back from imposing the lockdown until it was evident that the population would accept what a month previously had been unimaginable changes to its behaviour. For all the protests by Conservative backbenchers, the occasional arrests on beaches or in other public spaces have been largely symbolic.

The question is how far has the calculation of risk on the part of the general public changed.

There is a case for arguing that fear of infection has increased since the onset, despite recent evidence that the peak has been passed. In March we knew that Covid-19 was a serious form of flu. We did not know just how easy it was to catch it, just how unpleasant it was to be in intensive care, just how terrible a form of dying it was, and just how ineffective the government would be in key areas such as testing or the provision of PPE.

The government has been rightly criticised for allowing the Cheltenham Horse-racing Festival to go ahead in the week before it imposed the lockdown. A quarter of a million people jostled together on the racecourse. Now Cheltenham, an otherwise prosperous town, is a coronavirus hotspot. It is worth asking whether, were a similar event to be sanctioned this month, anything like this number of spectators would choose to attend. Gambling on horses is one thing. Gambling on your life is something else [this reminds me of the character of Sam the Gonoph in Damon Runyan's stories. Sam was a professional bookmaker who could set odds on any competition, even life itself, which he calculated was, in the round, 6 to 5 against].

There are two conclusions to be drawn. The first is that a successful navigation out of this storm will be more in the hands of we the people than our hapless governors. When we decide to change, change will be feasible, and it is unlikely to be much influenced by public service announcements and daily press conferences.

The second is that the debate which is now taking place will once more highlight the issue of the coherence of British society. We have temporarily forgotten the Brexit divide, but there are still immense variations by class, race and gender in the experience of Covid-19. Those locked in small flats, those for whom the shutdown is wrecking their businesses or family economies, will be a good deal less patient with the lockdown than the retired historian who is writing this, looking out at Spring unfolding in his garden.

- With regard to David Maughan Brown's entry yesterday on the Johnson interview in the *Sun on Sunday*, if Johnson's prospects were aligning with *The Death of Stalin*, the question, for those who saw the entertaining film, is who would be the Lavrentiy Beria of the event, the head of the secret police who attempted to take over after Stalin's death and was murdered by his henchmen? My money is on Michael Gove.

**Wednesday, 6 May 2020. Box of Provisions.**

Each Monday morning, before we are out of bed, an emissary of the government delivers a box of provisions to our front door.

The NHS vulnerable-stay-at-home-at-all-costs letter that I received at the beginning of the lockdown was accompanied by an instruction to log in to a government website giving details of my situation. I filled in the electronic form, and the next week, to our surprise and embarrassment, we received a free box of food and other necessities. By this time, we had found our way into the supermarket delivery system, but there appears to be nothing we can do to stop this charity. I have revisited the government site three times, ticking the box to say I have an adequate supply of food, but with no result. Amidst all the shortages and failed targets, this service is working like an unstoppable clock.

A neighbour takes the untouched box to a local food bank. There is thus a small subsidy taking place from the State to this necessary facility. Otherwise, the contents of the box, which vary only slightly each week, represent what an individual (I don't think the machine knows I have a wife) officially needs to survive on for seven days. This week's box contained:

500g pasta

2 kg potatoes

500g white rice

2 litres of skimmed UHT milk

1 litre apple juice

5 clementines

5 apples

1 ¼ lb of carrots

185g tin of tuna chunks

200g tin chopped pork [last week it was corned beef]

Large white-sliced loaf of bread

6 mini bars of chocolate chip cookies

450g Ready Brek

2 x 500g Bolognese sauce

3 x 400g tins of Heinz tomato soup

2 x 425g tins of Heinz baked beans

800g tin of mushy peas

8 sachets of Maxwell House instant coffee

12 breakfast tea bags

500ml Dove bodywash

1 Dove hand soap

2 loo rolls

Historians in some future time may examine these boxes as evidence of what the government thought people should be eating at the end of the second decade of the twenty-first century.

Apart from the pasta, rice and Bolognese sauce, I imagine something very similar was prescribed during the second world war and its immediate aftermath. Vegans, vegetarians, allergy sufferers, slimmers, religious minorities, might never have existed.

**Thursday, 7 May 2020. Snitching.**

One of the major questions of the crisis is the substance of the apparent strengthening of 'community spirit'. My local television news spends its allocated half hour briefly reporting the daily death toll in the region, then running a series of heart-warming stories about informal and organised efforts to support those suffering in some way from the lockdown. What will not be clear until the crisis is over is how permanent this shift in behaviour is, and how far it conceals much less commendable behaviour. Statistics on rising domestic abuse are already giving pause to more optimistic accounts.

On the debit side of the balance sheet was a recent story in the *Guardian*: 'Police say they have received 194,000 calls "snitching" on people alleged to have broken the coronavirus lockdown.'[6] Neighbours were reporting neighbours, expecting that fines or other punitive action would follow. The Chairman of the West Yorkshire Police Federation complained that 'the force has been dealing with a rise in domestic abuse reports at a time when people are living in close quarters without much chance to leave the house, and that there had been a rise in calls from people reporting others for potential flouting of regulations.'[7] Further south it was reported that 'The avalanche of complaints about twice-a-day jogs or overly frequent trips to the supermarket has been such that the Thames Valley Police Commissioner Anthony Stansfield felt obliged to go on the BBC and urge citizens to stop "tattling on one another."'[8] Elsewhere in Europe, more draconian regulations have been matched by more active tale-telling. The mayor of Rome has set up a website for people denouncing those who breach the quarantine regulations. In Spain it is said that 'snitchers' are not only reporting infractions but taking direct action against rule-breakers.

There is in fact nothing new in this behaviour. Nearly three decades ago I wrote a history of poverty and the state in the twentieth century. The Great Depression was the nearest modern equivalent to the current collapse of the economy. Large sections of the working population were forced to rely on state benefits to survive. From 1931 they had to complete a rule-bound Means Test to get support. I wrote in my book:

> The Means Test placed a monetary penalty on a whole range of domestic behaviour. Questions which had always formed the substance of rumour and gossip, such as who had an illicit source of income or a hidden cache of savings, who had bought what luxury or sold what necessity, now had a larger resonance. The greatest source of information on alleged transgressions of the new regulations was not the inspecting officers, whose

public enquiries were generally met with silence, but private and frequently anonymous depositions from those who lived and worked alongside the claimant. As Orwell discovered, 'there is much spying and tale-bearing.'[9]

The modern 'snitching' could just be seen as evidence of widespread support for government regulation and a collective anxiety to reduce the threat of infection. There is, however, a long and less benign tradition of reporting misbehaviour to the authorities. Such behaviour is a consequence of two conditions. Firstly a stressed citizenry, facing threats they cannot individually manage. Secondly a suddenly enhanced state, possessing, at least in the short term, immense powers over income and behaviour. Historical studies of the totalitarian regimes in twentieth-century Europe, particularly German fascism and East European communism, have long established how far the police authorities relied on networks of informers. The Stasi in East Germany raised reporting by neighbours and family members to a bureaucratic art-form.

There is, with reason, much concern about whether computer apps will cause an invasion of privacy. Less attention is being paid to more basic forms of surveillance, which will flourish for as long as this crisis lasts.

**Monday, 11 May 2020. Digital visitors.**

This morning the President of a European university was talking to me in my sitting room. Later in the day he returned with two of his senior colleagues. The conversations were joined by a Greek Cypriot, a Frenchwoman, a Croat and a Catalan, all of whom, given the lazy privilege of the British, talked in fluent English.

Last year, before the flood, I agreed to be part of a team organised by the Institutional Evaluation Programme of the European University Association. IEP maintains a list of international auditors and is commissioned by universities, or sometimes complete university systems, to review their organisation and strategies. The standard practice is for the team to make two site visits of three or four days and then submit a written report.

The first visit to the current institution should have taken place just as the European lockdowns were imposed. Instead, it was agreed to undertake the exercise remotely, which permits some estimation for the future of conducting international business in such a way. So far, the gains are:

- No real loss in the focus of the interviews.
- No loss in organising the programme, in timing meetings. Ease of adding new meetings.
- No problems with the platform, in this case Microsoft Teams, which works transnationally, and also enables documents, such as rapidly revised agendas, to be shared between the team members. Vision better than sound.

- No time wasted in travel. In this case it would have taken half a day in each direction, door to door. So for the two visits, that's two days of my life free for reading books, digging the garden .

- No costs to the IEP, and ultimately to the reviewed university, of such travel, plus accommodation and meals during the visit.

And losses:

- Opportunities for informal discussions amongst the team members as they spend long days together, from breakfast to dinner. It's these discussions which inform the next interviews, and frequently frame the final report.

- Opportunities for intervening in group discussion. Difficult to catch the eye of the chair, to know when it is, and is not, the moment to make a contribution.

- Opportunities for spending quality time with interesting academics from the four corners of Europe.

- Opportunities for travel. I am one of those odd people who actually enjoy the abstracted solitude of airports and planes, and however tight the schedule, there is always some chance to see faraway cities, and perhaps sample their food [except in Macedonia where every night we were handed a menu in a different restaurant, then served exactly the same pre-ordered meal as before].

- Opportunities for getting a physical feel for the institutions you are visiting. Turning up at the Macedonian university and being shown the bullet holes from the last civil war did help the team to understand the institution's strategic priorities.

- Opportunities for my wife to move about our house freely while I am working. It was built in around 1450, before it seemed necessary to soundproof one room from another.

Days of online conversations in front of me. I rather fear that the opportunities in terms of efficiency, if not pleasure [except Macedonia], are going to outweigh the losses. This project will be completed in terms of its purpose, but with no larger gain. Would I do it again, given that I am free not to? No.

**Tuesday, 12 May 2020. Time and the Crisis.**

Brenda in Hove's thoughtful May 9 entry 'In Transition' focussed on lives suspended by the crisis, with no certainty about what would happen when they were recommenced. There is a more general point here about time and the pandemic.

Much of the media commentary, in print and particularly on television, assumes that the experiences that are being described are entirely novel. Whilst there have been flu epidemics in the relatively recent past, these exist only as a distant memory. Individuals are presented as if they are encountering bereavement, loneliness, overcrowded interiors, children home from school (there were endless school holidays in olden times), poverty, unemployment, illness and fear of illness, for the first time in their lives. Of course, the intensity of these events has suddenly increased, but for the most part individuals are navigating the crisis on the basis of established maps of expectations and behaviours, however much these now need to be modified.

The degree of familiarity varies. In hospitals, for instance, there are cohorts of doctors and nurses for whom death is an event they have been trained to cope with. There is now more of it, staff are at much greater risk, and negotiating between dying patients and distraught relatives has become more complex, but if the chosen specialism is, say, cancer, it comes with the territory. On the other hand, there are those who made the career choice of, say, orthopaedics, perhaps because patient mortality was rare, who have been suddenly transferred to Covid-19 wards and are wholly unprepared for the experience. Similarly care home workers know all about death, and in my limited experience of my mother's final days, can be singularly unemotional about it. What is new, again, is the scale and the threat to their own lives.

For a retired but still labouring historian, it is the case that I have been locked down, with occasional escapes, for years, and from day to day, barely notice the change. How I have spent my past, what I have chosen to do, how I have learned to celebrate the merits of my way of life and manage its demerits, are fundamental to my present experience and how I will emerge from it.

My point is not to diminish the drama and the scale of suffering. Just that if we are to understand the coping strategies that are being adopted, we need to know about the skills, capacities and plans which in their different ways, everyone is bringing to the struggle.

•        Readers of my May 6 entry on Box of Provisions will be pleased to know that in spite of a further attempt to stop the service, a new box was delivered yesterday morning. Off it goes to the food bank, though I am sorely tempted by the loaf of sliced white bread sitting on top. Such degenerate food has been banned in our household for decades. But it remains a secret pleasure. There are some things, like eggy bread or bacon sandwiches (doubly forbidden), for which soft, chemically-infused white bread is just essential.    Otherwise, the relentless efficiency of this service amidst the chaos remains a puzzle. There will, however, be some for whom the box is the difference between eating and not-eating, so it is perhaps as well that it keeps coming.

**Wednesday, 13 May 2020.  Children of the Aftermath.**

As much as we are all wondering how we will get through to the end, we are also contemplating how we will be changed by the experience. From hospitals to universities, managers of complex, rule-bound organisations are astonished at how behaviours set in stone for decades have been transformed in a matter of weeks, and are speculating about how long such a metabolism of change can continue.

There is another way of considering the aftermath. I have a new great nephew, born on May 1st in a village on the shores of Loch Lomond, a great niece due next month in York, and if all goes well I shall have a new granddaughter, born to my son and his wife towards the end of

August in East London. The brave post-pandemic world will be the one in which these children will take their first steps and form their identities and ambitions.

In this regard, I have a shared experience. I was born early in 1949, when Britain was still in the midst of reconstruction after VE day which we have just celebrated. The bomb damage in the major cities was yet to be cleared. Rationing was to continue for a further five years. Whilst we now celebrate the heroic construction of the welfare state, life in those years was hard. The winter of 1946-7 was one of the coldest on record, causing and compounded by serious fuel shortages.

Looking back, what strikes me most about my childhood was how much my perspective was cast towards the future. This was partly because my own family had not suffered greatly in the war. There were no fatalities, no battlefield injuries still blighting civilian life. It was partly because I spent my early years in parts of the country which had not experienced physical damage (in Stoke-on-Trent, where my father's family came from and which we frequently visited, the story was that the Luftwaffe had flown over the city, concluded that it had already been bombed, and passed on).

And it was partly because as a small child I was the direct and immediate beneficiary of the Welfare State. I was conceived in the same summer that the NHS began its life. My father was a junior civil servant, seconded to Blackpool after the war to work on planning the new system, then promoted to run the first office of the Ministry of

Pensions and National Insurance in the north midlands town of Banbury and then in Oxford. I was in every possible way a child of the new provision, and I can still remember walking with my mother to collect my welfare orange juice from the clinic and my reading books from the children's library next door. Later came free education all the way up to my Cambridge doctorate.

If I have hope for the new members of my family, it must be based on two aspirations. Firstly, that they should be lucky in the homes into which they are born, as I was in mine. Where there has been death from Covid-19, where the outcome of the pandemic is of embittered lives, undermined health, shattered finances, long-term unemployment, it will be so much harder to form confident, optimistic identities.

Secondly, that we do in fact create a new world in which, once more, the wellbeing of every child, physical and educational, is front and centre of our collective action. It is a matter of addressing the inequalities which continue to disfigure our society three quarters of a century after the reforms of the 1945 Labour Government. And is a matter of ensuring, by signs and by facts, that each child feels itself the most important and cared-for person not just in its immediate family, but in all the places in which it develops as a person. I had that sense in my beginning. I grew up looking forwards, learning about the Second World War and its suffering only much later, mostly through history books.

Whilst as adults we must never forget what we have lived through this year, these growing children should never be held back by it.

**Thursday, 14 May 2020. The divided golf course**.

A month ago, on April 14, I wrote a piece on 'Borders', describing the 'insane' prospect of different lockdown regulations on either side of national borders within the UK.

Now it has come to pass. The picture above is the view from the bottom of my garden.[10] Below the field is the Severn, hidden by the trees on the bank. Almost unnoticed in the current crisis, we have been enjoying a warm, dry Spring and the river is unusually low for this time of the year. Beyond it, across a few more fields, is Wales, with The Breiddens in the distance. Were I to go for a walk on the hills, as we often did in peacetime, I could now be stopped by the police. It is legal to drive to take exercise in England, not in Wales. It is permissible for people to go to any kind of work in England, not in Wales. There is a golf course in the border village of Llanymynech, a few miles away, where 15 holes are in Wales, 3 in England. According to the new rules, only the English holes can be played.

Some of this is just a trivial irritation. But there is a more serious event taking place. The leaders of Scotland, Wales and even Northern Ireland, have publicly condemned Johnson's broadcast on Sunday, where he announced a partial, if very confused, relaxation of the rules 'in the UK'. The nation leaders were quick to point out that they had not been consulted about the new regime and did not agree with it. They were free to go their own way and intended to do so. This is partly a matter of local calculation about the state of the pandemic and the risk of relaxing the lockdown. It is also a consequence of the growing perception that the Westminster government is fundamentally incompetent. The electorates of the other nations are looking to their own representatives for a road map out of the crisis, and practices are likely to diverge still further in the coming months.

The coronavirus pandemic did not invent the break-up of the UK, but amongst the consequences will be a significant acceleration of that process. And the full effects of Brexit are yet to come.

**Friday, 15 May 2020. Fish!**

My household will not go hungry in this crisis. We have sorted out the supermarket home delivery system. The shelves of Sainsbury's are open to us. But food lacks surprise. No meals out. No entertaining at home. No takeaways in the countryside (we are two miles outside the delivery radius of the enterprising restaurant in Shrewsbury which is sending out prepared meals).

One of the benefits of living for many years in the same place is that you get to know the local sources of good things. The best meat comes from Churncote Farm Shop. The best vegetables from Pomona at the foot of Castle Hill. The best fish from Barkworth's stand in the covered market. The fish in fact is no better than fresh. The variety is limited. It is an abiding mystery to me why markets in France, often hundreds of miles from the sea, are so much better stocked than in those in a country where nowhere is more than fifty miles from water. All these shops are shut at the moment and were they to open I remain 'shielded' from the rest of humanity and unable to go out on a Saturday morning to see what I can find.

So with food, as with travel and many other pleasures, there is nothing to do but read about it. This week I have been going through, for a history project, Henry Mayhew's *London Labour and the London Poor* of 1861. Mayhew was an ethnographer *avant la lettre*, fascinated by the rituals and behaviours of the common people. He also loved to count where he could. At one point he turns his attention to Billingsgate, the London wholesale fish market on the banks of the Thames. Its business had recently expanded as the new railway network brought in fresh supplies from the coast. Mayhew set out to calculate, for the first time, the annual turnover of the market:

Table, Showing the Quantity ... of the Following kinds of Fish sold in Billingsgate Market in the Course of the Year

| | |
|---|---|
| Salmon and Salmon Trout | 406,000 |
| Live Cod | 400,000 |
| Soles | 97,520,000 |
| Whiting | 17,920,000 |

| | |
|---|---|
| Haddock | 2,740,000 |
| Plaice | 33,600,000 |
| Mackerel | 23,520,000 |
| Fresh Herrings | 1,225,000,000 |
| [Sprats | 4,000,000 (by measure)] |
| Eels | 9,797,760 |
| Flounders | 259,200 |
| Dabs | 270,000 |
| Barrelled Cod | 750,000 |
| Dried Salt Cod | 1,600,000 |
| Smoked Haddock | 19,500,000 |
| Bloaters | 147,000,000 |
| Red Herrings | 50,000,000 |
| Dried Sprats | 288,000 |
| Oysters | 495,896,000 |
| Lobsters | 1,200,000 |
| Crabs | 600,000 |
| Shrimps | 498,428,648 |
| Whelks | 4,943,200 |
| Mussels | 50,400,000 |
| Cockles | 7,392,000 |
| Periwinkles | 304,000,000 |

You read it correctly. That's over a billion fresh herrings consumed by Londoners in the middle of the nineteenth century (with a population of some two and a half million). Almost five hundred million oysters and shrimps.

That's fish!  Enjoy the sight.


**Monday, 18 May 2020.  The Bad News and the Good News.**

Last week two differing visions of the post-Covid-19 world were published.

The first was by the distinguished political philosopher John Gray in his 'Unherd' blog (thanks to my friend John Naughton for this).

He answered the question in his title, 'How Apocalyptic is Now?' with a resounding affirmative.  The pandemic fitted into an established pattern:

> history is repeatedly punctuated by discontinuities in which what was gained is irrecoverably lost. Whether because of war or revolution, famine or epidemic — or a deadly combination, as in the Russian Civil War — the sudden death of ways of life is a regular occurrence.  Certainly there are periods of incremental improvement, but they rarely last longer than two or three generations. Progress occurs in interludes when history is idling.

After dwelling at length on the millions of lives lost after the Russian Revolution, ranging from civil war to state-induced famine, he reached the modern day full of pessimism:

> Much in the way we lived before the virus is already irretrievable... More than government-enforced policies, public attitudes will prevent any reversion to pre-Covid ways. Covid-19 may not be an exceptionally lethal pathogen, but it is fearful enough. Soon temperature checks will be ubiquitous and surveillance via mobile phones omnipresent. Social distancing, in one form or another, will be entrenched everywhere beyond the home. The impact on the economy will be immeasurable. Enterprises that adapt quickly will thrive, but sectors that relied on pre-Covid lifestyles — pubs, restaurants, sporting events, discos and airline travel, for example — will shrink or disappear. The impact on the 'knowledge classes' will be far-reaching. Higher education operates on a model of student living that social distancing has rendered defunct. Museums, journalism, publishing and the arts all face similar shocks. Automation and artificial intelligence will wipe out swathes of middle class employment. Accelerating a trend that has been underway for decades, the remains of bourgeois life will be swept away.

By contrast, the American writer Rebecca Solnit wrote a long op ed piece in the *Guardian*. She listed multiple examples of how the crisis had been met by community action in different parts of the world, including Britain, and looked forward to a transformed society: 'I sometimes think that capitalism is a catastrophe constantly being mitigated and cleaned up by mutual aid and kinship networks, by the generosity of religious and secular organisations, by the toil of human-rights lawyers and climate groups, and by the kindness of strangers. Imagine if these forces, this spirit, weren't just the cleanup crew, but were the ones setting the agenda.' As with Gray, she viewed the crisis as a turning-point in history, but with a quite different outcome:

> The pandemic marks the end of an era and the beginning of another – one whose harshness must be mitigated by a spirit of generosity. An artist hunched over her sewing machine, a young person delivering groceries on his bicycle, a nurse suiting up for the ICU, a doctor heading to the Navajo nation, a graduate student hip-deep in Pyramid Lake catching trout for elders, a programmer setting up a website to organise a community: the work is under way. It can be the basis for the future, if we can recognise the value of these urges and actions, recognise that things can and must change profoundly, and if we can tell other stories about who we are, what we want and what is possible.[11]

Take your pick. What may be said is that such speculation, though understandable, is premature. The Chinese Premier Zhou Enlai is said to have replied 'too soon to tell' when Richard Nixon asked him whether he thought the French Revolution was good thing.[12] So also with our present drama in this third week in May 2020.

What may also be said is that Gray's determinism seems out of place. Post-modernism has taught us to mistrust cyclical views of history, the notion that liberalism, imperialism, capitalism, the proletariat, Corbyn's Labour Party, must eventually prevail, irrespective of individual intention. Gray's negative presentation of this trope, that all plans for progress will regularly be overthrown by versions of the apocalypse, belongs to that tradition.

If a more benign vision is to transpire, it will be the outcome of conscious, determined action in the aftermath. Covid-19 by itself will not guarantee progress.

**Tuesday, 19 May 2020. Pickled Eggs.**

Last week the invaluable Office for National Statistics published a survey of gardens in the UK.[13] The headline news was that one in eight homes lacked a garden, another measure of the wide-ranging inequality of experience in this crisis.

It is possible, however, to take a glass half-full, or seven-eighths-full, view of this finding. It seems to me astonishing that on this over-crowded island, so long after the invention of high-rise living, the great majority of people in Britain want to live in a property with a fenced fragment of nature attached to it and are able to do so. For the locked-in elderly the proportion of those with access to private outdoor space is even higher at 92%.

The size of the patch of land is not really the point. Obviously half an acre is a luxury to be enjoyed if it can be afforded. But each of my children, living in their first houses in London, take immense pleasure in the small rectangles of grass and surrounding borders beyond their back doors. The two that have young offspring have room for a sandpit, a paddling pool on hot days, a portable wigwam to play in. It's been a kind of rite of passage for them to start acquiring the horticultural knowledge and skills that they saw their parents possess and practice when they were themselves growing up.

Possession and use of a garden are matters of private choice. It is a measure of the relative transience of the Covid-19 pandemic is that we have not been instructed to 'dig for victory' as was the case in the Second World War (although today Prince Charles has launched a 'pick for victory' campaign to help the commercial fruit growers). Despite occasional gloomy forecasts, we have not been told to grow our own food to survive. In the First World War the pressures of urban slums were relieved by the provision of over half a million allotments following the Smallholdings and Allotment Act of 1908, which required local authorities to purchase or lease land upon which their communities could grow flowers and food.

Gardening is a necessary pleasure. As we begin to reduce the lockdown, garden centres have been amongst the first to be allowed to re-open, albeit with appropriate distancing measures. That much of their retail space is out of doors makes them a safer proposition than, say, clothing shops, but the queues that immediately formed once the relaxation was announced were testament to the pent-up demand. As I noted in a previous entry, the fact that in the northern hemisphere the pandemic has coincided with Spring not Autumn has helped to make the crisis bearable, but it has also created a lively market for plants, fertilizer and other sundries.

As with any recreation, gardening also performs the function of providing substitute dramas and anxieties, to distract from the larger problems. Last week the major misfortune in my life was not some coronavirus-related event, but a sharp May frost which decimated fifty cosmos plants that I had grown in my greenhouse and just planted out in the garden. Then there is the mole which has started digging up a lately sown patch of grass. In a Zoom session with my home-schooling seven-year-old granddaughter, I asked her to research humane remedies for moles. She came back later in the day with information that putting pickled eggs down their holes should keep them at bay.

But where, in the midst of a lock-down, am I going to obtain pickled eggs?

**Wednesday, 20 May 2020. Lessons in time.**

Yesterday the Today programme included a meditation by the novelist Ian McEwan on the coronavirus pandemic as 'an experiment in subjective time.' For those not engaged in vital work, or managing the minutely structured task of teaching unschooled children, the experience, he argued, has altered our perception of time: 'Bleached of events, one day like another, time compresses and collapses in on itself.' The consequence has been 'an exponential growth in introspection, day- dreaming, mental drifting, especially about the past.' We find ourselves 'tumbling backwards through time', achieving a new understanding of ourselves as we embrace without guilt a stillness in the midst of our days.

All of which is both eloquent and true. Those who have erased their diaries for months ahead have to learn for the first time in their long lives new ways of justifying the use of time. There are different kinds of choices in its management, and, above all, the choice of not managing it all. As anxiety about the unfilled hour recedes, so we can, as McEwan argues, form a calmer sense of who we have become and what matters to us.

And yet.

There are contradictions lurking in McEwan's eloquent prose.

In the first case, the form contradicts the content. This was an exactly timed slot in the country's premier current affairs radio programme. It lasted precisely five minutes, sandwiched between an item on Brexit and another on government financing of industry. The studio manager will have controlled the event with a stopwatch as the programme headed towards its 9 a.m. conclusion. McEwan will have been given the task of turning his prose into time – 150 words a minute is the BBC norm - and by pre-recording the talk, the programme presenter was relieved of the task of disciplining the speaker. Nothing can have been more time-infused than this disquisition on its absence.

And then there is McEwan himself. His experience of time may have changed with the lockdown, but he remains a professional writer. Unlike those who earn their living in more structured contexts, he has a lifetime's experience of controlling the use of the unforgiving hour. Finishing novel after novel requires, in P. G. Wodehouse's famous dictum, 'the application of seat of pants to seat of chair.' You do not wander through the day, jotting down the odd sentence, waiting for inspiration to strike. You devise a timetable that suits your temperament and circumstances, and stick to it all the more rigidly in the absence of external compulsion. I don't suppose for a moment that McEwan has stopped doing this, just because he can't see people at present. He will still be setting his clock, starting at his desk, just as he has always done.

I am myself a writer, of stories with footnotes. Three books published in the last five years. I start relatively early in the morning, and work in seventy-five minute-blocks, stopping for a coffee and then starting again. I did this before the pandemic and I am doing it now.

So, four minutes before the next break, this entry ends.

**Thursday, 21 May 2020.  Being Local.**

In my corner of our village are three households containing five adults. Fields containing three horses, thirteen sheep (newly shorn) and six bullocks (newly arrived) separate us from the rest of the community. Our neighbours are in the middle course of their lives, have no resident children, and are taking great care of themselves.  They pose no threat whatever to my health or that of my wife.

The question of the moment is how far that small bubble of security can be pushed out.  What distance can I move before the risk of infection becomes tangible?  That assessment is founded on information.  I know from informal contacts and the parish website that there is no Covid-19 not only amongst my immediate neighbours, but throughout the village. Beyond that, what is the data?

At present, the daily record is maintained at city and county level.  The 'rate of infection' (total infections divided by population multiplied by 100,000) for Shropshire is 233.2 as of yesterday.  Given that there are probably more sheep than people in my county, it might be expected that the rate is relatively low.  But the nearby cities of Manchester and Stoke-on-Trent at 267.0 and 275.6 are not significantly higher.  There are curious anomalies in the national picture – Oxford is 390.1 whereas Cambridge is 175.7 – but these can be left for geographers to explain at some later date.

The absence of sufficiently granular data on infection, and yet more critically, on transmission, is crippling the strategy of emerging from the lockdown, both as a public policy and as a guide to individual action. The Scottish public health expert Devi Sridhar said in the *Times* on Saturday that 'We have to listen to people who want to make an informed choice. The thing we are really missing and which I think could be transformative is local-level data. If people knew in their neighbourhood, whether in Glasgow or in Edinburgh, or if they are in a rural area, what the rates of transmission were, that would help.'[14]

At this point, the local is only possible if the right actions are taken at the national level. In particular the programme of test and trace has to be established before confidence can be invested in neighbourhood changes in behaviour.

The situation has been compounded by a wrong sense of national self-sufficiency. I have no competence at all in software development, but from extensive experience of senior management in complex higher education institutions, I do know one truth in this area. If the choice is between an off-the-shelf programme, which may lack full functionality but is already up and running, and a software product which may deliver every desired outcome but is yet to be written, then there is only one answer. This the more so when the new product would have to be produced at great speed, and failure would cost lives. The NHS has decided to write its own track and trace programme, rather than install the simpler and operational Apple / Google app. To no-one's surprise, it is already in trouble and missing deadlines. At this level, the bespoke solution is a mistake.

So we are left with a patchwork of responses to the national (English) policy of opening schools on June 1, and with companies in trouble because sections of their workforce have declined the invitation to go back to work (today Dyson reports such difficulties).

And for ourselves in our corner of rural Shropshire, the local remains micro for the foreseeable future.

**Friday, 22 May 2020. Fast Food!**

As part of the hesitant relaxation of the lockdown regulations, some of the fast-food chains have been experimenting this week with reopening their restaurants. McDonalds has unlocked thirty-three drive-through outlets in London and south-east England. Burger King, KFC and Nandos are said to be exploring the challenge of selling food whilst observing safety measures.

It's a glimpse of pleasure, the possibility of going out for a meal, whether or not these particular outlets are entirely to taste. But in my shielded lockdown, this is still a forbidden promise. So as last Friday, we must be content with reading about food, again relying on Henry Mayhew's *London Labour and the London Poor* of 1861.

After reviewing the markets for fruit, vegetables and fish, he turned his attention to the 'street-sellers of eatables and drinkables.' Once more he found a trade of enormous vigour and variety. He recognised that the demand was not necessarily for the most nutritious food. 'Men whose lives' he wrote '… are alternations of starvation and surfeit, love some easily-swallowed and comfortable food better than the most approved substantiality of a dinner table.' 'Easily-swallowed and comfortable food' is a perfect description of McDonalds and their rivals, however much their menus are deplored by nutritionists. And like the fast-food outlets of the modern day, it was essentially cheap, though far more varied. The following feast was delivered to the penny economy of the London poor in the mid-nineteenth century:

> The solids then, according to street estimation, consist of hot-eels, pickled whelks, oysters, sheep's trotters, pea-soup, fried fish, ham-sandwiches, hot green peas, kidney puddings, boiled meat puddings, beef, mutton, kidney, and eel pies, and baked potatoes. In each of these provisions the street-poor find a mid-day or mid-night meal.

> The pastry and confectionary which tempt the street caters are tarts of rhubarb, currant, gooseberry, cherry, apple, damson, cranberry, and (so called) mince pies; plum dough and plum-cake; lard, currant, almond and many other varieties of cakes, as well as of tarts; gingerbread-nuts and heart-cakes; Chelsea buns; muffins and crumpets; 'sweet stuff' includes the several kinds of rocks, sticks, lozenges, candies, and hard-bakes; the

medicinal confectionary of cough-drops and horehound; and, lastly, the more novel and aristocratic luxury of street-ices; and strawberry cream, at 1d. a glass, (in Greenwich Park).

The drinkables are tea, coffee, and cocoa; ginger-beer, lemonade, Persian sherbert, and some highly-coloured beverages which have no specific name, but are introduced to the public as 'cooling' drinks; hot elder cordial or wine; peppermint water; curds and whey; water (as at Hampstead); rice milk; and milk in the parks. (159)

That's Fast Food! Enjoy the sight.

**Tuesday, 26 May 2020. Lockdown Fortnight**.

All of us are looking towards the future, seeking to understand how we can draw lessons from the crisis and build upon them.

This is my modest proposal.

From 2021 there shall be a legally-defined annual **Lockdown Fortnight**.

The **Lockdown Fortnight** will fall in the last week of June and the first week of July. During that period, with exceptions listed below, every household will be required to observe full lockdown.

The **Lockdown Fortnight** will have four functions:

- It will serve as a memorial for the tens of thousands who lost their lives in the 2020 UK pandemic, and for the health workers who risked their lives in supporting the afflicted. Clapping is not enough;

- It will serve as an annual reminder that we need to be prepared for the recurrence of a global pandemic. Countries, such as South Korea, that had an active memory of the SARS epidemic, were much better prepared for Covid-19 than those without such a memory. During the lockdown the government will be required to make an annual statement of preparedness;

- It will create a pollution-free interval to remind us of what we have lost and have a right to regain;

- It will provide a planned break from the distractions of late modernity in order that individuals recollect themselves and the importance of their immediate social networks (and also do the necessary home repairs that otherwise are left undone across the year).

Because it will be planned and of a fixed duration, the disorder and stress of the current crisis can be largely avoided. Before the **Lockdown Fortnight**, supplies can be purchased, encounters with family and friends can take place, hairdressers can be visited. Any other practical difficulties can be borne for only fourteen days.

During **Lockdown Fortnight,** the only permitted movement will be such as can be conducted on foot, or on a bicycle (powered or otherwise). The only long-distance travel will be pilgrimages to the shrine of St Cummings the Martyr in Durham (and/or Barnard Castle).

The **Lockdown Fortnight** will be timed for the period of maximum daylight in Britain. It will incorporate the May Bank Holidays which will be moved forward for this purpose. The school summer half terms will be extended to two weeks and also be moved to this period.

The event is partly based on the Potters Fortnight, which was still functioning when I started work at Keele University. This was a relict of an industrial holiday, when the pot banks were shut for maintenance, and when, before the 1956 Clean Air Act, it was the only time when you could see across the city.

Exemptions to the **Lockdown Fortnight** will be:
- Health and related workers, though A and E business may again decline if the pubs are shut.
- Hospitality workers serving overseas visitors, who will be welcome to bring their currency to Britain and spend it at otherwise un-crowded hotels and bars (on production of a passport). This will represent a temporary but annual reminder of what we have lost with Brexit-inspired hostility to all foreigners. Britons travelling abroad will have to leave and return before and after the lockdown.

- Home-working will be permitted although no household will be allowed more than 10 hours video conferencing a week (5 work, 5 social). Wherever possible factories should arrange their annual maintenance for this period (see Potters Fortnight above).

- Sporting fixtures will be closed (the football season will be over), except Wimbledon on the grounds that it provides televised entertainment for those in lockdown.

The **Lockdown Fortnight** would be disruptive, but perhaps we have learnt this year that unbroken continuity of event and practice can oppose wisdom and self-knowledge. There may be a small net hit on the national GDP, but everything now is a balance between cost and benefit. See above for the gains.

The regulations will be rigorously policed by the Priti Patel Compassionate Enforcement Agency.

**Wednesday, 27 May 2020. Solitude and Loneliness.**

In my diary entry for April 8, I wrote that:

'Enforced isolation has an ambiguous effect on the two experiences. On the one hand it has made solitude a still more valued practice…On the other hand, it has made loneliness still more threatening.' I concluded that, 'Where the balance will finally be struck in these contrasting effects of isolation remains to be seen.'

Now the evidence is beginning to appear to answer this question. The crisis has stimulated the creation of a number of major research projects across the social sciences, which have been planned, funded and put into practice in a remarkably short space of time. One of the largest of these is the UCL Nuffield Covid-19 Social Study. This is a questionnaire-based survey which currently has 90,000 respondents. It is not a representative statistical sample of the population, but is large enough to generate substantial conclusions. The research team, led by Daisy Fancourt and Andrew Steptoe, have a sophisticated grasp of the concepts and categories of mental health, and are publishing weekly bulletins of their findings.

The 'Covid-19 Social Study Results Release 8', on 13 May, was particularly interesting.[15] Table 21 measured the incidence of 'Loneliness' on the industry-standard UCLA loneliness scale. This was unchanged across the lockdown period at around 5%. This is the same level that more cautious observers and social historians have projected across the entire post-war period, and about a quarter of the claims made in the Government's current loneliness strategy. Whatever else it is doing, the Covid-19 epidemic is not causing an epidemic of loneliness.

The team found that the condition was 'higher amongst younger adults, those living alone, those with lower household income levels, and those with an existing diagnosed mental health condition. They are also higher amongst women, people with children, and people living in urban areas.' It was correspondingly lower than 5% amongst those over 60, those with higher incomes, those without mental health conditions, and those living without children.

Table 27, by contrast, measured 'Activities missed during lockdown.' At the top of the table, not surprisingly, were 'Meeting up with family' and 'Meeting up with friends.' Half way down was 'Having time alone.' This was the solitude measure. The analysts broke down the emotion only by age. The younger the respondent, the more likely they were to be lacking time alone.

What is really interesting is the volume. Just over thirty per cent of the population were included in this category.

In other words, after an extended period of lockdown, solitude is being sought by six times as many people as are experiencing loneliness.

**Thursday, 28 May 2020. How the old are reacting to lockdown.**

Many of us are daily resisting the pressures to place us in a box called 'the elderly'. With the hard medical realities this is not easy. There is no question that as you pass into your sixties, then into successive decades, the risk of dying from Covid-19 shows a sharp linear increase. With matters of emotion and behaviour, on the other hand, there are grounds for resisting such age-determination. Nonetheless the social scientists now conducting detailed research into how people are coping with the crisis have a tendency to group their findings into age brackets.

Following yesterday's examination of solitude and loneliness revealed in the Nuffield / UCL Covid-19 Social Study, here are the findings more broadly about the interaction between age and experience (most of the data shows little change over the lockdown period). Whilst the figures are statistical facts (subject to the issues of category definition and sample quality), the explanations of cause and consequence are matters of judgement. So feel free to interpret these findings.[16] The two categories used are 60 and over, and 18-29 year-olds

The elderly are **more** likely than the young to:

- Comply with Government guidelines
- Show confidence in Government
- Have feeling of life satisfaction
- Have a sense of control of finances, family relationships, future plans
- Be concerned about meeting up with family
- Be concerned about going to cultural venues

The elderly are **less** likely than the young to:

- Experience depression and anxiety
- Employment stress
- Financial stress
- Have thoughts of death or self-harm
- To have been physically or psychologically abused

- Experience loneliness
- Be concerned about meeting up with age-group friends
- Be concerned about going out for a coffee, drink or meals
- Be concerned about having time alone

Some of the differences are smaller than others. There is virtually no variation by age in taking exercise or experiencing face to face contact.

Taken in the round, the striking feature is the lower incidence in the key categories of depression, anxiety, stress and loneliness amongst the older population, despite their much greater exposure to serious illness and death in the pandemic, and their greater likelihood of being locked down.

**Addendum.** Since writing this, *The Times* has today published results of a reworking by a team from Exeter, Manchester and Brunel Universities of a BBC survey of 2018 which questioned 46 thousand people from 237 countries about their experience of loneliness. As with the UCL evidence, the new research demonstrates that loneliness falls rather than increases with age.[17]

**Friday, 29 May 2020. Flowers!**

On May 19 I discussed the very high level of domestic gardens in this locked-down country. It is a practice with a long and much-described history. During the eighteenth and nineteenth centuries, specialised plant-rearing spread out from country houses to the mass of the population. By the beginning of the Victorian period there was a large industry of specialised nurseries, supported by a burgeoning literature which in its way supplied as much useful and timely information as Monty Don's Gardener's World. The 1803 edition of John Abercrombie's *Every Man His Own Gardener,* for instance, ran to 646 pages of monthly tasks, followed by another hundred pages cataloguing plants and then a thorough index.

Artisans joined together in associations which offered annual prizes. A survey of the industrial north in 1826, identified fifty auricular and polyanthus shows annually, together with twenty-seven tulip, nine ranunculi, nineteen pink and forty-eight carnation competitions.

I have on past Fridays, supplied stay-at-home and street food from Mayhew's *London Labour and the London Poor* of 1861. Here now, for those who like me still cannot get to garden centres, is the London trade in plants as sold in the Covent Garden and Farringdon wholesale markets. In this case the volumes are not the point; there were numerous nurseries on the edge of the capital also supplying a substantial market. But Mayhew's table does describe the basic tastes of Londoners in garden flowers:

| Primroses | 1,000 | Polyanthus | 1440 |
|---|---|---|---|
| Cowslips | 1200 | Daisies | 1400 |
| Wallflowers | 1920 | Candytufts | 1200 |
| Daffodils | 1200 | Violets | 2400 |

| | | | |
|---|---|---|---|
| Mignonette | 3800 | Stocks | 2880 |
| Pinks & Carnations | 800 | Lilies of the Valley | 288 |
| Pansies | 1080 | Lilies and Tulips | 280 |
| Balsam | 640 | Calceolarii | 600 |
| Musk Plants | 10560 | London Pride | 720 |
| Lupins | 1600 | China-Asters | 850 |
| Marigolds | 10560 | Dahlias | 160 |
| Heliotropes | 1280 | Michaelmas Daisies | 432 |

Most of these plants, in one form or another, are the staple of modern nurseries. It could be argued that gardens constitute one of the strongest links between the present and the past. In most other areas – diet, clothing, occupation, health, mortality, warfare, politics, religious belief (in particular) there is a void between our own times and a period even as recent as the Victorian era. But less so in the practice of growing flowers (and vegetables). John Clare (1793-1864), the great peasant poet of nature, owned half a dozen gardening books, including Abercrombie, and had a deep interest in the latest developments in horticulture. Were he to find his way into my garden, he would recognise many of the plants as versions of those that he grew, and would take an informed interest in later imports and introductions.

Above all Clare would understand why I spend so much time between my hedges, and what pleasure it gives me, with or without the current inconvenience.

**Monday, 1 June 2020. Unshielding.**

So a new month, the beginning of meteorological Summer, and the un-lockdown begins.

There is a special concession for the 'shielded', who, like me, have not been out of their house and garden since the last week of March (except for a medical check-up). My thanks to David Maughan Brown for pointing out the irritating misuse of the verb 'shield.' On the other hand, 'extremely vulnerable' would appear to be a phrase with meaning. Now we appear to be slightly less so.

The advice on the government website, updated yesterday, is as follows:

> People who are shielding remain vulnerable and should continue to take precautions but can now leave their home if they wish, as long as they are able to maintain strict social distancing. If you choose to spend time outdoors, this can be with members of your own household. If you live alone, you can spend time outdoors with one person from another household. Ideally, this should be the same person each time. If you do go out, you should take extra care to minimise contact with others by keeping 2 metres apart. This guidance will be kept under regular review.

This is of course just for England. Over the border, shielded or not, I can still be arrested if I drive more than five miles into Wales. The change is scarcely a revolution, but it has raised two profound concerns.

The first, which has been immanent throughout the crisis, is that the category of 'extremely vulnerable' covers a whole host of conditions. It places in the same situation those with only a marginal extra risk and those who should not be out of their home under any circumstances – Covid-19 is scarcely the only threat to those whose immune system is completely shot. Without detailed medical advice, which is generally not available (as I know myself), it is next to impossible to make the judgment call about going out of doors.

The second is that the change, and the broader relaxation for the unshielded, is driven more by political convenience or economic urgency than by medical reality. The 'R' rate is still perilously close to 1, and the improvements in the infection rate are at best patchy across England. No one was convinced when the Number 10 briefing came out with the tortured explanation that the country, whilst at level 4 of risk (where everyone should be in lockdown) is 'transitioning' towards level 3. Further, whilst London may be getting safer, the rest of the country is not necessarily doing so. Over the last ten days, the infection rate for Shropshire has *increased* from 233.2 to 253.2. The scores have also risen from 275.6 to 301.8 in nearby Stoke-on-Trent, and from 267.0 to 288.2 in Manchester.

As critics have pointed out, we need a much more nuanced approach to the vulnerable, and we need in place an effective track and trace system before we make any significant change to the lockdown. This was argued in an excellent article on Friday by Devi Sridhar, chair of global public health at Edinburgh University, and her colleague Yasmin Rafiei:

> What we suggest instead is a general strategy of suppression, where governments make a commitment to keeping daily new cases as low as possible through an active testing-and-tracing programme and real-time monitoring of transmission. At the same time, the government should advise those in 'shielded groups' about their individual risk, as well as provide them with data about transmission within their communities, and then leave these individuals to make an informed decision about how and when they would like to engage in society.[18]

Just so.

In the meantime, the changes are bringing some joy.

My five-year-old grandson was so pleased about the prospect of going back to school (four days a week from this Thursday) that during the hour-long family Zoom meeting on Sunday he insisted on wearing his school uniform throughout.

And I have a Finnish friend who tells me that in her country the relaxation of the two-metre rule has been welcomed, as it enables people to go back to their natural distancing of five metres.

**Tuesday, 2 June 2020. Solitary Confinement.**

Solitary confinement as a device for punishing and reforming prisoners was introduced in Britain in 1842, with the opening of Pentonville Prison. It was believed that if the prisoner was kept in isolation, visited only by the prison chaplain, he would meditate on his sinful life and over time re-build his moral being. It was recognised that the regime placed a dangerous stress on the mental health of the prisoners, who were subject to frequent inspections by medical staff to monitor their condition. From the outset the regime was criticised for its inhumanity, most notably by Charles Dickens, but the State clung to the device, albeit in a weakened form, throughout the nineteenth century.

Solitary, or separate, confinement finally disappeared between the wars, but it has lately returned not as a deliberate penal policy, but as a by-product of the growing crisis in the prison system. After 1990, a 'punitive turn' in the political discourse led to a doubling of the UK prison population. Following the financial crash of 2008-2009, the expanding numbers collided with a long-term retraction in public expenditure. Prisoners were locked in their cells because of infractions of the rules, or to protect them from other prisoners, or because there were insufficient staff to monitor them when they congregated with others.

On 30 May 2018, Her Majesty's Inspector of Prisons sent an 'Urgent Notification' to the Ministry of Justice on conditions in Exeter Prison. He was particularly concerned about the 'designated segregation unit' where 'there was a special cell which was completely bare and contained no furniture, toilet or bed. Prison and regional managers had approved the use of this cell for those judged to be so vulnerable as to be in need of constant observation, and it had been so used 17 times in the previous six months. There was supposedly an inflatable bed available for use in this cell, but it could not be found by staff during the inspection, and inspectors saw video of a prisoner on constant watch being located in the cell without it.' Other prisoners were discovered to be in self-imposed solitude: 'We found prisoners isolating themselves in their cells,' the inspectors reported of Birmingham prison, 'refusing to emerge because of their fear of violence.'

Everyone with an interest in prison reform knew that there were only two solutions to the crisis. Either the State invested an unfeasible amount of money in new prisons and more officers, or it significantly reduced the prison population in order to let the existing staff do their jobs properly. Caught between their traditional commitment to law and order, and their continuing embrace of austerity, successive Conservative governments were unable to commit to either course of action.

Then came Covid-19, and suddenly a pathway opened up. It would be possible to make a significant start on reducing prisoner numbers under the cover of the medical crisis. On April 4, just a fortnight after the lockdown began, the Ministry of Justice said that up to four thousand prisoners would be eligible for the end of custody temporary release (ECTR) scheme, in addition to freeing pregnant women and mothers of babies. The government also committed to releasing vulnerable prisoners, of whom there are about 1,200, through compassionate release.

But, as so often in the current crisis, the target was missed, and by such a margin as to suggest that the Ministry of Justice had completely lost its nerve. By the end of May, seventy-nine prisoners had been released under the ECTR scheme, together with about twenty-two pregnant women and mothers of babies.

Faced with the contagion spreading throughout the packed prisons, the regime imposed draconian lockdown conditions. With social distancing impossible in the overcrowded buildings, solitary confinement returned for more than twenty-three hours a day and all prison visits were suspended. On its own terms it worked. Deaths in prisons have been lower per head of population than had been feared. To date, twenty-two prisoners and nine staff are known to have died of Covid-19. But the psychological suffering has been immense. Since lockdown conditions were introduced on 23 March, there have been nearly as many suicides as medical deaths. Five suicides were reported in the last week of May[19], which compares with eighty over the whole of 2019, itself a figure which would have shocked the Victorians. As we debate the opening of schools, the Children's Commissioner has complained that children in prisons are only being allowed out of their cells for less than an hour a day, with destructive consequences for their education.

Amidst the coronavirus crisis, there are visions of building a better world. The prisons represent an inexcusable missed opportunity.

**Wednesday, 3 June 2020. Miscounting.**

The puzzle is why Matt Hancock thought he could get away with it.

Everyone knew that his claims for the level of coronavirus tests included multiple swab tests for the same individual, posted tests, pregnancy tests, driving tests, eyesight tests (the last two another form of double counting in Cummings land).

Yesterday he received a magisterial rebuke from the chair of the UK Statistical Authority, Sir David Norgrove:

> Statistics on testing perhaps serve two main purposes [lovely use of mock diffidence in the 'perhaps']. The first is to help us understand the epidemic, alongside the ONS survey, showing us how many people are infected, or not, and their relevant characteristics. The second is to help manage the test

programme... The way the data are analysed and presented currently gives them limited value for the first purpose. The aim seems to be to show the largest possible number of tests, even at the expense of understanding. It is also hard to believe the statistics work to support the testing programme itself. The statistics and analysis serve neither purpose well.[20]

Hancock and his fellow ministers seem to have forgotten that in earlier moments of virtue, previous governments have set up a series of bodies to keep them numerically honest – the UK Statistical Authority, the Office for Budget Responsibility, the Office for National Statistics (ONS), amongst others. These are staffed by competent, principled, number-crunchers who appear at times to take a positive pleasure in pointing out the official misuse of data.

It is not that Norgrove himself is new to the game. On 17 September 2017, he wrote to the then Foreign Secretary, one B. Johnson, about the Brexit Bus:

I am surprised and disappointed that you have chosen to repeat the figure of £350 million per week, in connection with the amount that might be available for extra public spending when we leave the European Union. This confuses gross and net contributions. It also assumes that payments currently made to the UK by the EU, including for example for the support of agriculture and scientific research, will not be paid by the UK government when we leave. It is a clear misuse of official statistics.[21]

The explanation of these repeat offences is not innumeracy, but rather a varying approach to the function of figures. In the case of the bus, Cummings had correctly calculated that it did not matter if the numbers were challenged. The mere act of discussing the claim, up to and including Norgrove's letter, anchored in the public mind that there was a substantial cost to EU membership.

Similarly, Hancock, desperately trying to defeat the coronavirus, seems to have calculated that the only way to mobilise action is to set and report huge targets, so as to create a boiling mass of activity amongst those charged with delivering outcomes. As anyone involved in running large organisations knows, there are more sober, disciplined, forms of project management, but Hancock seems entirely to lack the mental or practical resources to use these.

I came across this process when working on my book on solitude. As I reached the present, Theresa May published the world's first strategy for tackling loneliness. When I examined the figures she was using, I found that her claim that 20% of the population was lonely was contradicted by data in the same document from the ONS, which had calculated a figure of 5% (the same figure as lately reported by the Nuffield / UCL study discussed in the diary entry for May 27). But it was the larger headline figure that featured in the press release accompanying the strategy, and in the subsequent public discussion.

Statistical accuracy was subordinated to the need to dramatize a newly foregrounded social condition.

It was not difficult for a toiling researcher into the past to work this out. Historians can count when they need to. Guess what is the subject Sir David Norgrove's Oxford degree.

Look it up if you don't believe me.


**Thursday, 4 June 2020. Repentance.**

As an historian, I've had a nagging feeling that something is missing from the menu of responses to the Covid-19 pandemic.

Where is the National Day of Fasting?

In part, my sense of omission merely reflects the secular bubble in which I live. When I enquire, I find that the World Evangelical Alliance designated 29 March 2020, as a Global Day of Prayer and Fasting. 'The theme of the initiative', explained the Alliance, 'is 'Lord help!' Its impact on Britain passed me by. On the last Sunday of the month there must have been more people watching their diet because of their waistline than as a form of spiritual apology.

There is a long Christian tradition of responding to outbreaks of infectious disease in this way. Fast days were instituted in Britain during nine plague pandemics from 1563 to 1721. The theological rationale derived from the concept of special providences and divine judgments. Natural disasters were seen as God's punishment for the sins of a community, and required petitionary prayers and promises of repentance if they were to be averted.

During the nineteenth century the growing salience of medical explanations of infectious diseases marginalised this reaction. According to Phillip Williamson, an authority on this subject, a decisive moment came in 1853, when the Home Secretary Lord Palmerston publicly rejected proposals for a fast day against an outbreak of cholera, arguing that the solution lay in better sanitation and public health. Now the churches have left the centre of the stage. Whilst car showrooms have just been re-opened, religious buildings, together with public houses, remain closed for at least another two months.

My view of the marginal role of the Church of England was increased by its response to the Flight out of London. The Bishop of Manchester, David Walker, was reported as threatening to sever relations between church and state. 'Unless very soon we see clear repentance,' he said, 'including the sacking of Cummings, I no longer know how we can trust what ministers say for @churchofengland to work together with them on the pandemic.'[22] I don't know why the church of Cranmer and the Prayer Book is now reduced to a twitter hashtag, nor can I understand why any bishop should suppose that Johnson is going to repent of anything. It's like asking him to take up ballet dancing or synchronised swimming; it's just not something he has ever done, knows how to do, would ever want to do.

And yet. As a Christian, the Bishop had a perfect right to speak of repentance. It is central to the spiritual rule book of his calling. There are values, and a structure of faith, forgiveness and redemption to cope with their inevitable infraction in a fallen world. For all the political excitement, Cummings encountered a basic moral dilemma. Unlike his employer, he is, by report, a deeply committed family man. When the virus entered his home, he was faced with a choice between the wellbeing of his immediate social unit, and that of society more broadly. His panicked solution may have been the wrong one, but he is scarcely the first to make such an error.

In the event, repentance would have been not only morally but also politically the better course of action. If in the Number 10 rose garden Cummings had explained his actions and then asked for forgiveness for a mistaken judgment, most of the subsequent damage to his government, and, more importantly, to the public's trust in the state, would have been avoided.

We still have a shared moral discourse, the remains, in part, of a Christian heritage. It is worth reinforcing.

**Friday, 5 June 2020.  Aaron's Walnut Tree.**

Back in early April, I wrote a piece lamenting my barren walnut tree.

A metre-long stick had arrived from a garden centre, and despite the most careful planting, had refused utterly to grow.  All around it, Spring burst into life.  The forsythias, lilacs and wisteria bloomed, the fruit trees blossomed, the daffodils, tulips and roses flowered, the lawn grew, even the adjacent beech hedge, always the last to move, had become a shiny green wall.  Still, every morning when I went glumly to inspect its corner of the garden, nothing had moved.  Then one day, a definite swelling of the buds, and, earlier this week, finally shoots and leaves (*pace* Lynne Truss).

Readers will recall the Biblical story of Aaron's rod during the plagues of Egypt:

> Moses went into the tabernacle of witness; and, behold, the rod of Aaron for the house of Levi was budded, and brought forth buds, and bloomed blossoms, and yielded almonds. (Numbers 17: 8).

Thus with my rod.  'Almonds' may have been a translation error for walnuts.  At a time when rational, quantifiable evidence about our present circumstances and future prospects is in such short supply (see 'Miscounting' on June 2) foundation myths, metaphors, parables, have a particular attraction.  Insight and comfort can be afforded by such verbal constructions, particularly when they are enshrined in authoritative documents.

So what does my walnut tree *mean*?

Clearly there are opposing interpretations. On the positive side, the tree represents the triumph of persistence over doubt (my life-partner was heard to pass discouraging comments about the entire enterprise of walnut trees during the barren weeks). It represents the unshakeable rhythms of nature in the face of man-made misfortune. It represents an investment in the future, however uncertain our present times.

On the negative side, look more closely at Aaron's achievement. His rod produced blossom and fruit. Mine has grown only leaves, late in the season. No walnuts until at least next year, no serious crop for some years beyond that. We're not there yet. So also, most probably, with defeating Covid-19. Even in those countries which appear to have suppressed death and infection, there is no security that the plague will not return, whether as a small upturn or a full-blown second wave. It will be around next Spring, and could well be a permanent presence in all the future that we can see.

But that is the point of such stories. They can contain opposing meanings. As also, when it comes to it, most current statements from the Government.

**Monday, 8 June 2020.  Numbering the days.**

Besides his weekly column in the *Observer*, and sundry research activities at Cambridge, my friend and former colleague John Naughton is maintaining a daily blog, Memex1.1, to which is attached a short oral diary.  Both are well worth attention.  And the oral diary begins with a shock.  Yesterday: 'Sunday June 7.  Day Seventy-eight.'

Seventy-eight?!  If asked I would say perhaps a month since the lockdown began.  Likewise with this diary.  About twenty since the site was established.   But I count back and find that this is my fiftieth piece (unlike John I don't write at weekends).

Time has collapsed.  We have only a distant sense of it passing.  This is the immediate consequence of erasing our diaries when Johnson confined us to our homes.   In my case, out went working trips to Cambridge and London and Ireland, a short holiday on the West Coast of Scotland, and various visits, planned and not-yet planned, to and from family and friends.  Events to embed in the memory the succession of days and weeks.

In response to this common experience, it has been reported that increasing numbers of people have been occupying their spare hours by anchoring their present in the history of their own families.  Some years ago, on behalf of the OU History Department, I manned a stall in the 'Who Do You Think You Are' show at London's Olympia, where tens of thousands of people paid £22 a head to wander past stalls helping them with their genealogies. Next to my table was 'Deceased.Com', a database of tombstones, which remains a favourite electronic address. My pitch was that if you want to understand what it means to have a family tree, you need to study some history of those times. I didn't get as many customers as my neighbour.

Now I too have paid my shilling to Ancestry.co.uk, the largest of many online resources for this activity. In my filing cabinet are the paper records assembled by my parents at a time when such research meant physically visiting archives and buying copies of birth, death and marriage certificates. I have long meant to put these in electronic order for the sake of my children and those that come after them.

Besides providing a template to set out the family tree, the value of the resource, I have discovered, is not the now digitised census records, which only provide one line of information and for the most part had already been visited by my parents. Rather it is the access it provides to the work of other amateur genealogists. Each of my forebears, going back to the late eighteenth century, also feature in up to a dozen other family trees which have already been industriously assembled. The past is now a networked world. All I have to do is call up one of these lists, and most of my work is done.

I have filled out the detail of a story I already knew. That my parents were the first in their families to break out of the ranks of the labouring classes. That amongst their forebears were a scattering of skilled workers – a postman, a policeman, an overman miner - but at the beginning of the nineteenth century, most were just farm labourers. In what way their wives and daughters contributed to their family economies is almost never recorded.

Above all, across the six generations or so that can be traced, my family is utterly English. There is some movement out of a common point of departure in Sussex to the new employment opportunities in the capital and the north Midlands, but no hint of a connection even with Wales and Scotland, let alone further afield. Marriages were contracted by people of the same social standing, usually in nearby villages and towns.

Until, that is, my children's generation. My brother and I, who went so far as to take wives with a Scottish heritage, have sons- and daughters-in-law from Japan, France, Ireland, and Iran by way of the United States. These alliances are for the most part the consequence of higher education and attendant gap years, experiences wholly denied my forebears.

Just as my family tree largely conforms to what I know to be the broader demographic transition in Britain, with an evolution from large Victorian families to the tight two and three-child units of the twentieth century, so also this sudden internationalisation of the Vincent tribe may well be the common experience of the generation born in the closing decades of the last century.

If so, it will do much to explain why the young are so unattracted by the petty nationalism of Brexit, whilst the old cling to the world contained in the carefully-assembled family tress.

## Tuesday, 9 June 2020.   Here and not here.

Too many of the accounts of our present circumstance draw a hard line between what we are doing and not doing.  We are inside our houses not out in public spaces.  We are permitted to share the company of certain people and kept apart from all others.  But it is the essence of our human condition that we are not confined to such binary choices.

We have imaginations, the capacity to create and inhabit worlds apart from the actual present.  We all know this.  In better times, it is how we deal with that reality, offering us escape, solace, explanation.  In the lockdown, the media are full of devices for getting us to places that we are currently forbidden to enter.  Books are recommended that will expose us to the holiday locations we might have visited this year (headline in yesterday's *Guardian*: '10 of the best Latin American novels – that will take you there.') Television programmes, magazines and digital outlets let us wander through the gardens and art galleries that are now closed.  Food and sport journalists recycle stories that can at least remind us of pleasures denied.  And the imagination for its own sake, more important than ever, is succoured by print and electronic media.

My wife and I, inveterate readers and consumers of film and theatre, are at home in these parallel universes. Nonetheless we grieve the physical absence of our grandchildren, going through changes which we can only witness in weekly Zoom meetings. Unless Johnson and company sort out the mess their incompetence has compounded, we will miss the first sight of a new grand-daughter in a couple of months. Yet even this basic dichotomy of presence and absence can be bridged.

On Sunday we tuned into our weekly family get-together to find that my London-based elder daughter, her partner and her five and eight-year old children, had something to show us. For some weeks past they had been secretly building a scale model of the house and garden of the parents and grandparents they could no longer visit.

Everything that mattered had been re-constructed. The black and white house with cotton-wool smoke coming out of its chimney. The car (a sportier model than our ageing Volvo) in the drive behind the gate. In the garden were flowers (miniature versions of the actual flowers now blooming), fruit trees, a vegetable plot, a greenhouse, a paddling pool, a swing, a sandpit with real sand, two wigwams. There was even a miniature wheelie-bin which the children help me fill when they are staying. Around the perimeter was the River Severn, now alarmingly close to the property, but a reminder of its existence in our country life. *Rus in Urbis* if ever there was.

They still want to come and see us. We for our part felt still more strongly the pain of their absence. But nevertheless, it was such a joyful achievement, such a demonstration of how the creative spirit can bridge the gap between what is and what is not in our locked down world.

**Wednesday, 10 June 2020.  Staying alive.**

If we are to learn the right lessons from the pandemic, it is crucial that we are careful with the meaning of words.

Monday's *Guardian* carried a disturbing headline: 'Epidemic of Loneliness'.[23]  The phrase was much deployed in the public debate about loneliness in the years leading up to the present crisis.  It had two sets of meanings.

The first was a general metaphor.  It just meant that loneliness was a large and negative event.  If we say that someone received an 'avalanche of complaints' we do not mean literally that they were covered in a mountain of rocks, just that they experienced a lot of trouble.

The second was more serious.  It was at the centre of an attempt to medicalise a social condition, linking the experience to other crises such as smoking and obesity.  By this means the effect was dramatized, and campaigners hoped to appropriate longstanding concerns with major public health issues.

Critics were concerned about this use of language. Whatever it is, loneliness cannot be caught by someone breathing on you. It seemed an inappropriate descriptor before the present crisis, and now it would appear indefensible.

But in the *Guardian* article, no less an authority than Professor Martin Marshall, President of the Royal College of General Practitioners, was cited as saying: 'The Covid-19 pandemic is also creating an epidemic of loneliness, not just for older people, and sadly there are some people who will fall through the net.'

The story was actually about the tragic discovery of individuals who had died alone, either of Covid-19 or of another condition for which in their lockdown they had failed to seek treatment. A pathologist cheerfully described them as 'decomps', 'people found dead at home after not being heard from for a couple of weeks.'

There are many ways in which ill health can be exacerbated by the experience of enforced and unwelcome solitude. It is known that those living alone are less likely to seek medical assistance, even in normal times. Associated forms of depression, or melancholy as it was once termed, can lower immune systems and increase vulnerability to a range of serious illnesses. Conversely, various kinds of disability can have the effect of turning chosen solitude into an imprisoning loneliness.

It might be expected that these interactions will increase the incidence and danger of loneliness in the present crisis, although there remains little quantitative evidence that this is happening on a significant scale. The Office for National Statistics yesterday published its latest report on the experience of coronavirus in which it confirmed that the numbers 'feeling lonely often / always' in the lockdown remained at 5%. As in earlier surveys, the old seemed more resistant to this condition than the young.[24]

With the total UK death rate now passing sixty thousand, lives will have been lost in every kind of social setting. The evidence so far suggests that locked-down interiors, whether care homes or private residences, present the greater risk. A recent Wall Street Journal analysis of the US population found that the virus had spread more widely in the most crowded households, irrespective of population density.[25]

When the final calculations are made, it is likely that those dying alone because they are alone will be far exceeded by those dying in company because they are in company. Solitude has its compensations, and staying alive may be one of them.

**Thursday, 11 June 2020.   Free and not free.**

In the lockdown, I have tried to be sensible. I have maintained my hours of work despite the absence of timetabled commitments. I have written diary entries. I have resisted drinking all of our not very capacious wine cellar. My one besetting sin has been newspapers. Deprived of hard copy I have set up online feeds from the *Guardian*, *The Times* (for an alternative view), the *Financial Times* (for hard evidence) and the *New York Times* (for the rest of the world). Unlimited words, limitless time consumed.

Much of the knowledge thus gained has not illuminated my life. Today I learn that there is a looming shortage of marmite (caused by a decline in beer brewing, who knew), and mounting anxiety about the closure of public lavatories.

Occasionally, however, there is a story that seems to encapsulate all that is now going wrong. Yesterday, an article headlined: 'Lockdown eased to allow lonely to meet another household.' It was part of the good news narrative that Johnson is trying to promote. Day by day things are getting better. In every other regard it brings no comfort.

First, there is the nominative disarray I discussed yesterday; the confusion in this case between those living alone, and those who are lonely. A third of UK households are occupied by one person. Some of those are lonely; most are not. All of them with grandchildren are probably missing them.

Second, there is the small print. Everyone can go and see their grandchildren except those in lockdown, which includes all those over seventy. My wife and I, as it happens, are bang on the demographic average for the birth of our first grandchild (we were 63). But now we have more years and more grandchildren. Under the new regulations, we are too old to see them. It's as if the Government had announced with a fanfare that everyone was now free to play football, except those under thirty.

Third, there is the surrounding argument. The fifth paragraph of the same article reads: 'However, the government's claim to have made the right decisions at the right time on the pandemic was dealt a severe blow when one of the architects of lockdown said Britain's death toll could have been halved by imposing it a week earlier.' What has collapsed in the last few weeks is not the infection rate but public trust in the entire official management of the crisis.

Every recent decision, whether about schools, testing, opening shops, allowing grandparents out of the house, quarantining international arrivals, has immediately been met by criticism, counter-argument and in some cases legal action. The point is not so much the rights and Priti Patels of each issue, rather the belief that everyone is free to advance their own view and can find an 'expert' somewhere to back them up. Deference towards politicians, and towards those who advise them, has disappeared. In the early days there was a tendency to accept what we were told in the grave surroundings of No. 10. We needed to believe that those with power were doing the right thing, and anyway it was difficult for amateurs fully to understand the science and the projections. That comfort is no longer available.

The largest argument, referred to by the *Times* journalist, is about what was not done in February and March and how many tens of thousands of people died as a result. The Government's repeated hope that this kind of retrospective analysis could be left to a post-pandemic enquiry is in vain.

We are all historians now. And that is a measure of the trouble we are in.

**Friday, 12 June 2020. London. Gloomy, close and stale.**

The most famous literary description of lockdown is to be found at the beginning of chapter 3 of Dickens' *Little Dorrit*. Arthur Clennam, a middle-aged businessman, has returned to London from Marseilles to close down his late father's estate. He is gazing out of the window of a coffee shop, summoning the courage to visit his old family home:

> It was a Sunday evening in London, gloomy, close, and stale. Maddening church bells of all degrees of dissonance, sharp and flat, cracked and clear, fast and slow, made the brick and mortar echoes hideous. Melancholy streets, in a penitential garb of soot, steeped the souls of the people who were condemned to look out of windows, in dire despondency. In every thoroughfare, up almost every alley, and down almost every turning, some doleful bell was throbbing, jerking, tolling, as if the Plague were in the city and the dead-carts were going round. Everything was bolted and barred that could by possibility furnish relief to an overworked people. No pictures, no unfamiliar animals, no rare plants or flowers, no natural or

artificial wonders of the ancient world – all *taboo* with that enlightened strictness, that the ugly South Sea gods in the British Museum might have supposed themselves at home again. Nothing to see but streets, streets, streets. Nothing to breathe but streets, streets, streets. Nothing to change the brooding mind, or raise it up. Nothing for the spent toiler to do but to compare the monotony of his six days, think what a weary life he led, and make the best of it – or the worst, according to the probabilities.[26]

It should be noted that this was the perspective of a particular section of British society. That symbol of a more secular sabbath, the Sunday newspaper, had recently been invented – *Lloyd's Weekly Newspaper* in 1842, the *News of the World* in 1843, *Reynolds' News* in 1850. At the time that Dickens was writing, Henry Mayhew, whose surveys of food and flowers we have cited in earlier Friday diaries, was walking the London streets collecting material on the noisy world of the costermongers, which continued the week round.

Nonetheless it was a vivid account of the experience of the evangelical middle class of the time. As with the current lockdown, it was an essentially man-made event. In this case it replicated the response to a pandemic without the medical justification. And whilst the full observance of a day of church services and Bible reading was confined to a religious sect, their influence on the political process was such that they were able to impose their restrictions on the rest of society. What most annoyed Dickens was their success in closing the widening range of improving entertainments which had opened in the capital and elsewhere during the second quarter of the nineteenth century. Working a six-day week for the most part, Sunday was the only time that the bulk of the London workforce could take their families to visit attractions which were both entertaining and instructive. They deserved and would benefit morally from the opening of the British Museum and other venues.

In normal times, museums and galleries are now open on Sundays as are a host of more profane entertainments. But we continue to experience the Sabbatarian legacy, with larger shops closed before 10 and after 4 in order that we or their staff might attend a church service. As we begin to explore a return to a post-pandemic world, Sunday opening has become one of the many issues that were described in yesterday's diary, where Government proposals are provoking argument rather than consent. In order to boost the retail sector which has been so badly hit, a Minister has suggested that the Sunday trading laws be suspended for a year. The British Chambers of Commerce is in favour of the change, but Labour argues that it would favour supermarkets over the smaller shopkeepers, as does the chief executive of the Association of Convenience Stores. USDAW, the shopworkers' trade union, protests that 'the last thing the retail industry needs is longer trading hours, there is no economic case for this and it will put extra pressure on the retail workers who have worked so hard throughout this crisis.' Then there are associated disputes about whether any relaxation of social contact should be allowed, and if so, what distance should be kept between people.

We need a Dickens fully to describe the times we are living through. And we need a basis for agreeing change, without setting interest against interest, class against class.

**Monday, 15 June 2020. Prince Philip again**.

This is the same story told by David Maughan Brown on June 10, from the same perspective.

I too was a Deputy Vice Chancellor when the Royals came to my university. I too ended up spending time with the Duke of Edinburgh (we both occupied, after all, the same rung in our organisations).

There was some flummery. Ladies in Waiting really exist, and are indeed well-dressed women who stand around waiting to be useful. One of them told me that the Queen was excited about the bus we had hired to transport her from one side of the campus to the other, because she had never in her life travelled on one. Perhaps Ladies in Waiting have a hidden sense of humour. I was gravely instructed in how to ask the Queen if she wanted to use the loo. Unfortunately I have now forgotten the exact form of words, but as she and I are now in perpetual lockdown, the occasion is unlikely to arise in the future.

After an opening ceremony, we divided our forces. The Vice Chancellor, Janet Finch, took the Queen to see some new buildings, and

I escorted Prince Philip to inspect a display of work by staff. He treated them as equals, interrogating the meaning of graphs, demanding to know the evidence for their conclusions. Aggressive, but in the way that academics are to each other.

Then I walked him down to our main hall. 'Has the campus ever been planned?' he asked me. I told him not initially, but a master-plan was developed in 1962. 'Are its results showing yet?' he asked (this was now four decades later). Fair question if you know the Keele campus.

We entered the hall, in which were gathered a hundred local dignitaries, standing around in groups of ten. We had arrived before the Queen, but Philip suggested we tour the room without her. I had a crib sheet and introduced him to each individual in turn. 'This is Mr. Blenkinsop of Allied Ball Bearings, this is Mr. Greatbach of the Greatbach Pottery …'. When we got to the end, the Queen appeared, and Philip said he would show her round, leaving the crib sheet with me. He introduced the Queen to Mr. Blenkinsop and every subsequent person, without missing a name. I was astonished at this feat of memory in a man who was by then into his seventies. 'How did you do that?' I asked him. 'Ties' he said. 'I remember each tie and the name and activity attached to it.'

I think now, as I thought then, that this was a display of professional competence of a high order. A little like that shown by nurses and doctors and social workers and teachers as they go about their business in the coronavirus crisis. Quite unlike that displayed by our political leaders, the product of a democratic system which we thought was a better form of government than royalty.

And I say that as a life-long republican.

Dickens and Sundays, note 1.

The *Guardian*, as it happened, ran a piece by Peter Fiennes the day after mine, on Dickens and Little Dorrit and the lockdown. It broadened out into a discussion of his way of life at the time, with the beginning of his public readings, a walking tour of the Lake District, his constant pacing of the London streets. 'Dickens of 1857', it concludes, 'would have had trouble enduring the lockdown.'

Dickens and Sundays, note 2.

It was reported in *The Times* on Saturday that Boris Johnson 'is facing a cabinet backlash over plans to suspend Sunday trading laws after three ministers, including the chief whip, warned against it.' Another of those three was the nanny-raised Jacob Rees-Mogg, in his capacity as Leader of the House of Commons.

**Tuesday, 16 June 2020.  Bedtime Stories.**

There are three ways of identifying the impact of the coronavirus:

- Pre-existing problems exposed by the pandemic
- Pre-existing problems exacerbated by the pandemic
- Pre-existing problems which the response to the pandemic failed to fix

In the UK, the prison system sits under all three headings.

Her Majesty's Inspector of Prisons has just published a report on three women's prisons, Bronzefield, Eastwood Park and Foston Hall.[27]  It focusses on actions being taken to protect the prisoners from infection. 'We found', reported the inspector, 'that self-harm had increased from the high levels seen prior to the restrictions being implemented.'

In these prisons, and across the system, levels of self-harm, up to and including suicide, were already at an unacceptable level, and would have remained so without the impact of Covid-19.

As I discussed in my diary entry a fortnight ago, the key failure of the Ministry of Justice was not implementing a plan to reduce the size of the prison population, particularly those serving short sentences which would have included many women.  This is confirmed by the new report:

The two early release schemes in operation had been largely ineffective in reducing the population. Despite the process taking up significant amounts of management time, only six prisoners had been released. This was a failure of national planning.

Instead, the women prisoners were subject to a host of restrictions to protect them from the virus. They were kept in their cells for all but an hour in two of the prisons and half an hour in a third. Face-to-face education ceased, although it was noted that 'some limited one-to-one teaching support was given at cell doors.' Schoolteachers and university lecturers don't know what they are worrying about. All family visits were suspended, which 'had a particularly acute impact within the women's estate.'

Above all, in the case of prisoners 'with very high levels of need', who had been 'previously receiving significant structured support from a range of agencies', the services 'had stopped or been drastically curtailed at all three sites, creating a risk that these prisoners' welfare could seriously deteriorate.' The consequence was felt in all three prisons: 'Self-harm had risen since the start of the restrictions at Bronzefield and Foston Hall. The number of incidents was beginning to reduce at Foston Hall in May but remained above the level seen before the restricted regime was implemented.'

The report paints a picture of staff doing their best in impossible circumstances, working around obstacles as best they could, and in some cases finding new ways of alleviating the stress on prisoners. The inmates had phones which they could use in limited circumstances. At one of the prisons these were employed to help compensate for the absence of family visits.

'At Eastwood Park', the inspector reported, 'managers had established a scheme where prisoners could read a bedtime story to their children each evening.'

Makes you weep.

**Wednesday, 17 June 2020. Permanence and Planning.**

The clue is in the qualifier. The heads of civil service departments in the UK are called 'Permanent Secretaries.' They are in charge of bodies of public employees whose tenure is independent of changes in the political complexion of government.

Two of the most senior members of this cadre, Tom Scholar, Permanent Secretary at the Treasury, and Alex Chisholm, Permanent Secretary at the all-powerful Cabinet Office and formerly at the Department for Business, Energy and Industrial Strategy, were interviewed on Monday of this week by the Parliamentary Public Accounts Committee (PAC) on their preparations for a pandemic.

Dominic Cummings said earlier this year that he wanted to recruit to the civil service 'some true wild cards, artists, people who never went to university and fought their way out of an appalling hell hole.' Scholar, the son of a knighted civil servant, fought his way out of the hell hole that was Dulwich College public school and Trinity Hall, Cambridge; Chisholm struggled up from Downside public school and a degree (in history) from Merton College, Oxford. They are in charge of sections of a civil service that has so far resisted attempts to politicise its membership.

The question is, what are the demonstrable gains from this oasis of institutional stability? Over the last three years, there has been an obvious need for a locus of stable management of the affairs of a troubled state. There have been three Chancellors of the Exchequer since 2016, one of whom, Philip Hammond, ended up having the whip withdrawn and retiring from Parliament. The Department for Business has also had three heads, and the Cabinet Office, the central unit for co-ordinating the government machine, no less than five in four years.

What the PAC wanted to know, was whether the Permanent Secretaries had formed plans for the management of the economy during a pandemic, following the Cygnus simulation exercise in October 2016, which had modelled a scenario in which 50% of the population was infected by a flu-like virus.

It had cause to suppose that the civil service had a particular responsibility for this kind of planning. The politicians were living day-to-day through the prolonged crisis set in motion by the Brexit referendum in June 2016. Ideological commitment overwhelmed long-term thinking. Ministers ate, drank and dreamed of the pursuit of negotiating deadlines. Cohorts of civil servants were taken from their normal duties to work with Brussels, but compared to their political masters, there remained wide areas of the government machine with the time and space to engage with medium and long-term futures.

The answer to the Committee's question was that there had been no planning for the economic impact of a pandemic. The measures taken once the real thing arrived were made up as the crisis deepened. The chair of the PAC pronounced herself 'quite dumbstruck' by this omission. 'Could you do us a follow-up note on the lack of economic planning for the pandemic?' she said. Chisholm confirmed that he would.

Countries which have done best in this crisis have been characterised not by their particular political complexion, but rather by their capacity to have in place and then fine-tune long-term plans for crisis management.

When the history of the UK's lamentable performance is written, it will not be just the politicians who are in the firing line.

**Thursday, 18 June 2022.  Intrinsic and Extrinsic.**

I recently had a discussion with a Dean at a university I am reviewing about intrinsic versus extrinsic reward.

She was arguing that in her faculty, staff found such satisfaction in their teaching and research that external validation was not important.

There is a truth in this view.  One of the great privileges of a career in higher education is that it is full of people who found a passion in life, and a form of employment that enabled them to pursue it.  Most academic staff pay little attention to the exact length of a working week, or indeed very often to their maximum holiday entitlement.  They work long hours because of their commitment to the progress of their students, and their desire to push back the boundaries of knowledge in their chosen field.  A smart or lucky institution will align the enthusiasm of staff with the interests of the organisation without imposing a formal regime of mission statements and coercive strategies.

And yet, from a PhD onwards, every move is subject to peer review.  Projects are initiated and completed as part of a conversation with fellow researchers, and their response will range from the supportive to the terminally destructive.  And however much an academic's labour is driven by personal enthusiasm, mortgages have to be paid.  Everyone in the trade has either experienced or witnessed the colossal demotivation a failed or delayed promotion can cause.

There is a contrast with the passions that get you out of bed in this lockdown world. Where there is no remunerative labour to undertake, what is the purpose of the day's activities?

Take for instance gardening. My village takes part in a national open gardens scheme, where on a given summer Sunday, people can visit private gardens for a small fee which this year is donated to a nursing charity. We have always refused absolutely to take part, however worthy the cause. This is partly because in normal years we lack the time to arrive at a point of weedless perfection, but more fundamentally because what we grow is no-one else's business. We are happy to show it to visiting family and friends, but our pleasure in our achievement is, in management speak, entirely intrinsic. Even between the two of us, each has their own programme of work, and we choose whether to tell the other what we are doing and how well it is going.

There are, of course, those who treat gardening, or some other recreation, as a form of work or competition. Targets are set, outcomes are measured. A brother-in-law runs every Sunday, recording his performance on an app that allows him to compare his times with runners of the same age around the world. Gardeners have been forming themselves into societies and awarding prizes for fruit and vegetables for more than two centuries in Britain.

It is, nonetheless, one of the reasons why the pandemic lockdown has been bearable for those lucky enough not to be struggling with working and child-teaching at home. We have always pursued our recreations for our own satisfaction, and it is a minor matter that, in my case, the best of my garden will be over this year before anyone else gets to see it.

That said, were I to win a prize for my sweet peas at the Shrewsbury Flower Show, all my promotions and all my books would be set at nought.

**Friday, 19 June 2020.  Better Known.**

I have just recorded a contribution to 'Better Known', a podcast series in which the speaker recommends six people, places, objects, stories, experiences and ideas that should be better known.[28]

It was a challenging task.  Most of us carry in our heads our eight Desert Island Disks, revising them from time to time in the hope that one day we will be asked to make them public.  The brief for 'Better Known' was much wider, and coming in the middle of an avalanche of work, there was little time to ponder upon it.  I came up with five entries, and spent three quarters of an hour talking about them.

For places:

- Montaigne's Tower, in south west France.  The man himself, the first modern explorer of how an individual should live, is well enough known, but his tower, which we visit whenever we are in the Dordogne, is largely neglected by French visitors. Montaigne spent his days in one tower at the corner of a large courtyard, his wife in another (now demolished), and his mother in the main house (now rebuilt), a perfect arrangement for any family.

- St Peter's Church Melverley. A rare, perfectly preserved timber-frame church, constructed out of local oak in around 1405, every beam pegged to another without any fixtures, standing on a bluff with the River Vyrnwy swirling around it.

- The Stiperstones. A long rocky ridge, in sight of my house, with the remains of Britain's largest lead mine at its base, and long views across the Welsh Marches.

For objects

- Caroline Testout climbing rose. Named for a late-nineteenth-century French couturier, a splendidly blousy pink rose, with a faint scent. I have one growing over my front door, and any house would be improved by it.

For writings:

- Mayhew's London *Labour and the London Poor*, sometimes cited in these diaries

- The poetry of John Clare, the great peasant poet of the first half of the nineteenth century, the finest observer of the natural world this country has ever produced.

It is in some ways a counterproductive undertaking. The last thing I want is coach loads of tourists at Melverley, or Everest-like queues to ascend the Stiperstones. The writings are more secure. There will be a limit to the number willing to tackle the two million words in Mayhew's volumes, and Clare, quite simply, really should be better known, although his reputation is building, not least thanks to a recent biography by Jonathan Bate. Here is an evocative poem written in his asylum years on the topic of solitude, to which he returned frequently over his life:

> There is a charm in Solitude that cheers
> A feeling that the world knows nothing of
> A green delight the wounded mind endears
> After the hustling world is broken off
> Whose whole delight was crime at good to scoff
> Green solitude his prison pleasure yields
> The bitch fox heeds him not – birds seem to laugh
> He lives the Crusoe of his lonely fields

**Monday, 22 June 2020.  Reading and Solitude.**

The *London Review of Books* (LRB) sends me a digital advertisement: 'Improve Your Solitude. Engage with the world's best thinkers and writers, with Europe's largest literary magazine.'

In a practical sense the advert is wasted on me. I have been a subscriber since the happy day ten years ago when I retired from university management and swapped my subscription to the *Time Higher Education Supplement* for the LRB in the mistaken assumption that I would now have more time for reading books and reviews.

Since then, the LRB has been a mixed blessing. Most issues contain a piece that interests and informs, but not all. A great literary magazine makes you think you are a little smarter, a little better-read than you actually are. The LRB generally has the reverse effect.

Nonetheless its advert contained a basic truth. For those of us who are locked down without other responsibilities, there ought to be more time for reading. At the least it gives us a chance to replenish the shelves that we want to display behind our heads in ZOOM meetings (the prize for the politician for what clearly is the least-read, and smallest, background bookshelf goes to Iain Duncan Smith. No surprise there).

Books occupy empty hours. But they have never simply been the handmaiden of solitude. It took centuries after the invention of printing for the act of reading silently to yourself to become the standard practice. In the eighteenth century, women in particular read to each other as they worked at a household task, and one in a family read to the rest in the evenings. Increasing literacy and falling book prices in the Victorian era promoted private consumption of the printed word, but demand for books still outstripped the capacity to own them individually, and amongst the newly literate, children read to their less-educated parents and their parents to grandparents. In crowded households with unheated and unlit bedrooms, those who did read to themselves frequently had to do so amidst company. Books were less often the solace of complete isolation, and more the facilitator of abstracted solitude, the practice of withdrawing from others whilst still physically in their midst.

It is too early to take a final view of reading in the lockdown. Bookshops were shut until last week in the UK, book launches cancelled (including my own), as were book festivals. My wife and I were at the Dalkey Literary Festival in Dublin this time last year and had planned a return visit. On the other hand, the online trade was already well-established, and unlike food, and (for the most part) clothing, it is always possible to re-use what was purchased years ago. It is reported that sales of thrillers have risen, and also books about pandemics. My expectation is that the overall change will not be that great. For every household with more time on its hands, there will be several more in which the adults at least have lost every minute of solitary recreation.

In my case, where not much has altered in my daily round, the problem is as it always has been, the reluctance to take a book off the shelf after an entire day at my desk, reading and writing words. I'd sooner dig my garden.

**Add Mss (1). 16 June. Bedtime Stories.** No bedtime stories at Styal Women's Prison, where the stillbirth of a baby to a prisoner has been reported, the second in nine months. The medical staff failed to diagnose the pregnancy, and gave the prisoner paracetamol when she complained of severe stomach pains. Only twenty-three women across the system have been released under the scheme for pregnant prisoners and new mothers under the coronavirus pandemic (*Guardian*, 19 June 2020).

**Tuesday, 23 June 2020. Five Giants.**

This week, BBC Radio 4 is running programmes under the heading of: 'Re-think. People's Hopes and Dreams for the world post-corona.' It launched the series with a talk by Peter Hennessy on yesterday's World at One programme.

Peter Hennessy, Lord Hennessy, is, for those who do not know his work, the leading historian of modern politics in Britain. As a *Times* journalist and later an academic, he has written widely and authoritatively on the practice of government in Britain since the Second World War. His views repay attention. This is what he said:

It is possible that out of our experience of a cruel, capricious and deadly pathogen something of real and enduring value could emerge. That out of tragedy could come possibility and purpose. Is there a usable piece of our past to guide us, to give us hope? I think there is.

The Covid-19 experience has sharpened our sense of the duty of care we have one for another, that a state has for its people, all of its people, to a degree we've not felt collectively since World War II and its aftermath. We heard it week after week on Thursdays at eight when we clapped, cheered and rattled our pots and pans in salute to the NHS front line and other key workers. It was the sound of people, rediscovering themselves.

There are too many differences between six years of total war and the likely length of the Covid-19 emergency for easy comparisons to be made, but what we can learn from those war years is just how powerful and beneficial a never-again impulse can be if it is poured into the making of a new deal for the British people. The great World War II coalition led by Winston Churchill and Clem Attlee began to plan for exactly that on the back of what was and still is the most remarkable report ever produced for a British government. In late 1942, Sir William Beveridge, the leading social arithmetician of his day, identified what he called five giants on the road to recovery, and he put them in capital letters: Want, Ignorance, Idleness, Squalor,

Disease. The report was a best-seller. Beveridge's great insight was that all five giants had to be struck simultaneously if the hard crust of deprivation was to be shattered. After the war, governments of both parties were fuelled by a Beveridge-ite consensus for over thirty years.

Through the grim Covid weeks and months of 2020, can we see the possible outline of a new Beveridge, a new post Corona banner we can all rally round, a banner emblazoned with the heraldry of a new consensus? We can. I think there is a hard edged, not a fudged consensus to be crafted, using five priorities. Social care. Something must be done, and fast. A big public-private push on social housing. Getting technical education right at last after a hundred and fifty years of trying. Combating and mitigating climate change. Preparing our country and our people for the full impact of artificial intelligence on our productive capacity and our society.

If our politicians could pick up this new consensus and run with it, finding the right tone and pitch of language in which to express it, the early twenty-twenties could be one of the most creative and productive patches of our history and a worthy memorial to the Covid fallen. It has taken a pathogen for us to find and refresh our shared duty of care, but rediscover it we have.

More tomorrow on this vision. Others may wish to comment on his optimism, and on the five giants he has chosen to slay.

**Add Mss (2) May 21. Being Local.** 'The NHS has decided to write its own track and trace programme, rather than install the simpler and operational Apple / Google app. To no-one's surprise, it is already in trouble and missing deadlines. At this level, the bespoke solution is a mistake.' Thus it transpires. The only comfort is that in spite of the words spoken at the launch of the project, a computerised app seems no longer to be crucial, whoever designs it. A voice on the phone, preferably from the locality of the infected person, is what you need. And we have had telephones since 1875.

**Wednesday, 24 June 2020. Hibernation.**

Yesterday's public announcements, reinforced in my case by a personal letter from the NHS, have merely highlighted the collapse of trust in governing bodies in the UK.

According to Boris Johnson, the era of hibernation is over in England. Pubs and hairdressers will open, the two-metre rule is halved. The 'shielded' will be allowed to visit family from July 6, and permitted to roam freely from the beginning of August.

In better times, a public statement by the Prime Minister in Parliament, reinforced by a press conference attended by both the Chief Medical

Officer and the Chief Scientific Officer, plus an official three-page letter, should be enough. Who am I, a toiling historian, entirely innocent of a medical education, to dispute these authoritative statements?

But before I will move an inch from my current uneventful but secure lockdown I will consult every newspaper I can find, sundry blogs to which I subscribe, my neighbours, my friends (particularly two who actually are scientists), my younger brother who is playing a major regional role co-ordinating trace and test regimes and sits on the board of two hospital trusts, my grown-up children (especially), my lawyer, my astrologer, anyone who might be able to triangulate the official message. Then I will discuss the matter with my similarly sceptical wife, and between the two of us I expect we will decide to change nothing in our daily ritual until the consequence of the relaxation becomes evident in the infection rates (see Add Mss below).

This is tiring. A healthy democracy requires a questioning electorate, but only so far. If we are to get on with the business of our lives, we have to invest confidence in those to whom we delegate fundamental decision-making powers. The education we have received since the beginning of the year tells us that the administrative competence of ministers appointed not for their abilities but for their position on Brexit is low, that the government machine which should support them is not firing on all cylinders (no controlling 'deep state' here, any more than there is in the USA), that the Prime Minister is careless of detail and the truth, and that the scientists and medical specialists argue with each other, including about the current topic of the safe rate to relax restrictions.

And if we are to get on with the business of our lives, we have to walk down a street or enter a public building without viewing every stranger as a potential threat to our health and wellbeing. Amongst the many inherent contradictions in the new policy is allowing alcohol to be consumed in a 'mitigated' form. Someone somewhere has forgotten that the point of drinking is that is a means of throwing off the 'mitigations' of the daily round. It promotes personal interaction, reduces inhibitions, and in extreme but far from uncommon cases, leads to profoundly anti-social behaviour (there is a reason why the business of Accident and Emergency Departments has sharply declined in the pandemic lockdown).

In the end the calculation of risk will be largely personal. In two months we expect the arrival of a new grand-daughter a hundred-and-fifty miles away in London. It is likely to be that event, not further iterations of official advice and guidance, that will cause us to emerge from the burrow in which we have been sleeping.

**Add Mss 3. June 10 Staying Alive: '**When the final calculations are made, it is likely that those dying alone because they are alone will be far exceeded by those dying in company because they are in company.' In Australia a lifting of the lockdown has been suspended in large parts of Melbourne because of a resurgence of infections blamed on family gatherings and birthday parties.

**Friday, 26 June 2020.  Mr Worldly Wiseman.**

*Pilgrim's Progress* has featured in the recent entries on Beveridge and the Welfare State.  For those who do not keep the text by their bed, here is a taste of John Bunyan's writing.  The first part of the book was published in 1678, following twelve years in Bedford prison for refusing to cease unlicensed preaching.

Christian abandons his family and the City of Destruction and sets off, carrying his burden, to find salvation.  Along the way he encounters a series of temptations and dangers:

> Now, as *Christian* was walking solitarily by himself, he espied one afar off come crossing over the field to meet him, and their hap was to meet *just as they were crossing the way of each other.* The gentleman's name that met him was Mr. *Worldly Wiseman*, he dwelt in the town of *Carnal Policy*, a very great town, and also hard by from whence *Christian* came....

> Worl. ... *I see the dirt of the* slough of Despond *is upon thee, but that* slough *is but the beginning of the sorrows that do attend those that go on in that way: hear me, I am older than thou, thou art like to meet with in the way which thou goest, wearisomeness, painfulness, hunger, perils, nakedness, sword, lions, dragons, darkness, and in a word death, and what not?*

*These things are certainly true, having been confirmed by many testimonies.*

Worl. *Why in yonder village (the village is named* Morality) *there dwells a gentleman, whose name is* Legality, *a very judicious man, (and a man of a very good name) that has skill to help men off with such burdens as thine are, from their shoulders, yea, to my knowledge, he had done a great deal of good in this way: Ay, and besides, he hath skill to cure those that are somewhat crazed in their wits with their burdens. To him, as I said, thou mayest go, and be helped presently. His house is not quite a mile from this place; and if he should not be at home himself, he hath a pretty young man to his son, whose name is* Civility *that can do it (to speak on) as well as the old gentleman himself...*

So Christian tuned out of his way to go to Mr. *Legality's* house for help: but behold, when he was got now hard by the hill, it seemed so high, and also that side of it was the next way side, did hang so much over, that *Christian* was afraid to venture further, lest the hill should fall on his head; wherefore there he stood still; and wotted not what to do. Also his burden *now* seemed heavier to him than when he was in his way. There came also flashes of fire out of the hill that made *Christian* afraid that he should be burned: here therefore he sweat, and did quake for fear. And now he began to be sorry that he had taken Mr. *Worldly Wiseman's* counsel; and with that he saw

*Evangelist* coming to meet him; at the sight also of whom he began to blush for shame. So *Evangelist* drew nearer and nearer, and coming up to him, he looked at him with a severe and dreadful countenance...[29]

As the pandemic visits our lives, we are all us faced with 'wearisomeness, painfulness, hunger, perils,' to say nothing of 'nakedness, sword, lions, dragons, darkness, and in a word death, and what not.' The characters, Mr. Worldly Wiseman, Mr. Legality, Civility, and the places, Carnal Policy and Morality, may find their counterpart in people and locations you know yourself.

**Monday, 29 June 2020.  Lonesome George and the Cowboy.**

I enjoyed Nike in Katerini's account of sleeping with an owl and a snake by her bed.  In her culture, these are choices full of classical meaning.  In my own more prosaic world, I do not instinctively turn to such mythical objects when in need of guidance or security.

I was raised in a Protestant denomination.  Methodists focus on words, whether spoken, read, preached or sung.  They do not employ three-dimensional symbols to embody spiritual verities or to keep us safe from Bunyan's lions, dragons and darkness.   I do, nonetheless, keep two objects on my desk to guard my endeavours, albeit of an altogether more humdrum nature.

The first of these is a small, carved, wooden tortoise whose provenance I have long forgotten. I explained the connection between this animal and the lot of the long-distance writer in the entry for April 29. I have an engagement with tortoises beyond the ownership of my pet Herodotus (Nike may note that I was stretching for a classical association). Ten years ago, whilst still a university manager, I was sent to give a keynote speech at the remarkable Loja University in central Ecuador. The organisers arranged for the speakers to visit the Galapagos Islands before the conference started. There I met Lonesome George, the last known Pinta Island giant tortoise, just two years before his untimely death at the age of 102.[30] It is one thing encountering a tree that has survived over centuries, it is quite another gazing eye to eye with a creature that has moved so little and seen so much over so many years.

My second penates is quite different and much slighter. It is a mass-produced, 6.5cm high plastic model of a cowboy, six shooter in each hand. I don't know where I found it, but it speaks to me at some unconscious level. I must have owned such a toy as a small child. Now it stands at the opposite pole to my other desk guardian. The tortoise represents the slow daily slog that all scholarly writing requires. But I have read book after article after manuscript where the routine has overwhelmed inspiration. Each page represents a dutiful journey between evidence and interpretation, all true, all hard won, but lacking any spark in either the prose or the argument. It is far from easy to sit down day after day and attack the project, putting to flight mediocrity of thought or writing. My cowboy with his guns reminds me of that requirement.

So it has been during the pandemic. The tortoise element has not been so difficult. For those already living in semi-lockdown, surrounded by sufficient creature comforts, the prohibition on movement has not seemed a practical problem. The real threat is avoiding the descent into the Slough of Despond which faced Bunyan's Christian. Deprived of the stimulus of events, travel and fresh company, it becomes a challenge to generate the spark of energy and creativity during a day that begins and ends in the same place as the one before.

I have to find the six-shooter in me, up for whatever drama and danger I can manufacture.

**Tuesday, 30 June 2020. Loneliness and Life Satisfaction.**

We are living through a time of drama. Every week brings a new crisis, reported or anticipated.

History will record a belated response in the early days leading to thousands of avoidable fatalities, critical shortcomings in PPE, scandalous death-rates in care homes and amongst the BAME population, widespread failings in introducing test and trace procedures, the complete failure of the NHS testing app. Today we have the return of lockdown in Leicester and later this week there is the predicted disaster of choosing a summer Saturday night to open all the pubs in England for the first time in three months. And so it will continue in the face of a still unknowable virus and a government of still uncharted incompetence.

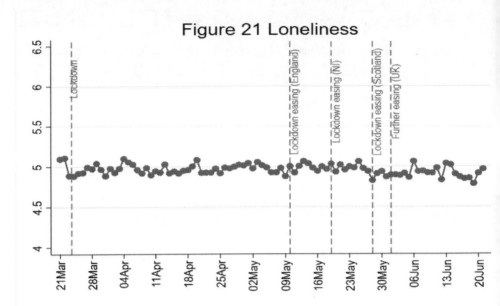

Figure 21 Loneliness

And yet, if attention is paid to how people are feeling about the crisis, a very different picture emerges. In my entry for May 27, I drew attention to the social surveys which have been launched at great speed in response to the coronavirus. One of the larger enterprises, the UCL Nuffield Covid-19 Social Study, has now published four further weekly reports, displaying consistent data over three full months of the pandemic.[31] The questions in the survey cover basic attitudes and emotions in the lockdown. Each topic has its own trajectory since the last week of March, and its own variations by age, income, and living conditions. But standing back from the detail, what is most striking is the absence of change over the period.

Graph after graph proceeds in an even line as each week passes, sometimes on a slightly upward trajectory, sometimes downward. What is missing almost completely is the kind of volatility that we read in the headlines each day. 'Loneliness' (see above) has been almost completely flat since the last week of March, unaffected by the recent marginal lifting of the lockdown. 'Life satisfaction' has gradually risen from 5 to 6 on a 10-point scale [it should be 7.7]. 'Happiness' [you may not know what that is, but here it is measured by the Office for National Statistics wellbeing scale], has been at or just under 6, again on a 10-point scale, with very small fluctuations. Levels of depression and anxiety have been higher than in pre-Covid times but have gradually declined through the Spring and early Summer. Confidence in the English government showed one of the largest short-term changes, falling from 4.5 to 3.5 on a 7-point scale at the beginning of May, but has since levelled out. Notwithstanding this decline, willingness to comply with guidelines has barely altered, slipping over three months from almost 100% to just over 90%. The sharpest fall has been in worries about food security, which began at around 60% of the population and are now only a little above zero.

The scale of the sample, which involves 90,000 respondents, inevitably has a dampening effect on variability. Individuals who have lost their jobs, or have been ill, or have suffered serious bereavement, will scarcely report so uneventful an experience. Nonetheless the absence of sudden change across the population in such fundamental areas as depression or life-satisfaction is a necessary corrective to the melodrama played out on the front-pages of the newspapers.

When the scores are broken down by issues such as income or living conditions, there are generally only minor differences. In most categories the young are suffering more than the old, the poor more than the rich, but often the differences are small. Much the largest variable on almost all issues is a prior diagnosis of mental ill-health. Again, the scores show little change over the period, but there are significant gaps between the graphs of the well and the unwell. On key issues such as depression, anxiety, loneliness and happiness, the mentally fit are between half and three times better off than those who entered this crisis already in trouble.

According to a report by the charity Mind this morning, almost two thirds of those with a pre-existing mental health problem said it had become worse during the lockdown.[32] When we consider where the effort should be placed in alleviating the consequence of the pandemic, the mental wellbeing of the population at the outset of the crisis will require particular attention.

**Wednesday, 1 July 2020.  Telling the numbers.**

My job as a Pro-Vice Chancellor at the Open University, working with Brenda Gourley, covered many areas, as befitted so protean an organisation.

Two of my responsibilities, ten years on, still influence all our lives.  I inherited the task, central to the OU from its creation, of working with the BBC to promote learning across society at large, as well as our own students.  And in what had become a digital age, I initiated the transfer of OU learning materials to a free-to-use site we called Open Learn.

The Radio 4 programme, *More or Less*, has just finished a series which has coincided with the coronavirus outbreak.  Its brief is to interrogate and illuminate the figures by which we understand our lives, some official, some generated by other organisations.  The programme is sponsored by the OU and listeners can follow up its broadcasts by going to the Open Learn site and engaging with further learning materials.

This morning, *More or Less* conducted a retrospect of its coverage of the pandemic from the first cases in Britain.  The emphasis was exclusively on what has gone wrong, particularly in England.  Data published in the last few days has demonstrated beyond doubt that we have the worst record in Europe, and over the long run are likely to be overtaken only by the disastrous populist regimes of Brazil and the United States.  The programme both summarised official data and demolished claims made along the way by Matt Hancock and Boris

Johnson, particularly with regard to the tragedy in the care homes, which have accounted for 43% of all excess deaths.

Throughout the crisis ministers have sought to postpone any historical reckoning until some later date, when a leisurely public enquiry can accumulate the evidence and reach a conclusion long after the guilty parties have left office. We are supposed to focus only on the future. The *More or Less* programme was broadcast the day after Boris Johnson's 'New Deal' speech in which he attempted to re-set the agenda of public debate, shifting the narrative away from the pandemic towards the glorious 'bounce forward not bounce back' economic agenda. It's not going to work. We are all of us historians now. We want to understand what went wrong, and, critically, we have multiple channels for helping us do so, including, directly and indirectly, the OU.

Amongst the comparisons made in any retrospective is with China, whose response, after a critical delay, has ultimately been much more effective that the UK's. The vast difference is in the level of public debate. It is more than possible that in a free society, the outbreak in Wuhan would have been spotted before it escaped to infect the rest of the world. And there is no prospect whatever of Chinese citizens now discussing what long-term improvements should be made in the management of pandemics. For all its ramshackle systems the British state is still exposed to the informed, Radio 4-listening, OU-studying, public

Much of the *More or Less* programme focussed on the missing fortnight in March, when the government failed to act on the information that was building up in Europe. It concluded, however, with a new scandal, the failure to inform local health officials of test results in their areas. The Labour MP Yvette Cooper tweeted today: 'Our local public health teams, council, NHS doctors & managers in Wakefield have had to fight for months to try to get this data. In public health crisis, most important thing is knowing where infection is. Appalling & incomprehensible that basic info hasn't been provided.'

Indeed it is. A functioning democracy needs debate not just at the national level but in local communities, which in turn requires the appropriate data to be made available at that level.

**Thursday, 2 July 2020. On Isolation and hunger.**

Those of us in lockdown feel, of course, isolated from our friends and family. We count the days, which in the present uncertainty stretch before us without limit, until we can share our lives with them.

This fragmentation of the population is reflected in other dimensions. Sitting inside our houses, patrolling our weedless gardens, we don't see, literally don't see, anything of how the rest of the country is experiencing the pandemic. Amongst the consequences of confining to their homes the fit and active of seventy and over, is depriving the community of a host of active volunteers who could both witness and respond to cases of need.

It is very easy to turn off our sensors and concentrate solely on our own misfortunes. One effect of the lockdown is to throw attention onto the most trivial grievances. The major event last Saturday in my household was the failure of Sainsburys to deliver the supplements in the weekend papers we had ordered. No book reviews, no television guides. It quite spoilt the day.

If you look for it, however, there is evidence that out there, people are going without more than just newsprint. There are those deprived of their income because they don't qualify for the furlough payments. There are the daily increasing numbers who are being fired in anticipation of the closure of that scheme. There are those who legally have 'no recourse to public funds' because they have a right to live here but not to benefit from the welfare state. There are those who had been barely getting by in the gig economy who are now wrestling with intricacies and inadequacies of universal credit. There is the group described by the money expert Martin Lewis as experiencing a 'financial catastrophe' as their businesses have failed leaving them with no safety net of any kind.

The consequence is not just some kind of social poverty, but basic physical deprivation. The Food Standards Agency has just published a report showing that since the pandemic began between 6.3 and 7.7 million adults had reduced their meals or missed them altogether because of lack of money, and that between 2.7 and 3.7 million adults sought charity food or used food banks.[33]  The food banks themselves have found it difficult to meet the increased demand, despite a 'Food Charities Grant' the government has established to provide them with short-term assistance.

Just now, my wife and I are living in a two-person fenced community. We must be grateful, I guess, that so far the material sufferings of so large a minority seem not to be reflected in the crime figures.

**Add Mss 4.   OU brings down French Presidential candidate.** Further to yesterday's discussion of the work of the Open University, the verdict has just been reported in the trial for embezzlement of the former French prime minister and presidential candidate, François Fillon, and his Welsh-born wife Penelope.  Up to a million euros were paid to Penelope over a number of years for office support that she never undertook.  The offence first came to light in a newspaper interview with Penelope back in 2007, when she admitted in passing that she was too busy to work for her husband.  The reason she gave for her lack of time was that she had just started an OU course in English literature.  She told the journalist that she was studying for a second degree because 'her five children viewed her as "just a mother"'.  She wanted to show them she was 'not that stupid' (my own mother, in her time, took an OU degree in her sixties for much the same reason).  Both action and motive seem more than sufficient to acquit Penelope Fillon of the charge she faced.  As it is, she has been given a suspended sentence of three years.

**Friday, 3 July 2020. Cherry Ripe.**

'Cherry Ripe' is a great example of the interpenetration of polite and popular culture in Britain. The seventeenth century lyric poet Robert Herrick based his famous poem on the cries of costermongers (whose successors featured in Henry Mayhew's study), selling fruit in the streets of London. Herrick's lines became part of the literary canon:

> Cherry-Ripe, ripe, ripe, I cry,
>
> Full and fair ones; come and buy.
>
> If so be you ask me where
>
> They do grow, I answer: There
>
> Where my Julia's lips do smile;
>
> There 's the land, or cherry-isle,
>
> Whose plantations fully show
>
> All the year where cherries grow.

In 1824 the composer Charles Horn set the poem to music, and the song immediately became a hit in London. It was particularly associated with the contralto Madame Vestris, who as both an actor and a theatre manager was an influential figure on the Georgian stage. A year later the immensely successful comedy *Paul Pry* began a record-breaking run at the Haymarket Theatre. Its popularity was enhanced by inclusion of Cherry Ripe, sung by Madame Vestris, although it had nothing to do with the plot. From the theatre, it escaped back into the streets. In 1841, the writer Charles Mackay, reflecting the growing sensitivity of middle-class householders to street music, gave a jaundiced account of the inescapable presence of Horn's song:

> About twenty years ago London resounded with one chorus, with the love of which everybody seemed to be smitten. Girls and Boys, young men and old, maidens and wives, and widows, were all alike musical. There was an absolute mania for singing, and the worst of it was, that, like good Father Philip, in the romance of 'The Monastery,' they seemed utterly unable to change their tune. 'Cherry ripe!' 'Cherry ripe!' was the universal cry of all the idle in the town. Every unmelodious voice gave utterance to it; every crazy fiddle, every cracked flute, every wheezy pipe, every street organ was heard in the same strain, until studious and quiet men stopped their ears in desperation, or fled miles away into the fields or woodlands, to be at peace.[34]

The popularity of the song owed much to Horn's melody, but it also reflected the perennial attraction of the subject. Nothing speaks more eloquently of the wealth of summer than the pure red fruit. The photograph [not reproduced in this version] is some of the crop from our garden this year. The larger bowl contains sweet 'Stella' cherries. They grow on a large tree we planted more than three decades ago. It is too tall to net, so we just share the crop with the blackbirds who nest in the adjacent hedge to ensure the shortest journey to their breakfast each morning. The smaller bowl has sharper morello cherries from a fan-trained tree on a wall, now carefully netted after the birds stripped it bare last year.

The sweet cherries became a clafoutis earlier this week, and the remainder we eat between and after every meal for as long as they last. The morellos were bottled yesterday and will be cherry brandy by Christmas. At least we have something to look forward to amidst the collapse of all plans and expectations.

**Monday, 6 July 2020. General Montgomery and my mother.**

In his Memex 1.1 blog yesterday, my friend and colleague John Naughton reproduced the letter sent by General Montgomery to the troops about to launch the D-Day landing in 1944, which has turned up in the papers of his wife's father. 'The time has come to strike the enemy a terrific blow in Western Europe' it begins.

I too have seen a copy of the message, sent not to my (as yet unmarried) father, who was on a ship off the coast of West Africa, but my mother, who spent the war in an anti-aircraft unit, plotting incoming planes and V-bombs[35] – you may have seen the films in which uniformed young women push models across a map on a table before the order is given to the anti-aircraft gunners. She was moved down to the south coast as part of the preparations for D-day and was sent the letter.

Her technical role in the war always puzzled me. During her life as my mother, she never once showed the slightest interest in, or affinity for, machines or science. Her OU degree taken in her retirement was in literature and the social sciences. I once asked her how she had been recruited for such a role. She told me that when she was called up, she was given an aptitude test, which was to construct something out of meccano. She had spent her childhood playing with her younger brother's set, made a model in no time, and was sent off to track aircraft.

In the same way my father, a civil servant in later life with no responsibility for radio technology at work and no competence in it at home, was a chief petty officer in the navy specialising in the arcane skill of listening to Japanese morse code. Global conflict took people to places they never visited again, and caused them to learn capacities which died upon the instant peace was declared.

There are two possible conclusions to be drawn from this wartime experience.

Either we humanities people have deep inside us a technical capacity which it requires a well-organised world war to bring out. I have my doubts, but who knows. Or major ventures, think of Bletchley Park, think of NASA, succeed by bringing together all sorts of skills, some scientific at a high level, but many others which have nothing to do directly with the science but nonetheless are crucial to the outcome of the project. My new book on the history of solitude is dedicated to an aunt by marriage, who died not long ago, and who was at Bletchley

Park in the war. Later in life she was, again, a literary woman, who eventually published books of fiction, poetry and a memoir. She was sent to Bletchley because she was (a) very bright, (b) had security clearance, and (c) had fluent German. Not a codebreaker, but, along with many others in the huts, critical to the outcome.

So, perhaps, with the skills discovered or mobilised to counter Covid-19. Except, as world wars go, this has not been well organised. That is to say not by the British. The Germans have beaten us hands down.

**Tuesday, 7 July 2020. Anti-Vax.**

After half a year of the pandemic, we should be immune to shock at the responses to it.

But this morning there is published a finding which is startling and depressing in equal measure. A survey conducted by YouGov, an entirely reputable polling organisation, has found that almost one in six British adults will 'probably' or 'definitely' refuse a coronavirus vaccination when one becomes available. Another 15% say they are not sure what they will do.[36]

We expect this kind of anti-science in the United States, where according to the latest research, only a third of the population believe in secular evolution, a century and a half after *Origin of Species*.[37] But Darwin is our man, indeed my man, born and educated in Shrewsbury (his parents, for an unexplained reason, are buried in the churchyard of Montford parish church, just down river from my village and some distance from the town where they lived). Surely we are beyond so irresponsible a rejection of medical research.

In the popular history of medicine, Edward Jenner lines up with Alexander Fleming as a hero-discoverer of life-saving remedies. In 1796, as every textbook tells it, he vaccinated James Phipps, the eight-year-old son of his gardener, with cowpox, which gave him immunity to the disfiguring and frequently lethal illness of smallpox. Crucially Jenner not only applied a remedy which was already being investigated, but conducted a series of tests to prove that it had worked with young Phipps and later triallists. There then followed the first public legislation in the field, with Vaccination Acts in 1840, 1853, (the first to make the vaccination of children compulsory), 1867, which tightened the regulation, and 1898, which introduced a conscience clause for parents still opposed to the practice.

The last of the 19th century Acts reflected the power of the anti-vaccination movement which had grown up as regulations were introduced. In the present moment, Leicester is in renewed lockdown, at least in part because of the failure of sections of the population to observe social distancing advice. Here is the same city in 1885, with up to 100,000 anti-vaccinators marching with banners, a child's coffin and an effigy of Jenner: 'An escort was formed, preceded by a banner, to escort a young mother and two men, all of whom had resolved to give themselves up to the police and undergo imprisonment in preference to having their children vaccinated...The three were attended by a numerous crowd...three hearty cheers were given for them, which were renewed with increased vigour as they entered the doors of the police cells.'[38]

The Victorian era was notable not so much for the progress of medical science, which for the most part was more successful at diagnosis than therapeutic intervention, but for the growth of mass literacy, which turned every citizen into a consumer of the printed word. With newspapers came advertisements for every kind of quack medicine. With the Penny Post of 1840, came the machinery to distribute products by mail order, using stamps as currency. The most credulous were not the newly literate farm labourers whom Jenner had treated, but the confident, educated middle classes. In 1909 the British Medical Association, alarmed at the success of patent medicines, conducted an inquiry into the market:

> It is not, however, only the poorer classes of the community who have a weakness for secret remedies and the ministration of quacks; the well-to-do and the highly-placed will often, when not very ill, take a curious pleasure in experimenting with mysterious compounds. In them, it is perhaps to be traced a hankering to break safely with orthodoxy; they scrupulously obey the law and the Church and Mrs. Grundy, but will have their fling against medicine.[39]

Facebook and other sites, which bear a criminal responsibility for the resistance to orthodox medicine, are merely the inheritors of a long tradition of self-medication weaponised by commercial forces and facilitated by communication systems. The medical profession itself has not always been as secure a bastion against these pressures as it might wish to be seen to be. It took twelve years for *The Lancet* finally to retract the article it published in 1998, falsely claiming that the MMR vaccine caused autism.

•

It is, of course, possible that if and when a vaccine is made available, there will be less resistance to it than is now threatened. History offers scant comfort that this will happen.

**Wednesday, 8 July 2020. The Community Reassurance Team Hotline.**

Late yesterday afternoon, as the rain clouds were beginning to obscure the Welsh hills, the phone rang. It was Catherine from Shropshire Council, calling me because I was on the NHS list of those shielding from the coronavirus. She had three questions.

The first related to the announcement that from the end of the month, the shielded were no longer to receive their weekly food boxes. Could I cope with this? I told her that I would not go hungry. I had stopped the delivery of the boxes some weeks ago and was being supplied by supermarket home delivery. Nonetheless I was impressed by her concern. When last did the government take a decision that might cause you harm, say a reduced service or an increased tax, and then ring you up and ask if you minded about it? This is a good precedent.

The second was whether my house was fitted with a smoke alarm. I was puzzled by the question, but then wondered if the lengthening list of coronavirus symptoms now includes spontaneous combustion. You will recall that this was the misfortune that befell the alcoholic rag and bone merchant Mr. Krook in *Bleak House*. Dickens insisted that he had documentary evidence that such a death could occur, and there has been debate about it ever since. I assured Catherine that we had two alarms and she seemed pleased with the answer.

The third was whether I would like the number of the newly established 'Community Reassurance Team Hotline.' I was entranced by the prospect.

'Hotline' perhaps not so much. Since the term was introduced to the English lexicon, referring to the dedicated line American and Russian Presidents use to try to prevent a nuclear war breaking out, as in *Dr Strangelove*, the word has lost much of its urgency. Every over-stretched public or commercial body offers such a service in order to keep clients and customers at bay. A 'coldline' is a number which you ring, is never answered, but it doesn't matter. A 'hotline' is a number which is never answered, but it does matter.

'Community' is more promising. Although, like hotline, it has lost much of its meaning in recent years, it is enjoying a renaissance in the pandemic. The local Parish News has just resumed its monthly delivery. It has a centre spread of all the services being performed across a distributed rural population of some 800 people. Twelve separate activities are mentioned, too many to list here, but they range from 'those who kept in contact with people living alone and/or self-isolating' to 'everyone who shopped and collected medical supplies for those unable to go out' [which includes our neighbours collecting our prescriptions] to 'the Groves who have made the Montford pond area a delightful wild life oasis and a resting spot for walkers and riders'. This is real.

'Team' is good. If the helpful Catherine is relocated to the parking fines division, it is comforting to know that a multi-skilled group of officers stands ready to continue the service.

But 'Reassurance' is the prize. No official body has ever offered me this.

I need reassurance that my children will keep their health and their jobs, and that I will recognise my grandchildren when next I see them. I need reassurance that the shops, restaurants, theatres, cinemas that I once enjoyed will still be there when I go out. I need reassurance that when I do mix in company, it will not immediately constitute a lethal threat to my health (see 'shielded' above). I need reassurance that the apparent incompetence of every level of English government above the local is a mirage that will dissolve in the summer sun.

And now all I have to do is pick up the phone to get it.

But only in Shropshire. I'm sorry for the rest of you.

**Thursday, 9 July 2020. Build, Build, Imprison.**

Here's a happy tweet from the Ministry of Justice: 'We are building 4 new prisons to: Improve rehabilitation. Help local economies. Support construction industry to invest & innovate. Part of our £2.5bn plan to create 10k additional prison places. Delivering modern prisons & keeping the public safe' (thanks to my colleague Ros Crone, for this).

Each line has a helpful little illustration. The one for the construction industry has a crane and jib which at first sight looks just like some gallows. Next time perhaps.

The prison population of England and Wales has almost doubled over the last twenty-five years. According to the figures for 3rd July, the current population of 79,522 is just over two thousand less than the 'Usable Operational Capacity'.[40] The press release accompanying the tweet stresses that the new cells will be an 'addition' to the present stock, presumably taking into account the need to replace prisons no longer fit for purpose. They will be on top of already planned new prisons at Wellingborough and Glen Parva, which are to provide 3,360 places by 2023. The announcement reflects an expectation that prison numbers will expand still further in the coming years.

Last February the then Justice Secretary of State, David Gauke, announced a policy of abolishing custodial sentences of fewer than six months. But he took the wrong view of Brexit, lost his Cabinet post, was thrown out of the Conservative Party and is now out of Parliament. His junior minister in charge of prisons, Rory Stewart, stated that 'We should be deeply ashamed as a society if people are living in filthy, rat-infested conditions with smashed-up windows, with high rates of suicide and violence.'[41] He was quickly promoted to a Cabinet post at the Department for International Development, since abolished (do keep up!), before he was himself abolished, following Gauke's trajectory out of office and out of Parliament because of his opposition to Brexit (and to Johnson personally).

As noted in my diary entry for June 2, the Ministry of Justice failed to implement an early undertaking to make an emergency reduction of 4,000 in a prison population threatened by mass infection in confined spaces. Now cause and effect has been reversed. The response to the virus demands growth not contraction. The overriding need is to get the economy moving. The MoJ's press release explains the broader purpose of the announced expansion: 'Thousands of jobs will be created overall in the areas surrounding prisons during construction and once they have opened. This will provide a major spur to local economies and support the construction industry to invest and innovate following the Coronavirus epidemic.'

This is the new mantra of 'build, build, build' given form. There seems no good reason why the Government should stop at 10,000. We need to be world class at something, and setting aside the United States, we are already well ahead of advanced countries in the proportion of the population in prison (the British figure of 140 per 100,000 is almost double the German rate). Each new prison takes undesirables off the streets, cures unemployment, boosts the private sector (only one of the new prisons is certain to be run by the state). What's not to like?

Quite a lot, according to a new report from the Parliamentary Human Rights Committee.[42] It has just demanded that the government 'should end the Covid-19 visiting ban on children in England and Wales whose mothers are in prison and consider releasing those who are low risk… The committee said it had heard heartfelt evidence from children prohibited to visit their mothers during the outbreak which had exacerbated problems and posed a serious risk to an estimated 17,000 youngsters.' It further called for the 'early release for those mothers who can safely go back home with their children.'

The Committee is on the wrong side of history.

**Friday, 10 July 2020. Le temps des cerises.**

Following my piece on 'Cherry Ripe' last week, my friend Marie contacted me about the French national song on the same topic. She writes:

> I was interested to see your post on cherries and the popularity of the song 'cherry ripe'. In France too we have a very popular song about cherries. 'Le temps des cerises,' a sweet and wistful song about the fickleness of girls and the transient nature of the cherry season. It's a lament for lost love and maybe the lost ideals of the Revolution as well. It was composed by Jean Baptiste Clément in 1866 and was popular during the time of the Commune rebellion. In fact, Clement who supported the Commune, later dedicated it to a nurse helping the wounded on the barricades during the 'semaine sanglante' in 1871 when the French government pitilessly overthrew the Commune.

> The red colour of the cherries became a symbol for the shed blood of the Commune martyrs and the nostalgic longing for the cherry season was equated with a yearning for social change. It is well known even now and was often sung by left leaning singers and heard at socialist meetings. Barbara Hendricks sang it at François Mitterrand's memorial ceremony in 1996 in front of the Opera Bastille. I imagine a large part of the crowd would have sung along and been sad.

People of my age think of their grandparents when they hear it and feel a lump in their throat.

These are the verses:

Quand nous chanterons le temps des cerises (Quand nous en serons au temps des cerises)
Et gai rossignol et merle moqueur
Seront tous en fête
Les belles auront la folie en tête
Et les amoureux du soleil au cœur
Quand nous chanterons le temps des cerises
Sifflera bien mieux le merle moqueur

Mais il est bien court le temps des cerises
Où l'on s'en va deux cueillir en rêvant
Des pendants d'oreille...
Cerises d'amour aux robes pareilles (vermeilles)
Tombant sous la feuille (mousse) en gouttes de sang...
Mais il est bien court le temps des cerises
Pendants de corail qu'on cueille en rêvant !

Quand vous en serez au temps des cerises
Si vous avez peur des chagrins d'amour
Évitez les belles!
Moi qui ne crains pas les peines cruelles
Je ne vivrai pas (point) sans souffrir un jour...

Quand vous en serez au temps des cerises

Vous aurez aussi des chagrins (peines) d'amour !


J'aimerai toujours le temps des cerises

C'est de ce temps-là que je garde au cœur

Une plaie ouverte !

Et Dame Fortune, en m'étant offerte

Ne pourra jamais calmer (fermer) ma douleur...

J'aimerai toujours le temps des cerises

Et le souvenir que je garde au cœur !


And here is 'Le temps des cerises' sung by Yves Montand in all its lovely melancholy.  Do listen:


https://www.youtube.com/watch?v=edXFWik4ODA


**Monday, 13 July 2020.  Whydunnit.**


In my entry of June 22, I speculated on the fate of reading books in the lockdown.  Now the bookshops have opened and the books sales monitor Nielsen has started to generate data on sales and reading habits.


I turn out to be at once atypical and absolutely on trend.


I wrote then that for all the extra time forced upon those in lockdown, I was not reading much more for pleasure.  I was still spending too much of my working day wrestling with print, and it was rather my garden that was gaining from my additional leisure.

Not so with the wider public. The increase in hours spent with a book has been dramatic. Before the lockdown, UK adults averaged 3.4 hours a week reading. By the beginning of May that had increased to 6.1. hours. This must be the largest single growth in functional literacy ever recorded in so short a period. It has since declined marginally, but in spite of the gradual relaxation in competing recreations, it is still running at 5.9 hours.

The extra reading has been reflected in the business of the bookshops which reopened on 15 June. Although the high street has in general reported significantly lower demand than the same time last year, Waterstones and its competitors have seen sales rise by a healthy 19% over the same period.

There have been gains in various genres, including contributions to the Black Lives Matter debate. But the largest growth has been in crime novels, up 120,000 for the last two weeks of June over the same period last year.

So with my own reading. I have been buying the works of the American writers James Lee Burke (New Orleans) and Michael Connolly (Hollywood) and re-encountering Simenon, some in collections I have had for years, some in the excellent re-translated novels Penguin have just finished publishing.

It would be tempting but facile to suppose that this increased interest in murder reflects the tensions caused in families forced to endure each other's company over several months, without escape to the office or the schoolroom or other company. In fact, as a range of national and international agencies have reported, such tensions, where they exist, have been reflected not in literary habits but actual domestic violence, particularly involving men unable to escape their demons and women unable to escape the threat they pose.

The pleasure in crime fiction answers a different need. The genre is wide, and the detail of homicide varies. For the most part the focus is not on the act of murder, but on the solution to the mystery. This is particularly the case with Simenon's policeman. In most of the novels the drama is not whodunnit but why. Take, for instance, *Maigret and the Tall Woman*, which I have just finished reading in a new translation.

Maigret is contacted by the wife of a hapless safe-breaker - the tall woman of the title whom Maigret had first encountered when she was earning a living on the streets of Paris. Her husband has disappeared after finding a body of a woman in a house he was burgling. It takes little time to locate the house, identify the victim, and determine that the victim's husband, a prosperous dentist, either himself or in conjunction with his controlling mother, had murdered her. Much of the rest of the book is taken up with an epic interrogation of the dentist as Maigret establishes not so much the fact of guilt as an explanation of the psychological tensions within the dentist's household which had resulted in the fatal shooting.

So with our current crisis. What we need above all is to narrativize a drama which has broken all the rules of expected behaviour. Already the stories are being written about the fateful early weeks of the pandemic, incomplete and contested though the evidence is. In the meantime we find some solace in a literary form where the crime is stated and, in the last chapter, an explanation is found.

Whether the culprits will go to jail is another question. Maigret, famously, lost interest when the charge was brought. He had done his job once he understood how the event had happened and how people had behaved in the way they did.

**Tuesday, 14 July 2020. Directors of Public Health.**

Here's an idea. The health of an area is a complex matter, interacting with a wide range of public services and private behaviours. Why not appoint a senior figure in each local authority who can work across the three connected fields of protection, improvement and health care. The role would advise elected members and senior officers and liaise with national bodies such as Public Health England and NHS England.

It has taken a long time for Matt Hancock, the Minister of Health, finally to accept that 134 such figures already exist. The post of

Director of Public Health (DPH) was created as part of the Lansley reforms of the Cameron government in a creative attempt to compensate for the damage caused by the abolition of regional health authorities. According to NHS England, 'Directors are responsible for ensuring that public health is at the heart of their local authority's agenda. Using the best and most appropriate evidence, they determine the overall vision and aims for public health in their locality. They then manage the delivery of those objectives and report annually on their activities.' As the Department of Health's own website puts it, their role embraces both long-term issues such as obesity and health inequalities and short-term reactions to 'outbreaks of disease and emergency community and emergency preparedness.'

The turning point in the deployment of the Directors of Public Health came in the second week of May, two months after the country began to grapple with the coronavirus outbreak. The scandal of the infection and mortality rates in care homes forced central government to recognise that it simply did not have the capacity to determine how to prioritise a testing programme. It turned to the Directors of Public Health because of their familiarity with provisions for the elderly in their areas, and their connections with other community agencies. A DPH was quoted at the time as saying, 'We've been pushing and pushing government to realise that we exist and that we are best placed to organise things like testing, alongside directors of adult social services, because we know our patch.'

Now, in an article in the *Telegraph* last Sunday, with the official UK death rate approaching 45,000, Hancock finally recognised that the coronavirus was a local event requiring interventions tailored to local circumstances. He wrote that 'now we can take more targeted local action and less national lockdown, to restore the freedom of the majority while controlling the virus wherever we can find it.'[43] The much-delayed track and trace system can only work if the Directors of Public Health are supplied with all the so-called 'Pillar 1' and 'Pillar 2' returns so they can fully understand the conditions in communities or workplaces that are giving rise to anomalies, and develop tailored actions for dealing with them.

With power comes responsibility. Central government has not lost its appetite for intervention and it was reported over the weekend as threatening to take over running Leicester council if it failed to deal with the crisis in the city. The Directors of Public Health are finding that their new powers are bringing with them an immense body of work, and an unwelcome exposure to the media. The Herefordshire Director did not appear at all comfortable yesterday answering questions on television about the outbreak in a farm, particularly why three of the workers had managed to abscond from the lockdown she had imposed.

Nothing will be easy, and it remains to be seen how permanent is the shift of authority from the centre to the periphery. But after so much confusion, wasted resources and unnecessary deaths, the belated change in policy can only be welcomed.

As the far-seeing Dominic Cummings almost said, 'Take back local control!' Just now I live not in the United Kingdom, nor in England, but in Shropshire. Home rule cannot come too soon.

**Wednesday, 15 July 2020. Connecting with Adobe.**

In my capacity as a temporarily returned member of the Open University History Department, I have just taken part in an online research seminar. As with most of my many video meetings in the lockdown, it achieved its basic purpose. A group of interested scholars was gathered together. The two presenters were able to outline their work, switching between their spoken account and various illustrative documents. Questions were asked and answered. We ended the session knowing more about the potential of using search engines to conduct textual analysis - in this case the deployment of the word 'nationality' in Hansard in the nineteenth century. It turns out that the technical challenge of the process somewhat outweighs the insights yielded into the political history of the period.

I thought by now I was if not the master then at least a competent user of video technology. However in addition to Zoom, Skype, and Microsoft Teams, I was now faced with Adobe Connect. As has been the case in first encounters with each of the technologies, the ten minutes before the session began was a time of mounting panic, with emergency downloads of apps, repeated attempts to get them to work, before, for no apparent reason, suddenly there was a connection and we were away. But Adobe Connect, at least in the version I had found, lacked the mute / unmute switch. So when the time came to ask my own penetrating question, I could neither be heard nor could I know that I was excluded from the conversation which was continuing without me. It was a kind of waking nightmare, when you know you are speaking, but not that no-one can hear you. Eventually one of the presenters noticed my gesticulating hands and, as the new language has it, let me in.

The world of virtual discussion has placed a new premium on listening. Physical face-to-face conversations have become a rare privilege, and those conducted electronically lack many of the visual clues by which we communicate meaning. In the case of an arcane branch of the digital humanities, this may not matter so much. But when it comes to medical consultations, it becomes much more important. I was talking yesterday to a nurse sent out from my surgery to conduct a routine blood test in my home. How are the practice staff managing with a limited number of physical consultations and the rest conducted on the phone or by video link? Not well she thought. You need to see someone, how they look, how they hold themselves, to understand what they are, and crucially, are not, telling you.

This applies particularly to the field of mental health, which as I discussed in the entry for June 30, is especially vulnerable in the pandemic lockdown. A newly qualified mental health social worker is interviewed in today's paper. Thrown in at the deep end, he has had to refashion his newly-acquired diagnostic tools. He is compelled to meet his clients virtually. 'The challenge,' he explains, 'and the negative side of that, is that I am not going into people's homes so I don't get to see the full picture. You can get a real sense of somebody within seconds of seeing them. People might be able to present quite well on the phone but be feeling quite unwell.' The pandemic has caused him to hone and refocus his skills: 'I have had to learn to practise with my ears open and really listen to people and hear what they are saying.'[44]

We speak of love at first sight, not at first hearing. To get even someone you know, let alone a stranger, fully to express themselves in words, is hard. Harder still is the patience and the attention required to understand what they mean.

**Thursday, 16 July 2020. Isolation and Bad Medicine.**

Today a front-page headline in *The Times*: 'Coronavirus vaccine hopes raised by success of early trials.'[45] Read closely this is more a 'good news because it's not bad news' story. Phase 1 of the Oxford vaccine trial has not thrown up any counter-indications, but the major test still lies ahead. The commercial partner of the project, AstraZeneca, is quoted at the end of the article cautioning that 'news on whether the university's vaccine worked was unlikely before data was gathered from much larger trials towards the end of the year.'

Nonetheless the story brings back into the focus the issue I discussed on July 7, of whether any vaccine would be effective in the face of opposition by a significant minority of the population, in Britain or elsewhere. An insight into the scale of the problem was supplied by an article in the *New York Times* last week by Anne Borden King.[46] She is an active opponent of the anti-vax movement, founder of the Campaign Against Phony Autism Cures and a consultant for the watchdog Bad Science Watch. She has also just been diagnosed with breast cancer, and shared the news on Facebook.

The consequence was an avalanche of advertisements on her Facebook feed for 'alternative cancer care', promoting 'everything from cumin seeds to colloidal silver as cancer treatments. Some ads promise luxury clinics – or even 'nontoxic cancer therapies' on a beach in Mexico.' There were, by contrast, no legitimate cancer advertisements.

This is not a new problem, either historically in print, as I explained in my piece, or in the internet age where the misinformation comes to you unbidden, or is seductively available via Google searches. What was particularly interesting about Anne Borden King's article was the connection she made with life in the pandemic. Under any circumstances a cancer diagnosis threatens a sudden loss of personal control as the patient is subjected to intrusive tests and invasive treatment. No matter how supportive friends and family try to be, there are few places as lonely as a hospital waiting room.

With the coronavirus restrictions, this sense of social alienation has got worse, which partly explains why fewer appointments for cancer treatment have been made and kept. 'During the pandemic,' writes

Anne Borden King, 'many of us are also isolated. Our loved ones can't come to our appointments or even visit us in hospital. Now more than ever, who is there to hold our hand?'

The pseudoscience cures offer an alternative sense of community, the claim that out there 'experts' are on your side, dedicated to supporting the whole person in the face of the fragmenting authority of official medicine. They promise to return a sense of agency to the individual, supported by a network of other enthusiastic users.

Facebook, under intense pressure to censor proliferating bogus coronavirus cures, has been slow to act. The only certain defence is to turn off the feed.

Which can only exacerbate the sense of isolation.

**Add Mss.** Yesterday I wrote about the enhanced importance of hearing clearly in the lockdown. Later in the day the BBC 'PM' programme ran an item featuring two representatives of the deaf community. They were responding to the newly announced policy (in England) of compulsory face-masks in shops. To communicate with others, they explained, they needed to be able to read a person's lips. This was impossible if the mouth was concealed by a mask. There were transparent masks on the market, but they tended to steam up. This is not a minor matter. According to the Government Digital Service, 11m people in Britain are deaf or hard of hearing.[47]

**Friday, 17 July 2020. The hissing of rats.**

Let me introduce you to Jim, encountered during a tour of Poplar and Limehouse in 1899. by one of the team employed by Charles Booth to investigate the social conditions of London:

> He is a navvy or bricklayer's labourer & besides being very handy is noted for his strength. Jim is herculean to look at, enormous chest, arms which looked as if they wd. burst his coat sleeves & huge hands, about 6ft high. His failing is drink & excess of animal spirits. He had an attractive manner & pleasant way of speaking but is said to be a 'fair terror' in the neighbourhood. He is now about 38 years of age: was married at 17 or 18, has a grown up son who takes after his father & has just been turned out of the army, also several small children. He married a wife who was a match for him & tried to bang him about. He left her, took up with another woman & his wife is now doing 6 months in Holloway jail for having tried to brain No. 2 with an empty champagne bottle.[48]

The cumulative result of the project was issued in seventeen volumes in 1902/3. Alongside the prose analysis Booth also prepared a series of maps of all the city streets, colour coded from black (lowest class, vicious, semi-criminal) to yellow (upper-middle and upper classes). These have just been republished in a handsome, remarkably inexpensive book by Thames and Hudson.[49] Such a topography of wealth and poverty in what was at the time the largest city in the world, had never previously been attempted. Now the modern reader can once more traverse the streets of London, many of which still survive, noting then as now the proximity of deprivation and privilege.

Or the reader can go on-line and accompany the investigators as they walk down every road and into every court, usually guided by a local policeman. Their manuscript notebooks are readily available at https://booth.lse.ac.uk. For the most part the rich were unseen behind their front doors, but the poor, living much of their lives on the streets, are a vivid presence. The details of their world lodge in the memory. Here, for instance, a policeman describes a fat refinery in Poplar:

> You should come down here of an early summer morning; if possible after a shower of rain: Rats, not in twos or threes or in 10s or twentys, but in thousands and tens of thousands: the street will be covered with them, so will be the yard of the factory; rats, not small rats but big & fat, the size of cats: you knock a [illeg.] with your book & away they go with a rush and a hissing sound from their feet upon the pavements that will make your blood run cold.[50]

At the end of one of the notebooks, the guiding policeman turns his attention to the threat of infectious diseases, particularly with regard to a tenement building in which whole families lived in single rented rooms:

Inspector Pearson thought that all statistics relating to deaths in [Queens] Buildings were one sided because as soon as any one was ill they were sent away to a hospital & not Report at home as they wd. be in a private house. In his opinion they are much more unhealthy than small houses & the danger of an epidemic spreading much greater – While the hospitals have room, he said, patients can be sent off & there is not much risk but supposing a general epidemic, & and no room in the hospitals, then 'buildings' become a death trap to their inhabitants.[51]

Substitute care home for the 'buildings' and you have an exact description of the disaster that has just befallen us.

**Monday, 20 July 2020.  Home Restaurant.**

We always knew that this would be the hard stretch.

When everything was shut and no-one was going anywhere, there was little sense of frustrated opportunity.  But now shops and restaurants are beginning to open, and the young and fit are getting out of the house.  Lockdown becomes daily less amusing.

So we consider food.  One discovery of this event has been the interplay of pleasure and spontaneity.  The best meals you cook for yourself are those for which you conceive an appetite one morning, go out and buy the ingredients and cook them in the evening.  When you are confined to an intermittent home delivery, each night you are faced with a vague intention conceived a week earlier when the order was compiled. All invention is lost, except insofar as there have to be unexpected workarounds because some essential ingredient has been left off the list.

Out in the countryside there is a trade between clean air, fine views, quiet roads on the one hand, and an absolute absence of takeaway services on the other. But then we read, in a restaurant column in one of the weeklies, that proper restaurants are delivering proper meals irrespective of distance and at a reasonable price.

One of these is the chain of six up-market bistros run by Gary Usher in Manchester and Liverpool. Usher has gained a reputation not only for the quality of his meals but for his approach to the business, launching ventures in unfashionable areas using crowdfunding, and adopting an ethical approach to employing his staff.

So, as if in a restaurant, we read the online menu and order the following meal: Starter: Burrata with charred spring onion dressing, fennel and chilli crisps; Main: Confit duck leg, red cabbage, mango and macadamia salad, tarragon bbq sauce; Braised featherblade of beef, truffle creamed potato, glazed carrot, red wine sauce; Desert: Yorkshire parkin, salted butterscotch sauce and clotted cream; dark chocolate and sea salted fudge.

Looks promising. An insulated, chilled box arrives exactly on time containing a host of labelled polythene bags.

Then the problem. The food has been half-prepared. There is not much that can go completely wrong. On the other hand, this is absolutely not a Marks and Spencer microwave job. Everything has to be separately reheated in different ways for different times, or unpacked and reassembled. If you have a basic kitchen competence, each activity is not so difficult. But, like a real restaurant, there is the question of timing. When you go out for a meal, the company usually makes a point of ordering different items from the menu, to compare and contrast, to enjoy your own choices and everyone else's. In this game, such behaviour is a fundamental mistake.

Like the professional chef I find myself having to prepare two multi-layered dishes for completion at exactly the same time, whilst my wife is busy with two other sections of the menu. At one point I am boiling bags on the stove, roasting in the oven, and grilling a duck leg, whilst at the same time preparing a salad and heating a sauce. All to a deadline. I have always regarded the new verb to 'plate' as an affectation used only by wannabe tv chefs, but on this occasion when I got to the last line in each of the extensive instruction sheets, plate is what I did.

And of course, when the meal was finished, no-one came to clear the dishes, or deal with the pots and pans and a small mountain of discarded food bags. We have a rule in my household, as in most, that we wash up before the day ends. Not this time.

It was an event (with candles and a good bottle of wine). Not to be missed. Or repeated, at least for a while.

**Tuesday, 21 July 2020.  On Hugging.**

Towards the end of my book on solitude, I addressed the argument that the internet was killing face-to-face speech.  A range of critics, particularly the American psychologist Sherry Turkle, claimed that immersion in digital technology was destroying both the incidence and the skill of talking one to another.

There was clearly substance in the analysis of current modes of interpersonal communication.  The problem was the temporal context for such a claim.  Those writing about the digital revolution tend to regard modern history as beginning with the introduction of the i-phone in 2007, the rest of history starting with the invention of the internet in 1983, and all the eras before that as the stone age about which little is known or needs to be known.

In fact, we have very little information about the volume of private speech earlier in the twentieth century, or at any time before that.  I ended my discussion by writing: 'Whether there was a moment in late modernity when peak conversation was reached and passed requires further investigation.'[52]  I would love to write a book answering this question, but I have yet to find the evidential base for doing so.

What is true of face-to-face exchange applies also to body-to-body contact. Commentary on the pandemic lockdown is full of concerns about restrictions on physical embrace. Again, there is a case to be made. In general terms, the anguish of suffering is nowhere better captured than in the difficulty the bereaved have found in offering bodily warmth to each other. In my own case, nothing expresses the pain caused by enforced shielding so much as my inability to hug my children and my grandchildren.

But beyond those extremes of emotional reassurance, what else have I and others lost in this regard? I am, after all, a child of my culture, and in the family of nations the English are renowned for the distance they keep from each other. The *Financial Times* columnist Simon Kuper writes, 'Americans won't touch strangers, the French won't talk to them, but the British neither touch nor talk to them.'[53] The more crowded our island has become, the more expert we have learned to be in avoiding physical contact in public spaces. The list of those whom we would expect to greet with anything more than a quick handshake is for most people very short.

These are cultural traits of long standing. Beyond my parents, I don't myself recall much if any physical contact when growing up even with aunts, uncles and grandparents, let alone friends and more distant relations. As an adult my greatest exposure to the flesh of strangers has been in the artificial context of a degree ceremony where hundreds of hot, cold, dry, sweaty palms are grasped as the graduands walk across the stage.

It may be that with more diverse metropolitan communities, full of people who have brought with them different expectations of physical contact, we have in recent years learned to be more relaxed about embracing others. On the other hand, the sharp rise in awareness of inappropriate touching has caused renewed anxieties. There is mounting evidence from social psychologists that hugging is good for you, releasing endorphins that improve physical and mental health. But still the instinct when seeking greater wellbeing is to get on an exercise bike, or occupy a private yoga mat. Mindfulness begins with listening to your breathing, not with engaging with the bodily rhythms of another.

When this crisis is over, we need to learn how to hug more and hug better.

**Wednesday, 22 July 2020. Where to work?**

A difficulty in writing these diary entries is that of generalising from a distinctly skewed perspective. All of us are different, but some occupy more specialised slots than others.

This fact applies in particular to one of the major questions in the pandemic, the future of work. Just about every office worker has been sent home. Now Boris Johnson wants them back in their place of employment, if only to restore the income flows of sandwich shops and the vendors of the clothes people think they need to wear when outside the house. So far, the indication is that many are declining the invitation, partly because it has been issued at just the moment when all schools are on holiday and childcare problems are once more multiplying, and partly because of very real fears about a renewed threat of infection in a country which has far from conquered the coronavirus.

Beyond these relatively short-term issues lies the question of whether the larger part of the workforce will want to resume their office lives. On the upside is no more commuting, more time with a family, no need to dress up at the beginning of the day (see above on vendors). On the downside there is mounting evidence that home-working reinforces inequalities (an office is an office; no one charges you rent for it, decides whether you can afford a desk), weakens already limited trade union protection (with some employers already exploring technologies that will monitor what happens in your home), and above all crowds out that part of your life which is not work.

I ought to be an expert on this topic. I have at least partially home-worked since my first pay-packet. Every word of every book and article I have published has been written in a room in whatever house we were living in. On the wall in my current study is a photograph of my son, when a small baby, wrapped in a shawl, lying in the open bottom drawer of my desk while I labour above him. He did have a cot. It was just that we had developed a very particular and privileged mix of work, child-rearing and domestic pleasures.

In my first university, where we raised our family, I had total discretion as to where, how and when I earned my living. We lived during the week in campus accommodation, ranging from a starter flat to a family house. My journey to work never exceeded an eight-minute walk. I could transfer myself from study to office and back as and when the need arose, or I just felt like a change of company. All the choices about where I was and what I was doing were mine. Other than turning up for timetabled teaching commitments and departmental meetings, I was, like most academics of my generation, at least in the humanities and social sciences, under no instruction at any point about my labour.

At Keele, the sum total of advice I received on how to undertake my work during almost three decades was as follows:

> Young lecturer, not yet completed probation, on meeting Head of Department in a corridor: 'Paul, you might like to know that my PhD has been approved.'
> HoD: 'That's good. You can take it easy now.'

Then I went to the Open University, the higher education institution where homeworking has long been the norm rather than the exception.

So what do I know about the challenges facing the modern office worker? Not much, except perhaps this one truth. Bullying employers and inconsiderate colleagues will always be a problem. The major challenge, however, is self-discipline. This applies not just to the decision when to start in the morning rather than sit around in the kitchen with another cup of coffee and an unfinished newspaper, but far more importantly, when to stop. There will be backsliding, but the real threat is self-exploitation, going back to emails in the evening or the weekend, never turning off to engage with the life of the home or with personal interests outside employment.

Go out to work. See more of your family.

**Thursday, 23 July 2020. Hobbies and the English.**

'As I write,' began George Orwell, 'highly civilized human beings are flying overhead, trying to kill me.' The time was 1941. Britain had been driven out of continental Europe and victory over Fascism was a distant and uncertain prospect. He set out to define what was 'distinctive and recognizable in English civilisation.' He found his answer not so much in the large generalities of freedom and courage but rather in the detail of everyday life:

> here it is worth noting a minor English trait which is extremely well marked though not often commented on, and that is a love of flowers. This is one of the first things that one notices when one reaches England from abroad, especially if one is coming from southern Europe. Does it not contradict the English indifference to the arts? Not really, because it is found in people who have no aesthetic feelings whatever. What it does link up with, however, is another English characteristic which is so

much a part of us that we barely notice it, and that is the addiction to hobbies and spare-time occupations, the *privateness* of English life. We are a nation of flower-lovers, but also a nation of stamp-collectors, pigeon fanciers, amateur carpenters, coupon snippers, darts-players, crossword puzzle fans.[54]

These were deeply embedded national pastimes. It was not just gardening, which has been discussed in earlier entries. Stamp collecting became a passion of schoolchildren and their parents almost as soon as the adhesive postage stamp was invented with the Penny Post of 1840. The term 'hobby' entered the national discourse at the end of the nineteenth century, with a magazine bearing that title launched in 1896. Amateur practitioners not just of carpentry but an immense range of decorative and useful objects multiplied, generating societies, a flourishing retail trade in supplies and a raft of publications. The crossword, imported from the United States in the late 1920s became a fixture in the back pages of newspapers. 'The range of pastimes, which are collectively known as hobbies,' observed Ferdynand Zweig his 1952 study *The British Worker*, 'is enormous and satisfies a great variety of interests.'[55]

As we face the largest peacetime crisis since 1945, we appear to be rediscovering the same passions. It has just been reported that B&Q, the chain of do-it-yourself supplies, saw a 42% rise in sales for May. As soon as the lockdown was eased, shoppers poured in to buy all the materials they required to improve their homes and gardens. They took away plants, compost, fence panels, and a wide range of decorating and building materials, causing a temporary shortage in wall plaster.

A recent survey found evidence of people re-awakening old skills or setting about acquiring new ones.[56] One individual described how he put into practice a long-dormant training in furniture making, another took up embroidery again as she sought relaxation from her job in the NHS, another decided it was time to fulfil a lifetime's ambition to learn the concertina, another rediscovered a childhood passion for playing the yoyo.

There is much discussion of how this pandemic will cause a revolution in how we live. On the evidence so far it seems more likely that we will return to all the comforting distractions that made the English who they are.

**Friday, 24 July 2020.   On Happiness.**

Four months pass. We remain fit and well-fed. But do we know we are happy?

Few ask that question unless the answer is likely to be a negative. And those that do find it difficult to consult any objective evidence.

However, the pandemic has provoked a wide range of studies in the social sciences as well as medicine. The largest of these, the 'Covid-19

Social Study', has been addressing the question of happiness in a series of reports.

The latest of these, published on 16th July, provides further evidence on the incidence of happiness across British society. The study deploys the methodology of the government's official body, the Office for National Statistics which regularly measures personal well-being under four headings: Life satisfaction; Feeling the things done in life are Worthwhile; Happiness; and Anxiety. Like Spinal Tap's amplifiers, total well-being scores 11 on a 1-11 point scale.

The Covid-19 study, which is concentrating on the experience of the lockdown, finds that overall happiness, though starting at a lower base than pre-lockdown, has been slowly but consistently rising over the period between 21 April and 14 July.

More interesting are the variations by condition. You are more likely to be happy if you are:

Older: we struggle against the label, but have had to wear it through the crisis.

Live with company: we have each other and we know we are not amongst the one in four couples reported in another study whose relationships have come under pressure in the crisis.

Have higher than average household income: there is much to be said for receiving a public sector, final salary pension on retirement; one of the last such pensions ever likely to be paid in this stressed economy.

Have no underlying mental health conditions: which is our good fortune.

Live in a rural area: as we do.

The only qualification is that the Welsh and Scottish are slightly happier than the English. But Wales is in view from the bottom of the garden, and my wife considers herself entirely Scottish, so we can work around that disability.

Still I wonder if I know what it is that I have.

And then, just after breakfast this morning, the phone rang. My younger daughter was in a car with her husband and two children on their way from London to Holyhead to catch the ferry to Ireland where her mother-in-law has a house by the sea in Cork. They were ahead of time, had changed their route, and would be calling on us within the hour (we live a couple of miles from the old Holyhead Road).

And so, for the first time since Christmas, we saw them in the flesh. The children, escaped from the car, played in the garden. If we could not embrace, we could at least talk face to face as we sat around a table in a rare burst of sunshine.

That was happiness.

**Monday, 27 July 2020.  Home Restaurant (2).**

I have long wondered whether there is an easier way of earning a living with my pen than writing history.  Anything will do that does not involve footnotes (as even these diary entries must have from time to time).

So I have decided to explore a career as a food critic.  Doesn't seem difficult. I have to eat every day.  There is a common experience (more or less), a common language (ditto), and to judge from the persistence of food columns in the lockdown, even when their writers were unable to get to restaurants, an inexhaustible demand for such prose.

And I have a specialist topic.  Restaurant meals at home.  Last week it was Elite Bistros, this time it is the Côte brasserie chain which has recently expanded across the country.  It opened a branch in my local town just before the coronavirus struck.  I'm not sure whether it's still there, but I can now buy Côte's meals online.

For Saturday dinner we ordered: starter (for two): marinated heritage beetroot with crème fraiche £4 50; mains: chicken and walnut salad £ 6 95, poulet breton with chips £ 7 95; desserts: lemon and Armagnac posset £ 3 50, crème caramel £ 3 50.  The service also has a bakery and a cheese counter, so we added a sourdough seeded batard and two croissants, a St Nectaire fermier and a chèvre buchette frais cendrés. The was a £4 95 delivery, charge, waived if the bill exceeds £80.

The website was easy to use, with every dish and product illustrated. The box arrived within the specified hour on Saturday morning.

Unlike the serious misadventure last week, cooking was straightforward. I wrote then that it was nothing like a Marks and Spencer meal. This, by contrast, was exactly such a product, better quality, not much more expensive, and requiring only time in the oven. Or rather several different time slots in two ovens at different temperatures, but not too great a sweat.

Five minutes unwrapping, half an hour watching the timer, and we sit down to eat.

What else to say? How do these food writers spin out a meal into a thousand words? There is no service to describe. You don't want to know about my kitchen, before or after cooking. Or my kitchen table (though if you do it was made by a friend out of elm blown down in the great gale of 1987). The beetroot was a surprisingly attractive reworking of a familiar vegetable. The mains were huge. I had ordered mine largely because I hadn't eaten chips since before I can remember, and these oven products were not great. The desserts were fine, the crème caramel leaving us with a little earthenware pot.

The real gain was the bread and cheese. On Saturday, had the year turned out as planned, we would have begun our family holiday in a gite on the shores of the Mediterranean south of Montpellier and west of the Camargue. There we would have enjoyed one of the basic pleasures in life, visiting the boulangerie every day for croissants and cakes, exploring the cheese stalls in the weekly markets. Now we could do it online, with a fine array of bakery products and regional cheeses (Côte advertises itself as a 'Parisian brasserie', but I have rarely stepped inside one, except in the pages of a Maigret novel where the alcohol-dependent policeman is forever visiting them during the course of his working day, or in the case of the 'Brasserie Dauphine' next to the Quai des Orfèvres, inventing the modern office takeaway by having beer and sandwiches sent up in the midst of a long case.)

The one demerit, as with Elite Bistro, is the pile of packaging left behind, although it is all supposed to be recyclable. The washable ceramic plate is one of those inventions that once made, is unimprovable. As also the metal pot. Food packed in, or still worse eaten out of, paper, plastic and cardboard, is an offence against civilisation and will be the death of this planet.

**Tuesday, 28 July 2020. I am not an Island.**

Over the weekend there appeared in the newspaper a preview article of the kind publishers like to commission as free advertising. It was headlined, 'I ran away to a remote Scottish isle. It was perfect.' The book in question was *I Am An Island* by Tamsin Calidas.[57]

As with my own project on solitude, isolated living in nature, a subject addressed by writers at least since Petrarch in the fourteenth century, is suddenly topical. A recent example of this genre is Sara Maitland's *How to be Alone*.[58] This new memoir should find a wide readership. There are, however, reasons for limiting its relevance to our present circumstance.

In the first place there is the headline (for which neither the author nor the publisher may have been responsible). It suggests that it is a narrative of a flight from the pandemic-ridden city to the sea-protected Hebrides. What is left of wilderness in Britain usually has communities living in them, who have not been enthusiastic about acting as refuges from the coronavirus. One of the first actions taken by the Scottish Government was to forbid the ferry company Caledonian MacBrayne from taking anyone to the islands who was not already a resident there. It was rightly fearful of an influx of infected escapees from elsewhere in Britain. On closer examination it transpires that Tamsin Calidas had moved to her island sixteen years ago. This is an insider's account.

Beyond this technical point are more fundamental issues. The book is about isolation as pain. In the summary we are introduced to the breakdown of her marriage on her island, debt, unemployment, bereavement, loneliness, and acute illness. The path out of this suffering involves a voluntary embrace of other forms of hardship, particularly swimming: 'I have swum in snow, in freezing rain with thick ice particles obscuring visibility, in crisp sunshine and in dense mist, and once with the wind chill dipping to -16C and the solid edges of the sea freezing.' This need not diminish the readership. At least since Robinson Crusoe, the numbers of those who have taken comfort reading about the solitary misfortunes of others, whether imposed or chosen, vastly outnumbers those who have directly endured them. But it does call into question the relevance of such a narrative to those who are seeking a more humdrum, and essentially benign pathway through the unexpected experience of enforced solitude.

Tamsin Calidas describes how she made the transition from breakdown to fulfilment by embracing the spiritual resource of nature: 'Some call this biodynamic living, and it makes sense. It connects the unique solitude of every animate or inanimate sentience, and connects it to an expansive, interconnected universe.' Again there is a long literary heritage for this kind of pantheism, given a classic expression in Henry Thoreau's *Walden* and restated in writings such as *A Philosophy of Solitude* by John Cowper Powys (1933). It still has a niche in our culture. People like to think of the countryside as restorative of health and spirits. However, our growing awareness of global pollution has made it increasingly difficult to conceive an untouched nature as a source of moral regeneration in the face of a corrupting urban civilisation.

At least in Western Europe and its surrounding seas there are diminishingly few opportunities to escape the trail of our destructive practices. We carry our responsibilities with us as we walk into what is now very rarely an unspoiled landscape.

**Wednesday, 29 July 2020. Having Babies.**

A Minister of Health, Nadine Dorries, is reported as speculating that nine months on from the start of the lockdown there will be a bulge in the business of the nation's maternity units.

Should we take her seriously? There are two levels of response to this question.

The first is *ad personam*. This is the same Nadine Dorries whose first book, published in 2014, was described by the *Daily Telegraph* reviewer as 'the worst novel I've read in 10 years. Only with imaginative effort might some readers of a mawkish disposition like *The Four Streets*. A sequel – may the Holy Mother protect us – is due in the autumn.' Undeterred, she appears to have written another fourteen novels, all of the same quality.

In the meantime, she earned a reputation in Parliament, as an especially thoughtless, publicity-seeking Brexiteer, opposed to gay marriages and abortion counselling. So it was when Johnson came to form his ministry-of-almost-no-talents, she was appointed a Minister in what would become the key government department for responding to the pandemic. Here she distinguished herself by becoming the very first

MP to be infected with Covid-19, getting diagnosed on the same day she attended a reception with the Prime Minister at Number 10.

Then there is the scientific evidence. Studies beginning with the 1889 flu epidemic in France and the 1918-20 global Spanish flu pandemic have long established that birth rates tend to fall rather than rise after a medical crisis. This applies also to natural disasters like major earthquakes. In the case of our current event, in a recent study people under 35 living in five European countries – France, Germany, Italy, Spain and the UK - were asked whether they intended to have children this year. Between 60 and 80% of respondents replied that they were postponing or abandoning altogether such a decision.

The reason for this caution is not hard to find. Parents seek as much security as possible for the early years of child-rearing. In the case of the Covid-19 pandemic, every forecaster is predicting the worst economic recession since as far back as records exist. The only question is about the speed of recovery. It is recognised that the aftermath of the 1918-20 pandemic, compounded by the Slump of 1929, depressed birth rates in Britain throughout the inter-war period.

What is different this time is the demographic context. I have always felt vaguely guilty that my three children have been a contribution to the unsustainable rise in the global population. Since 1970 the number of people on the planet has almost doubled to the current figure of 7.8bn and was thought to be heading towards 11bn by the end of the century. Now a new study by Washington University is predicting that the peak will be reached in 2064, and will be followed by a major fall in most populations outside Africa, with a halving in countries such as Japan and Spain. In Britain, the Office for National Statistics reports a 12.2% fall in the birth rate since 2012, giving a reproduction rate of 1.65 per woman, well below the level needed to maintain current numbers.

If these projections are even distantly accurate, they pose a major threat to the sustainability of modern economies. The old will no longer have enough people of working age to pay for their pensions and their health care. The long-term remedy will involve major changes in the notion of what a 'working age' is. Mine may be the last generation ever fully to retire.

In the short term there are only two solutions in the UK. Increase the birth rate by attacking child poverty, restoring Sure Start, improving nursery provision, reversing reductions in per-capita educational funding.

Or increase immigration. Not a policy favoured by Nadine Dorries.

**Thursday, 30 July 2020. The Wisdom of Aznavour.**

The lyricist Don Black (Born Free, Diamonds are Forever and an awful lot else), now a cheery eighty-two-year-old Covid-19 survivor, is interviewed in my paper. He has a memoir coming out. The journalist is anxious to discover the secret of his continuing good spirits. Black explains: 'Something Charles Aznavour once said always stayed with me: "A man will never grow old if he knows what he's doing tomorrow." I think that's true.'[59]

That, in a nutshell, is the problem in this lockdown for those of us who are fighting to resist the advance of age. The first thing we all had to do in March was to erase every planned event from our diaries for what looked like a few weeks and now appears, like diamonds, almost forever. My daughters have re-booked their flights to France so we can have the family holiday next July that should be happening now. It seemed a sensible thing to do, until this week when ministers started talking about second waves and re-imposing travel restrictions from the continent. Most days all that we can say about what we are doing tomorrow is that it is likely to be very similar to what we did yesterday.

So we go about inventing small tasks whose content has some purpose and whose completion we can control. Yesterday, on what was falsely promised to be twenty-four hours without rain, I finished varnishing the oak window frames on our extension. Today, as part of a research project on the history of silence, I will immerse myself in the recordings of the sounds of the same London streets in 1928, and those of this May which the enterprising Museum of London has just placed online. And I will write a diary entry, a task set and finished around breakfast time.

I don't doubt that Aznavour, who died recently at the age of ninety-four after a singing career which spanned seventy years, had plans for the morrow which embraced more than home improvements and long-distance research projects.  As it happens, on Friday we are finally getting away from the house to visit locked-down friends in Suffolk for the weekend.  Aznavour would have gone further.  According to his Wikipedia entry, in the last two years of his life he performed in: São Paulo, Rio de Janeiro, Santiago, Buenos Aires, Moscow, Vienna, Perth, Sydney, Melbourne and Haiti, Tokyo, Osaka, Madrid, Milan, Rome, Saint Petersburg, Paris, London, Amsterdam and Monaco.

Eight of those cities I have lectured in and recall visiting.  Perhaps Aznavour's dictum should be reversed.

A man will never grow old if he can remember what he did yesterday.

**Friday, 31 July 2020.  London Sounds.**

The enterprising Museum of London has just made available two sets of recordings of London noise.  The first is a series of gramophone records of street sounds made in 1928.[60]  The Museum claims that these were the earliest such recordings ever made, and that they have never since been heard in their entirety.  They were commissioned by the *Daily Mail* as part of its campaign against what it considered to be the unbearable noise of the modern city.  It wrote that:

'Those who cannot afford the time to travel about the city to hear for themselves how ear-splitting the traffic din has become will be able to have the noises brought to them so that they may be analysed and studied. It is confidently expected that a surprising proportion of them will be found to be wholly unnecessary and therefore preventable.'

The Museum then had the bright idea of organising a parallel set of recordings of the same streets this May, in the midst of the lockdown.[61] They are posted on its site as 'Silent London.'

Much to praise, except the title. The ten, five-minute recordings, listened to through earphones, are anything but silent. The recordings were made during weekday afternoons, and almost without exception they are dominated by the roar of street traffic. It is difficult to calibrate the relative volume of noise in the two sets of recordings. The 1928 sounds, taken from sometimes scratchy LPs with a voice-over describing what is passing the microphone, seem less invasive than the technically much superior modern recordings in which vehicles pass in stereo from one ear to the other. Only in Leicester Square, where there is limited traffic in ordinary times, is it possible to pick up occasional birdsong (particularly cooing pigeons at the beginning) and passing conversations.

By contrast the 1928 soundscape, which so exercised the *Daily Mail*, presents a wider range of aural events. The traffic is more varied, with steam lorries and frequent horse-drawn carts amidst the petrol-driven cars, taxis, buses and lorries. The bells and wheel-flanges of trams can be heard. And over the background roar there is music – a violinist playing with great clarity at the beginning of one recording, a boy whistling, a band including a clarinettist and a banjo-player, and a barrel organ, the mainstay of later nineteenth-century street players, still issuing mechanical tunes. There is a newspaper seller barking in a strident monotone.

So was the much-discussed phenomenon of the silent, locked-down city an illusion? Perhaps the May recordings were just made too late. My diary entry of 17 April described a 75-mile drive to Manchester where the traffic was lighter than usual but far from absent. The period of grace in central London, if it existed, may have been over before the Museum of London set up its microphones. I am told by a friend who daily walked through the streets in the early weeks of lockdown that birdsong could be heard loud and clear, though not much conversation between people keeping their distance. And always there were the ambulance sirens.

Perhaps it was and still is seriously much quieter in the side streets. Perhaps a half-empty thoroughfare, on which the traffic can flow freely, is intrinsically noisier than a near-gridlocked one where cars are mostly at a standstill (I assume traffic engineers know about this). There are other silences not picked up by road-side microphones. My son tells me that he remains daily mindful of the absence of planes on the flightpath to and from the City of London Airport which normally pass over his house.

I would like to imagine the possibility of walking about the capital listening to nothing noisier than birdsong, occasional conversations, and intermittent church bells. But I fear that at least in the daytime, the streets of London have never been that quiet since the fields were first built over.

**Monday, 3 August 2020.  Fixed point.**

We travel across the country, our first weekend away since Christmas. The trip was planned as a celebration of the ending of lockdown for the shielded, officially dated from August 1st. But as we drive, announcements are being made on the radio about the re-imposition of restrictions across a swathe of northern England.

On Radio Manchester, the Health Secretary Matt Hancock conducts a car-crash interview. The presenter, who seems not to be point-scoring, just puzzled, asks him:

'You said that people could go out of Greater Manchester to another area if they followed social distancing but, the government guidance online says you must not visit someone else at home or garden even if they live outside the infected areas, so can you clarify that for us?'

Hancock: 'Yes, I'll make it absolutely clear, which is that there's a distinction between the guidance and the law, I will absolutely get back to you with exact chapter and verse.'

Presenter (after two more minutes of further incoherence): 'Forgive me, but you seem a little confused.'

Had we set off on our journey from about thirty miles further north, we would, at this point, have had to turn around and go home. Hancock does at least seem clear that whilst the new rules / guidance / law means that people can meet outdoors, this does not include gardens, where, on a warm weekend, we did in fact spend most of the time with our friends. Later a newspaper reports that the Government is considering not only locking down the shielded again, but extending the category to include a larger section of the population. This is officially denied but that does not mean it will not happen within days.

So what is fixed in the fifth month? As we once more conduct a risk assessment about whether it is safe to go out, perhaps just this one point. The factor analysis which various bodies have been undertaking since the pandemic took hold, has produced a picture which is at once complex and very simple in terms of my household.[62] There are a range of indicators which make it more likely that infection will lead to hospitalisation and death. These include medical conditions such as diabetes, asthma, obesity, recent organ transplant, some forms of cancer, together with gender and race (particularly black and Asian). But standing out above all others is age, particularly from sixty onwards.

The chef Rick Stein was interviewed last week. He is seventy-four but said he still felt no more than forty, perhaps just a little stiffer. We all do this, taking decades off our birth years in terms of our physical or mental capacity.

We can still, within limits, choose the age of our state of mind. We can still, within limits, choose the age of our fitness. But when it comes to our body's resistance to infection, there is no gaming Bergman's chess player. It is the lesson we have been forced to learn in this pandemic.

Seventy, alas, is the new seventy.


**Tuesday, 4 August 2020. Keeping the Secret.**

After the performance of the confused Matt Hancock over the weekend (see yesterday's diary), the premium on a figure of trust and competence has risen still further.

Step forward Sir Paul Nurse, Nobel Prize winner, director of the Francis Crick Institute, former president of the Royal Society, chief scientific advisor to the European Commission. Here at last is a figure whom a local radio presenter would not be able to reduce to incoherence in a few short minutes.

His contribution to the Covid-19 debate on Sunday should be taken seriously. The issue to which he drew attention was excessive secrecy in government decision-making.

I have written a book on this subject.[63] I argued that the birth of the modern state following the 1832 Reform Act was accompanied by the development of the doctrine of 'honourable secrecy'. Politicians and civil servants controlled information on the basis not of law but culture. Honourable men could be trusted to decide what to say and when not to say it. For as long as the state machine remained small, this system worked, at least on its own terms. The government apparatus was, for its times, both competent and honest. But when, towards the end of the nineteenth century, the civil service expanded and drew in officials who were not gentlemen, and still worse, not men at all, then a law was required to discipline junior staff. The definition of what was a secret was left in the hands of senior officials and their masters. The continuing growth of the role of the state in everyday life eventually required further legal clarification, resulting in a revised Official Secrets Act in 1989, and the 2000 Freedom of Information Act (FOI).

But entrenched habits die hard. What bothers Nurse are two aspects of the old culture. The first is that despite twenty years of FOI, official information is still seen as the possession not of civil society but of politicians and their advisors. They are free to decide when to release it, and even to admit that it exists at all. In the words of Henry Taylor in 1836, 'A secret may be sometimes best kept by keeping the secret of its being secret.'

The second is the instinctive feeling that open debate impedes rather than enhances policy-making. It invites disruptive commentary by the ill-informed or the ill-intentioned. It distracts and delays the work of those charged with taking action. Better to leave the moment of full openness until some later inquiry.

Thus SAGE, the key advisory committee, chaired by two scientists who are now government employees, sought in the early stages to deny information on who were its members in case they were subject to unwarranted lobbying. Its advice on key areas of policy remains confidential. 'It sometimes seems' said Nurse, 'like a "black box" made up of scientists, civil servants and politicians are coming up with the decisions. ... It needs to be more open. We need greater transparency, greater scrutiny and greater challenge to get the best results.'[64] Rather than the scientific culture of critical debate informing government, the political process had muzzled science.

The consequence, as so often in the past, was that the wrong decisions were made and then covered up to prevent embarrassment. On the rolling shambles of coronavirus testing, for instance, Nurse charges that, 'They seemed not to want to admit that they weren't prepared, that they were unable to do the testing properly, because that would have been an admission of failure from square one.'

As in other areas the response to the coronavirus has exposed rather than transcended deficiencies in public life. And as elsewhere, this matters not just for the management of the crisis but for the future of society more generally. The pandemic is just one example of how complex policy decisions will need to be fully informed by scientific information which is itself a matter of constant debate.

The discovery of how far secrecy is still ingrained in the official mind is an open threat to us all.

**Wednesday, 5 August 2020. Dostoyevsky rules.**

In an addendum to the June 22 diary, I noted a further still-birth in a woman's prison. As ever in this rear-view country, a set of inquiries has been launched, but their findings have been pre-empted by a whistle-blower in the person of Tamsin Morris, a lawyer who previously managed the mother-and-baby unit at Styal Prison.

She revealed that four months before the event she had written to the local MP, the Mayor of Manchester, and the Ministry of Justice, raising concerns about conditions for pregnant women in prison. Together with the charity Birth Companions, she had drawn attention to the failure to record the number of women in prisons who are pregnant, the unavailability of appropriate termination procedures, inadequate pregnancy testing, and inconsistent antenatal services. Pregnancy tests were only offered on entry to the prison and could be declined by the prisoner. Thereafter there were no further tests, and no national record of pregnant women prisoners.

In the Styal case, no care was given until the prisoner unexpectedly went into labour. It is possible that in this prison, and across the sector, some minor reforms will follow. The question remains, as I argued in my entries for June 2 and June16, whether the coronavirus presents an unmissable opportunity to reform an essentially inhumane and destructive penal regime. As the pandemic persists so also does one of its more unacceptable consequences, the imposition of widespread solitary confinement in prison cells as the only available means of preventing mass infection.

We arrive at the end of the second decade of the twentieth century with, at best, a partially modernised version of the system that began to be constructed in 1842, with the opening of Pentonville. There has been a long debate about the function of incarceration. Proponents of rehabilitative justice have largely been defeated by the advocates of retribution.[65] Ever since the introduction of solitary confinement where the prisoner was supposed to repent and reform through a prolonged period of spiritual meditation, there has been scant evidence that rehabilitation works. After nearly two centuries of inquiry and adjustments to the system, the recidivism rate in England and Wales (the proportion of prisoners committing crimes on release) stands at 50% after one year. There is ample evidence not only that prison does not reform, but that the experience of incarceration is destructive of mental and physical health, especially with the renewed use of solitary confinement.

The prisons should be front and centre of public policy in this pandemic for two reasons. The first is that of opportunity. Dominic Cummings promises that a 'hard rain' is going to fall on the civil service. Were he to focus his iconoclastic tendencies on the Ministry of Justice, then history would indeed go round a corner. There are European examples of how to do it better. In Norway a much smaller proportion of the offending population is housed in civilised, small-scale accommodation where the prisoners are treated with a basic respect. The result is a vast reduction in both public expenditure and the recidivism rate, which stands at 20% over two years. In Britain, perhaps ten per cent of the current prison population needs to be behind bars to protect the rest of society. Outside, the plethora of electronic surveillance devices, which so alarm privacy campaigners, could be applied to the task of monitoring the behaviour of potential repeat offenders.

The second reason is more basic. Dostoyevsky's much travelled dictum still applies: 'A *society* should be judged not by how it *treats* its outstanding citizens but by how it *treats* its criminals.'

So also will be the verdict on how we have learned from this crisis.

**Thursday, 6 August 2020. Goggling at the box.**

According to a new survey by OFCOM, at the height of the lockdown in April the average person watched television for six hours and twenty-five minutes a day, up almost a third on the same month last year.[66]

With people locked in their homes, and those who could get out faced with closed cinemas and theatres, it was inevitable that there should be a rise in viewing. But six hours and twenty-five minutes? After reading the papers online, complaining about Johnson, taking care of emails, zooming relations and colleagues, walking round the garden, eating and drinking, complaining about Johnson, where are there so many hours left in the day?

Some of the answer lies in the flexible term 'watching'. In the late 1980s, with a television in every home, sociologists led by Laurie Taylor began to enquire into what actually happened when the screen was lit up. They found that in many households the television tended to be switched on permanently, providing the same kind of generalised warmth as the fireplace, but otherwise disregarded unless a particularly popular programme brought the family together. For the most part the life of the household went on much as before, with its members occupied with their particular concerns. They cited the response to their inquiry of a thirty-one-year-old housewife: 'We have it on but we don't sit watching it. We turn it on first thing in the morning when we come down and it's on till late at night. I'm out in the garden, doing the gardening, going back and forth – I'm not watching telly all the time – it's just there and it's on.'[67]

I am part of that vanishing generation which had no television at all until mid-way through my childhood (our first set was acquired from our cleaner when I was about nine). My responsible parents decreed that their children could only watch this enticing invention for an hour a day, leaving the rest of free time for homework, playing in the garden, talking to each other. This at least meant that we watched every last minute of our allocation and I still regard it as sinful to have a television playing to an empty room.

The Ofcom finding that there has been a surge in subscription television may mean something. We too have joined the art-house channels

MUBI and Curzon Home Cinema. These are vastly superior to the repetitive menu of Film 4. But they are a tough challenge at the end of another wearisome day. A current MUBI offering is described thus:

> Defined by its director as a work of 'futurist ethnography,' this gem of Brazilian underground cinema is a dystopian sci-fi at once witty and visually thrilling. Powerfully commenting on modern-day racism, Adirley Queirós' third film digs into the very heart of both past and present politics.

Instead we decided late yesterday evening to start watching a re-run of *The Blues Brothers* on Netflix. Stylish fun with a knockout cameo by Aretha Franklin.

And it only lasts two hours and thirteen minutes.

**Friday, 7 August 2020. Take a Pill.**

Big pharma is having a good war. It is generally accepted that the only way of ending the pandemic is the discovery of a vaccine, and its manufacture and distribution on a global scale by multi-national drug companies. Everything else is just dealing with the symptoms.

Companies like AstraZeneca are making deals with governments around the world to make available the first vaccines to succeed in the current trials. Never before have we been so aware of the virtues of their technological competence and organisational power.

There remain, however, areas where these companies stand to gain from the crisis in less welcome ways. The widespread disruption to established patterns of social interaction has raised fears that loneliness may be on the increase. As I have argued in earlier diary entries (especially May 27), the first batch of survey evidence suggests that acute loneliness, the kind that causes serious psychological suffering, appears remarkably stable in the pandemic at around five per cent of the population. Nonetheless the preceding moral panic, which produced inflated loneliness figures of over fifty per cent and referred to a widespread 'epidemic', has gained a new lease of life in a time when everyone's relationships are under strain.

The drive to medicalise what is a form of failed solitude is partly a function of how political change works. Pressure groups and concerned scientists have since the 1950s, compelled governments to intervene in a growing range of private behaviours which have demonstrable physical consequences, starting with smoking, and, in recent days, finally causing the overweight Boris Johnson to commit his administration to tackling obesity. Thus, campaigners claim that loneliness has worse consequences than smoking fifteen cigarettes a day, or having too large a waistline.

As a recent newspaper report has revealed, the discourse has thrown renewed attention on the search for a loneliness pill.[68] In Chicago,

Stephanie Cacioppo, co-researcher with the late Stephen Cacioppo, is continuing work on isolating a pharmacological treatment for social isolation. Another research group is investigating the prescription of oxytocin for loneliness sufferers. Whether these pills are a self-sufficient remedy or part of a psychotherapy treatment, the prospects for the pharmaceutical companies are immense. Whilst serious loneliness is a minority experience, the multiple transition points in late modernity mean that all of us at some point risk malfunctions in our social life. The current pandemic in this regard merely highlights the fragility of the networks of personal relationships that we all seek to maintain. If every time there is a failure of interaction, or a perceived danger of such an event, we could just pop a pill out of its foil sheet, how relaxed might we be, and how great the profit for the manufacturer.

There are of course complex ways in which medical conditions, including mobility or communication disabilities, can impact on interpersonal relations. Forms of acute depression can have a range of physiological consequences including damage to immune systems. There is a longstanding debate about whether and in what form pharmacological treatments should play a part in psychotherapy. None of these complexities are resolved by conceiving the existence of a loneliness pill or seeking to put one on the market.

Just as good solitude is a rest from the labour involved in effective social relationships, so bad solitude requires for its alleviation a wide range of public actions.

There is no pill that will resist the effects of the coming collapse in income and employment, or the continuing underinvestment in mental health and local support facilities.

**Monday, 10 August 2020. Keeping the Secret (2).**

No words from me today. Just a letter in Friday's *Guardian* from senior statisticians, on exactly the same theme as my piece on August 4, 'Keeping the Secret':

> The Covid-19 public health crisis has placed a sharp emphasis on the role of data in government decision-making. During the current phase – where the emphasis is on test and trace, and local lockdowns – data is playing an increasingly central role in informing policy.
>
> We recognise that the stakes are high and that decisions need to be made quickly. However, this makes it even more important that data is used in a responsible and effective manner. Transparency around the data that is being used to inform decisions is central to this.
>
> Over the past week, there have been two major data-led government announcements where the supporting data was not made available at the time.

First, the announcement that home and garden visits would be made illegal in parts of northern England. The prime minister cited unpublished data which suggested that these visits were the main setting for transmission. Second, the purchase of two new tests for the virus that claim to deliver results within 90 minutes, without data regarding the tests' effectiveness being published.

We are concerned about the lack of transparency in these two cases – these are important decisions and the data upon which they are based should be publicly available for scrutiny, as Paul Nurse pointed out in the *Guardian* (Secrecy has harmed UK government's response to Covid-19 crisis, says top scientist, 2 August).

Government rhetoric often treats data as a managerial tool for informing decisions. But beyond this, transparency and well-signposted data builds public trust and encourages compliance: the daily provision of statistical information was an integral part of full lockdown and was both expected and valued by the public.

As champions for the use of data in policymaking, set out in the Royal Statistical Society's data manifesto, we ask the government to recognise the importance of transparency and to promptly and prominently publish all data that underpins its decisions.

Prof Sylvia Richardson, Prof David Spiegelhalter, Prof Christl Donnelly, Prof Peter Diggle, Prof Sheila Bird, Simon Briscoe, Prof Jon Deeks

*On behalf of the Royal Statistical Society Covid-19 taskforce'*

On the one hand, secrecy is bred in the bones of the British system of government despite legislative reform. It is made worse by the arrogance of an 80-seat majority and the conviction that control over communication is essential in what amounts to a wartime endeavour. As was noted in an earlier diary entry (April 27), very few of the Ministers have a scientific background, including those at the frontline of managing the pandemic.

On the other hand, politicians, as they have stressed from the outset, are dependent upon the input of scientists. This means not just their knowledge, but how that knowledge is generated. Scientists proceed by evidence-based research, open to review and improvement by other practitioners. As Sir Paul Nurse and now the Royal Statistical Society complain, their culture is fundamentally at odds with those they are now working with.

With Johnson and Cummings in charge, there seems no likely resolution of this impasse.

## Tuesday, 11 August 2020.  Corrigendum.

On this my hundredth diary entry, I begin with a correction.  On August 7, I wrote: 'It is generally accepted that the only way of ending the pandemic is the discovery of a vaccine and its manufacture and distribution on a global scale by multi-national drug companies.'  A day later, a study conducted by King's College London and Ipsos Mori reported that only 53% of the British population was definitely or very likely to accept being vaccinated, whilst one in six said they would definitely be very unlikely to go ahead with such a treatment.

This finding is in fact very similar to a survey I discussed on July 6, based that time on a YouGov poll.

At face, the finding is deeply depressing.  It suggests one of two things.  Either the community spirit that has carried us through is decaying just when it matters.  The widely-observed initial lockdown depended on an act of collective altruism.  Those unlikely to suffer greatly from an infection controlled their social lives on behalf of the elderly and those with co-morbidities, who were much more vulnerable.  In the new study the young (16-24 and 25-34 year-olds) are twice as likely to refuse a vaccine as the old (55-75).

Or the proportion of the population prepared to disregard medical advice is much larger than we supposed.  It is not so much a matter of disputing a particular scientific finding.  There will always be argument about which remedy is most appropriate, even amongst researchers themselves. Rather we are faced with a Trumpian disdain for science altogether as a mode of advancing the truth. It is a wholesale rejection of the Enlightenment project, the notion that the natural world could be progressively understood through evidence-based rational discourse.

There is, however, a caution against despair. The opinion poll surveys are asking a hypothetical question. There is no vaccine, merely encouraging reports of several clinical trials. Conversely there are any number of bogus cures being widely discussed in books and online forums. John Naughton in his *Observer* column on Sunday traced in convincing detail how the algorithms on sites such as Amazon are promoting anti-vax literature with little to counter it.

As and when the vaccine is found, manufactured, and distributed to doctors' surgeries, then the whole debate will shift. Governments will stop issuing vaguely optimistic promises and get behind a determined programme of mass vaccination. If it is seen to work not just in random trials but in real populations, the proportion of refuseniks will surely shrink to a marginal though possibly damaging fringe (at least in the UK; all bets are off in the States, whoever wins the presidential election).

It may be that the poll findings are not so much a cause as a reflection of a collapsed optimism. I have been writing entries every weekday for nearly five months. During that time public spirit has made a transition from panic contained by collective endeavour to weary disillusion with every aspect of the official effort. We come to the end of the first period of the pandemic with the highest per capital death toll in Europe and the deepest projected economic recession. Whether it is a second phase or a renewed surge, there appears no end in sight to the level of infections, which climbed back over a thousand at the weekend. In England no-one believes the assurances of any part of government, from face-masks to care homes to test and trace to reopening of schools. Dominic Cummings' Flight to Durham in late March and subsequent non-apology in the Downing Street garden is held to mark the turning point in public confidence. He's still inside Number 10. It will take a real vaccine, actually and widely available, before spirits change.

But by that time, we will be mired in Brexit outcomes.

Enjoy the rest of your summer. I'm taking a break.

**Friday, 4 September 2020. The Rise of an Historian.**

Here's a question for you. Who is the author of this PhD?

This research takes a chronological approach, in order to trace both the development of policy and of the role of the JIC within central government. It explores the major crises of the period: the Soviet blockade of Berlin in 1948, the riots in East Berlin of June 1953 and the 1958-61 Berlin Crisis. Away from these crises, the thesis examines the picture that the JIC painted of

Soviet intentions and capabilities in Eastern Germany and of the development of the two German nations.[69]

The answer is the second, or joint second, most powerful man in the British political system. Should he wish so to do, the new Cabinet Secretary and Head of the Home Civil Service could describe himself as Dr. Simon Case. At a certain point in his late twenties, he decided not to publish his thesis and pursue a university career, although he has retained an association with academic life and is currently a visiting professor at King's College London. Instead, he passed the exams for fast-track entry into the civil service. Thereafter he rose rapidly, until he fell out with the then chief Brexit negotiator in 2018, and after three months working on the Irish problem left for what was surely the dead-end job of Private Secretary to the Duke of Cambridge. Now amidst the massacre of Permanent Secretaries, he has been recalled to active service.

The question for us all is not so much his indecent youth, as his academic qualification. Should we worry that the country is now being run by two historians in their forties?

A further degree gives only qualified assurance. I spent my adult life in the company of men and women with a doctorate, and supervised a fistful of students seeking to obtain one. I know whereof I speak. Demonstrated command of what is usually a very narrow field of knowledge is not to be confused with any level of general intelligence or practicality. I have worked with holders of PhDs whom you would not trust to write an online shopping list, much less unpack the groceries on arrival.

However, Case appears to have been an exception. His supervisor Peter Hennessy has said that 'He had a muscularity of intellect and masses of intellectual curiosity, plus precise organisational gifts which you don't usually see in students.' A historian who can tie his shoe-laces unaided is indeed a promising prospect.

The larger question resolves itself into a narrower issue: can he defeat 'hard rain' Cummings in the battle to politicise the civil service.

There are two grounds for hope, beyond the general fact that after the brutal dismissal of his predecessor, he is unsackable for the time being (unless Johnson goes the full Trump and dismisses all his senior officials every year).

The first is that his academic mentor was not, as in Cummings' case, Norman Stone, the most morally corrupt senior historian of the modern era (see Diary 27 April), but the upright Peter Hennessy (see Diary 23 June), the wisest and best informed of all historians of contemporary British politics. And Hennessy backs him: 'There is nothing flash or histrionic. He is one of those people you find every now and again in professional life who are so capable that you don't mess around with them because they are a level above.'

The second is that the completion of the long, lonely road of a Ph.D. in the humanities is at least a measure of persistence. This is someone who has demonstrated a capacity to take the slow road to achieving his goal. Cummings has never held any post for much more than a year and will be out of Number 10 before the end of 2021, for whatever cause. Case will outlast the man who despises the civil service, and with any luck will turn out to be its creative defender.

**Tuesday, 8 September 2020. Publick good and Private Mischief.**

I have been reading Daniel Defoe's *Journal of a Plague Year*, a narrative of the outbreak of bubonic plague in London in 1665.

Defoe addressed his subject much as Netflix might treat the current event. Carefully accumulated factual evidence was translated into a moving human document by means of a lightly fictionalised narrative structure. He wrote in 1722 about an event that took place when he was about five years old. His direct memory of the plague must have been slight, but as the son of a London tallow-chandler he grew up amidst a community for whom this was an epochal experience. He was one of the first modern journalists and accumulated as much factual evidence as he could find, making particular use of the contemporary Bills of Mortality which provided a weekly map of the spread of the plague across the city.

Defoe wrote to entertain, to make money, but above all to warn. The plague had broken out again in Marseille in 1720, and all Europe was on the alert in case it spread across the Continent once more. The *Journal* was history written to prevent its repetition.

In every major plague outbreak from the fourteenth century to the coronavirus, the central response of authorities has been to keep victims apart from those yet to be infected. Whether it was the forty-day quarantine invented by the Venetians in the fifteenth century, or our own mis-firing track and trace system, the task is to identify the sick and remove them from the company of the healthy. Until the late nineteenth century there was no accurate understanding of the biology of pandemics, but the coming of DNA analysis has made little difference to the essential common-sense reaction.

Neither has there been any alteration to the basic relocation of power from the individual to the collective at such a time of crisis. In 1665, the Lord Mayor of London imposed the drastic remedy of locking families in their houses when one of their members fell ill. Defoe was impressed by the ferocity of the policy:

> It is true, that the locking up the Doors of Peoples Houses, and setting a Watchman there Night and Day, to prevent their stirring out, or any coming to them; when perhaps the sound People, in the Family, might have escaped, if they had been remov'd from the Sick, looked very hard and cruel; and many People perished in these miserable Confinements, which 'tis

reasonable to believe, would not have been distemper'd if they had had Liberty, tho' the Plague was in the House ... But it was a publick Good that justified the private Mischief; and there was no obtaining the least Mitigation, by any Application to Magistrates, or Government, at that Time, at least, not that I heard of.[70]

So it comes to pass that the plague has arrived in my own small village. A twenty-year-old decided that he was owed a continental holiday. On his return he transmitted Covid-19 to his parents. Defoe's principle still applies. 'Publick Good' justifies 'private Mischief', that is to say the harm caused to the felt interests of individual citizens. Parties, large-scale social gatherings, foreign vacations, are personal luxuries we cannot afford. In Defoe's plague year the Magistrates stuck to their rule, despite the many attempts to evade it. As we must.

**Thursday, 10 September 2020. Smoking the Mail.**

Over the last six months, the main exposure of our home to the threatening outside world has been in the form not of visitors but deliveries of post, parcels and weekly groceries. The postman and other van drivers keep their distance. The problem is what to do with the letters and boxed items. We know that the coronavirus can linger on hard surfaces for at least twenty-four hours. This causes us to leave untouched uninteresting items such as mail shots and bank statements.

But we are less patient with anything that looks as if it will entertain us or improve our lives.

For guidance on how we should conduct ourselves in this regard, we can turn once more to Daniel Defoe. Alongside his *Journal of the Plague Year*, he also published the much less well-known *Due Preparations for the Plague, as well for Souls as Body. Being some seasonable Thoughts upon the visible approach of the present dreadful Contagion in France; the properest measures to prevent it, and the great work of submitting to it* (1722). This was a more overtly didactic work than the *Journal,* although it deployed much of the same material.

Among the topics he addressed was how to treat incoming mail. Thanks to the work of James Daybell and other historians, we now know that there was a widely-used postal service operating across Britain by the mid-seventeenth-century. It was deployed for business purposes, for connecting family members of the middling and upper classes, and for supporting an international network of scholars. At the Restoration in 1660, Charles II had established the General Letter Office, which was designed to create a state monopoly in the conveyance of letters. Operating with a very broad understanding of infection, Defoe regarded the service as a serious threat to health.

We now know that the bubonic plague was spread by fleas carried by black rats, and unlike fabrics sent about the country, the hard surface of paper was not likely to be a means of transmission. But it is now, so we should take seriously the *Due Preparations*. In the book Defoe cited the example (also referred to in the *Journal*) of a prosperous wholesale grocer in London, head of a household which comprised his wife, five children, two maid servants and an apprentice. The grocer took the precaution of keeping his doors shut in order to avoid physical contact, hauling any necessary items to an upstairs window by means of a pulley:

> Hitherto he had corresponded with several of his acquaintances and customers in the country, and had received letters from them, and written letters to them constantly, but would not do any business, or send any goods to them upon any account, though very much pressed to it, because he resolved not to open his doors, whatever damages he suffered.

> His letters were brought by the postman, or letter-carrier, to his porter, when he caused the porter to smoke them with brimstone and with gunpowder, then open them, and to sprinkle them with vinegar; then he had them drawn up by the pulley, then smoked again with strong perfumes, and, taking them with a pair of hair gloves, the hair outermost, he read them with a large reading-glass which read at a great distance, and, as soon as they were read, burned them in the fire; and at last, the distemper raging more and more, he forbid his friends writing to him at all.[71]

I can only commend this practice to you.

**Tuesday, 15 September 2020. 'very little Difference was to be seen.'**

Once the scale of the pandemic became clear, commentators of all perspectives began asking the question, how different would the post-coronavirus world look? Would individuals, societies, governments, embrace radical change, or would we do all that we could to reinstate familiar routines and pleasures?

Looking back in 1772, to the 1665 plague, Daniel Defoe was pessimistic about the outcome. 'But except what of this was to be found in particular Families and Faces,' he wrote, 'it must be acknowledg'd that the general Practice of the People was just as it was before, and very little Difference was to be seen.'[72]

At least part of the explanation for the transient effect was that the outbreak of bubonic plague was immediately followed by the Great Fire of London, which reset the programme of improvement on every front. We have already arranged for a cataclysm next year in the form of a no-deal Brexit, which in the UK at least may indeed wipe out all prospect of progressive change in the 2020s.

Nonetheless the question remains on the agenda, even if the point of conclusion is now receding into the distance. The large-scale Nuffield / UCL Covid-19 survey which I have written about before, has just asked its panel of now over 70,000 respondents whether they expect to change the way they live their lives once the pandemic is over.[73]

The results are deeply underwhelming. Whilst only ten per cent expect to return exactly to their previous life, a mere two per cent of the respondents assented to the proposition, 'I will entirely change the way I lived compared before Covid-19'. Over half the population thought that 'they were more likely on balance to return to how things were before' with about a fifth expecting to change things and over a quarter in between no change and some change.

When the survey focusses on the specific actions of those who wanted a new life, the poverty of aspiration becomes still clearer. Top of the list is an activity which perhaps has been created by the pandemic, giving more support to local businesses. But as the fourth most desired change is more shopping online, it seems unlikely that there is going to be a wholesale shift to buying the necessities of life from the grocer around the corner. Otherwise, the head of the chart is filled with such mundane ambitions as saving more money, exercising more, eating healthier food. About ten per cent report an intention to 'seek a new romantic relationship' but it is not clear whether this ambition has been communicated to an existing partner.

The problem with these sorts of enquiries is the absence of a pre-Covid baseline. In a culture which foregrounds the freedom of individuals to set their own future, it might be supposed that a desire for some sort of change is near universal. The content of the reported agenda looks a lot like the first week of any given New Year, when in the aftermath of over-consumption, resolutions are formed to live a more virtuous life.

These peter out as the days lengthen, leading to an outcome that looks very like Defoe's verdict.

The conclusion has to be that alongside staying alive and getting a virus test, we need to devote serious time to conceiving a new future. It will not occur by default, nor by responding to short-term inconveniences. The slogan 'Build Back Better' is now widely used by agencies, pressure groups and politicians (even B. Johnson, God help us) reacting to the crisis.

On the survey evidence, what better is remains out of focus and beyond what at present we seem able to imagine.

**Thursday, 17 September 2020. Sneak Culture.**

Boris Johnson has given an interview to this morning's *Sun* in which he is quoted as criticising the Home Secretary's encouragement to neighbours to report breaches of the 'Rule of Six' to the authorities. He told the newspaper that 'I have never much been in favour of sneak culture myself.'

Only readers of a certain age and a deep immersion in British boarding school literature will understand the meaning of a 'sneak culture'.

For illumination, let us turn to an iconic figure in such stories, the rotund person of Billy Bunter. In *Billy Bunter's Barring Out* of 1948, Frank

Richards' eponymous hero is encountering, not for the first time, a moral dilemma. Bob Cherry, a fellow pupil in the Remove at Greyfriars School, is facing expulsion after a bag of soot was inadvertently dropped on the head of the master, Mr. Quelch. Bunter announces to his classmates that he knows the culprit and intends to inform the headmaster. His proposal arouses immediate hostility:

'That's why—I—I—I mean, I—Look here, you fellows, I jolly well know who it was, and I'm going to tell the Head.'

'You can't do that,' said Harry Wharton. 'You can't give a man away—we don't sneak in the Remove. But you can tell us, and we'll put it to the fellow to own up.'

'And we'll put it pretty strong!' growled Johnny Bull.

'I'm going to tell the Head,' persisted Bunter. ''Tain't sneaking— I'm no sneak, I hope! Did you fellows ever know me do a rotten thing? I ask you!'

'Sneaking' constituted a fundamental breach of the public-school code. That Johnson should use the term betrays not just his upbringing but the juvenile way in which he conceives the restrictions his government has introduced. On the one hand there is an intrinsically repressive state, prone to impose regulation in order to entrench its power. On the other there is the community of the governed whose principal loyalty is to each other. There is no offence greater than reporting misbehaviour to authority.

In a grown-up world, it might be supposed that citizens and the state have a common interest in rules designed to achieve the urgent objective of controlling infection. If the agents of discipline, the police or local wardens, are seen as representatives of an alien regime, the prospects of observance diminish. There will instead be a corresponding increase in jolly japes like un-distanced drinking or non-face-masked shopping.

For Billy Bunter, as ever, the story ended badly:

'So you've wriggled out of it, you fat worm?' exclaimed Bob Cherry... 'Gentlemen, chaps, and sportsmen,' said Bob Cherry. 'It was Bunter all the time, and he seems to have pulled the Head's leg and got off. I'm glad he isn't bunked, but he's going to be jolly well bumped—'

'Oh, really, Cherry—!'

'Collar him!'

'Here, I say, you fellows—Leggo—Beasts—yaroooh!' roared Bunter, as he was collared.

Bump!

'Oh, crikey! I say—.'

Bump!

'Will you leggo?'

Bump!

'Whoooooop!'

Billy Bunter sat on Smithy's carpet, and roared.

Our own fat worm deserves no less.

**Monday, 21 September 2020.  New Life.**

We have a new granddaughter, conceived when coronavirus was only an unreported event in China.  'Shielding' has entered our vocabulary during the last six months, but no living being has been as protected from the raging storm as this infant growing in her mother's womb.

Now she is amongst us, three weeks old, small but perfectly formed.

There have been a host of  inconveniences surrounding her first few days.  My son found himself almost completely excluded from her birth, much as fathers were when I was born.  It took a fortnight's careful planning before my wife and I could drive down to London to greet her.  Distance was observed during the visit, masks were worn.  What effect so many half-covered faces is having on this intensely observing person we will only later discover.

These difficulties eventually will pass.  The bigger question is the longer term.  I grew up in a country still recovering from the material and human destruction caused by the Second World War.  My recollection of that era is entirely of the future that was being created in the 1950s.  My granddaughter might not feel so blessed.  She may instead experience a childhood over-shadowed by the re-fighting of wars of the previous decade.

About the yet longer term I have almost nothing to say. With an average amount of luck, this small child will live through the whole of this century. I simply cannot conceive what her surroundings will look like by the time she reaches my age. Climate change must constitute the greatest risk, but what in the end will be the balance between human neglect in creating the crisis and human ingenuity in responding to it, is beyond my calculation.

At least we have met. A cousin has just sent me a photograph of my paternal grandmother, Hannah, called Polly. She was a miner's wife, and died of TB, what used to be called consumption, at the age of forty, on my father's tenth birthday. I never knew even what she looked like. Cameras were uncommon possessions in her community. But it turns out that an image has survived, taken in a studio in Hanley. I gaze upon her face with fascination. She has thick dark hair, pulled back from a central parting. A strong, intelligent, humorous face. In what way have her looks found their way into my children? What was she like, and what part could she have played in my childhood, when she would only have been in her sixties and seventies?

I have lived long enough to encounter five grandchildren, and with this latest there is once more the prospect of getting to know each other, of exchanging views about what the world is like and how we might better live in it.

**Thursday, 24 September 2020. Log-stack.**

It's the autumn equinox, so we take delivery of a thousand kiln-dried logs to get us through the winter.

As the logs tumble out of the trailer onto our drive, we ask how business has been during the pandemic. Never better says the man from Logalog, a Shropshire firm specialising in high quality timber. In March, orders were three times higher than the same time last year.

Enquiring on the web confirms this report. 'Kindwood', a firm claiming to be 'the UK's first and only true sustainable firewood brand', experienced a 320% rise in sales at the beginning of the lockdown.

It's an oddly atavistic form of hoarding. It was to be expected that there would be bulk buying of modern essentials such as loo paper or pasta, and later handwash and face-masks. But not firewood, at the end rather than the beginning of winter (I find a report of a similar rise in demand in the Stirling Woodyard, Adelaide, Australia, but there at least the obverse seasons made this a more rational behaviour). There is something very primal about stocking up with firewood in the face of a looming national crisis, just as the days are lengthening.

Our heap of logs has then to be transported down the garden and carefully stacked. For this activity I rely on one of my favourite books, Lars Mytting's *Norwegian Wood. Chopping, Stacking and Drying Wood the Scandinavian Way.* This was a surprise hit when it was published in Britain in 2015. Its title fully reflects the contents. Chopping, and in particular stacking wood are treated as both a science and an art. There are wrong ways and right ways to construct piles that are stable, damp-proof and aesthetically pleasing. Mytting writes:

> You know exactly where you are with a woodpile. Its share price doesn't fall on the stock market. It won't rust. It won't sue for divorce. It just stands there and does one thing: It waits for winter.[74]

Or a pandemic.

Amongst the information the book conveys is the existence of a Norwegian law which requires every house over a certain size to possess a source of heating independent of the electricity supply. This makes a lot of sense. Most forms of warming a house depend on the national grid, either directly or in order to pump the water through a central heating system. In an arctic winter, if the electricity supply fails, families can freeze to death. Hence the importance of a log-pile (and a wood-burning stove, upon which Mytting is also a source of encyclopaedic advice).

Almost unnoticed in the catalogue of government incompetence, the British long-term energy strategy collapsed last week. Hitachi pulled out of building a nuclear power station in Wylfa, north Wales, calling into question the planned Sizewell C project. The only plant actually under construction, Hinkley Point C, is over time and over budget. The official policy is to rely on nuclear power to fill the gaps in renewable energy generated by the sun, wind or waves. If that strategy is correct, the consequence of the serial failings in implementing the nuclear programme will be that sooner or later in the UK, the lights will start to go out, and the central heating boilers to cease functioning.

Better stock up on logs. But do make sure they are stacked properly.

**Friday, 25 September 2020. On Saints.**

I read that Cardinal Giovanni Angelo Becciu has resigned suddenly over a scandal concerning the purchase of property in London.

This is, of course, not the first time that a large sum has been used to buy housing in the world capital of laundering illegitimate money. What caught my eye was the role in the Vatican played by the Cardinal, which presumably will be carried on by his successor. The corrupt prelate was in charge of the department that decides who will become saints.

It might be supposed that in this time of crisis, when the wrath of God is being visited on the children of disobedience, we are in sore need of such exemplary figures. Since the early days of the pandemic, there has been a chorus of praise in the media for the devotion, in particular, of health professionals who were risking their lives to save the afflicted.

The now discontinued collective applause on Thursday evenings was a diffuse recognition of their selfless dedication.

It is important, however, to look carefully at the criteria for canonisation in the Catholic Church. Besides leading an 'exemplary life of goodness and virtue worthy of imitation', and ideally having suffered martyrdom, the candidate also has to be shown to have performed directly or posthumously two miracles. Much of Cardinal Becciu's time will have been spent sifting out candidates who were exemplary moral beings but could not display the requisite number of verifiable miraculous actions.

A miracle is a divine event that has no natural or scientific basis. The latest English saint, Cardinal Newman, was credited with curing a man's spinal disease and a woman's unstoppable bleeding. I used to teach Newman's theology for a living as part of a Master's course in Victorian culture. He was the leading Christian intellectual of his generation in England, first in the Church of England, and then following his conversion in 1845, in the Catholic Church. None of his writings, and no scholarly examination of his career, ever featured a role curing the sick, but the Vatican managed to find two instances which could not be explained by medical science.

It could be argued that this kind of saint is nothing but a threat in our present difficulties. The public figure who by his own estimation mostly closely fulfils the criteria of performing actions that defy scientific reasoning is Donald Trump. Since the outset he has made predictions about the course of coronavirus and the efficacy of remedies (including bleach) that are not only unsupported by medical knowledge but in his terms are the more credible because they are the product of a higher grasp of the truth. Trump evidently believes that he has access to knowledge that has more authority than the reasoning of toiling scientists. So, by extension, the internet is awash with Covid-19 cures sold on the basis that they are superior to orthodox medicine.

We see it also in the pale imitations of Trump who govern our destiny in Britain. Whilst they must make a profession of listening to scientists, their narrative of progress is essentially magical. Johnson has made a series of proclamations about the course of the pandemic which have no basis in evidence-supported fact but are justified only by his professional hostility to 'doomsters and gloomsters.' Similarly, his hapless Health Secrecy has promulgated achievements and targets for track and testing devices (with a new app launched yesterday) that are the product of faith rather than rational calculation.

Now, more than ever, we should seek solutions that have a scientific basis. We want leaders of goodness and exemplary virtue; we have no use for saints.

That said, the odd martyrdom would not come amiss. St Dominic Cummings of Durham would be a good start.

**Monday, 28 September 2020.  Counting.**

Pandemics have always generated numbers.   Defoe structured his *Journal of the Plague Year* around the weekly Bills of Mortality which allowed him to track the progress of the disease from parish to parish across London in 1665.  We have the same ambition on a global scale. Today's figures are 32.85 million infections and nearly a million deaths.[75]

Less directly we can consider quantified measures of physical or psychological suffering.  A number of university departments and other agencies set up funded questionnaire-based enquiries with great speed once the scale of the event was recognised.  The largest of these, conducted by a Nuffield-funded team at UCL, has been discussed in earlier diary entries.

The best official source of information has been generated by the weekly reports of the estimable Office for National Statistics (ONS). Instead of creating a fresh bank of interviewees, it addressed new questions to its 'Opinions and Lifestyle Survey', an established, weighted sample of the population.

Amongst the issues measured by the Survey is the key experience of loneliness in the pandemic (solitude, the subject of my recent book, is almost never counted).   There is an obvious risk that repeated lockdowns are causing disruptions to social patterns leading to increased personal isolation.  Two basic truths are revealed by the tables, which apply not only to the coronavirus crisis, but to contemporary society more generally.

The first is that the instance of 'often/always' loneliness, the category where real suffering is to be found, started at around five per cent of the population, and has moved, at most, by a single decimal point over the last six months. Whatever else it is doing, the coronavirus is not making us much more lonely. Five per cent still represents around two and a half million people of sixteen and over, and is to be taken seriously. But in its most acute form, increased loneliness is not a consequence of the pandemic.

The ONS then asks a question which previously had not been systematically addressed: the relation between loneliness and disability. The results are striking. Those not suffering a self-reported disability have an 'often/always' loneliness level of only 2.8% in the 8-18 July 2020, sample, compared with an overall figure of 6.2%.[76] By contrast the disabled show a level five times higher at 14.5%. Separate categories of impairment display still higher scores – 19.7% for vision, 15.8% for mobility, 21.7% for learning, 24.7% for mental health.

It is not difficult to comprehend why these conditions should discourage or prevent levels of social interaction which individuals wish to undertake, or why they should make the experience of being alone so much more painful. There may also be a reverse causal flow, with, for instance, mental health problems exacerbated by a lack of human contact.

This confirms an argument I have made elsewhere, that those seeking to engage with loneliness across a broad front are missing the point. The experience is above all a function of specific forms of impairment, each with their own dynamic, each with a set of pressure groups and campaigners, and each having a destructive interaction with austerity-driven health and welfare policies over the last decade.

Here, as with other categories of suffering, the pandemic is exposing critical shortcomings in the provision of support for a range of disabilities, perhaps most importantly, mental health. Loneliness, in this sense, is a proxy for wider failings in our systems of medical and social care.

### Add Mss on Hoarding

Further to my entry on logs and panic buying, it is reported that Tesco has again begun rationing loo rolls, pasta and flour as shelves empty following the renewed lockdown restrictions. When this crisis is over, it will be possible to count the evolution of public anxiety by constructing a loo-roll purchase index.

### Wednesday, 30 September 2020. Snitching contd.

It is reported that more than 80 Conservative MPs are prepared to rebel against the imposition of new coronavirus laws. The MP Steve Baker has invoked Orwell's *1984* in his portrayal of a dystopian regime. The numbers are sufficient to defeat the Government and would represent a major reversal in its management of the crisis, at just the moment that deaths and infections are beginning to rise sharply.

The final straw was the overnight introduction of a new set of offences at the beginning of the week. Fines of at least £1,000 are to be imposed for a range of misbehaviours, including wrongly identifying someone as a contact of an individual who had tested positive for an infection.

There are several possible explanations for this expansion of the disciplinary state.

Just as the Minister of Health sought to blame the malfunctioning of testing on too many fit people using the system, now the failure of the tracking mechanism will be attributed to a shadow army of maliciously nominated non-contacts. Or ministers and officials have indeed identified a vulnerability in the structure of official surveillance. As I wrote in my entry for May 7, there is a long history of 'snitching' - using a new disciplinary mechanism to settle scores between neighbours. Introducing significant fines for infractions of regulations weaponizes local disputes. If you are irritated by the noise someone next door is making, now at the swipe of an app, you can shut them in their house for a fortnight, or expose them to a hefty fine.

There is evidence that with the coronavirus entering its second wave as the nights draw in, tempers in communities are fraying. Mediators who deal with neighbourhood disputes are reporting a sharp increase in business.[77] According to a provider of such a service in Manchester, 'The problems will get worse as people are home more. If the neighbours are being difficult and you can't go out because of the weather, that's going to cause a problem, whether it's breaking lockdown rules or someone trimming your hedge.' As the months pass, tolerance becomes frayed. The police 101 reporting line [for non-emergency issues] is said to be 'swamped' with complaints about people breaching the 'Rule of Six' that was introduced as the second wave began. Some of these reports are well-founded, driven only by a concern to protect public health. Others have less heroic motives. A mediator explained that 'in a tit-for-tat dispute, people will employ any kind of measure they can and make false allegations about breaches to settle a score.'

Or, finally, the new regulations are, as Steve Baker and other on the Conservative right are now claiming, the consequence of ministers and officials exploiting the shift of power from the individual to the collective that must happen in any pandemic. As the number of infections starts to rise again, they can amuse themselves by inventing new offences without any kind of Parliamentary scrutiny, in the latest case seemingly in the small hours of the morning.

It is a game without limits. Soon we will need a regulation fining those who maliciously report people for maliciously reporting their neighbours.

**2 October 2020.  All in Tears.**

In his *Journal of the Plague Year*, Daniel Defoe set himself a double challenge.  He wanted readers to engage with the scale of the epidemic, making critical use of Bills of Mortality.  It is likely that the death toll was double our current number, in population of a little over five million.  And he wanted readers to engage with the experience of dying. He appealed to their imaginations by deploying sight, smell and above all sound in his lightly fictionalised descriptions.  In a famous passage he wrote:

> *London* might well be said to be all in Tears; the Mourners did not go about the Streets indeed, for no Body put on black, or made a formal Dress of Mourning for their nearest Friends; but the Voice of Mourning was truly heard in the Streets; the shrieks of Women and Children at the Windows, and Doors of their Houses, where their dearest Relations were, perhaps dying, or just dead, were so frequent to be heard, as we passed the Streets, that it was enough to pierce the stoutest Heart in the World, to hear them.  Tears and Lamentations were seen almost in every House.[78]

It is one of the major differences in the modern encounter with a major health crisis.  Covid-19 is almost entirely a silent event.  A friend reminds me that when the streets of London fell quiet in the immediate aftermath of the March lockdown, all that could be heard, apart from birdsong, was the wail of ambulances transporting the sick to hospital.

But as traffic reappeared, the prominence of the sirens diminished. What was left was an escalating disaster which largely occurred without any kind of identifiable noise at all.

We live in a culture in Britain which confines the expression of grief to private spaces. Amongst the bereaved of what the Office for National Statistics calculates to be more than 50,000 victims, the tears are shed in the home. Double glazing keeps disturbing noise in as well as out. The only Covid-19 generated sound has been the Thursday-evening applause for health workers. Funerals too are in our own times orderly events where undisciplined grief is discouraged. And in the lockdown they were rendered into near silence by the severe restriction on the number of mourners.

Amongst the living, outdoor noise associated with the pandemic is mostly transgressive – gatherings in public houses or street parties that are at best a threat to collective health and at worst illegal. A justification for the new 10 pm curfew in pubs is that alcohol in crowded spaces causes people to shout more, thus dispersing infected droplets over a wider area.

Amongst the dying, there is a journey from the small sounds of coughing to the quiet of a hospital intensive care unit. Family members are excluded. Patients are sedated. At the last, only the rhythmic working of the ventilators can be heard.

The consequence is a greater division between the afflicted and those still going about their lives. Britain is not 'all in Tears'. Where an event generates serious noise, it is difficult to ignore. Now, the only aural disturbance to the peace of the fortunate are the messages broadcast on radio and television.

At least the Londoners of 1665, did not have Charles II regularly addressing them in the privacy of their homes.

**Tuesday, 5 October 2020. A New Child.**

We are sent a video clip of our new granddaughter, lying on her mat, looking up at her mother, and making greeting sounds. Her huge eyes focus, and her mobile mouth softly and deliberately responds to the person who is her universe. Just one minute and twenty-one seconds. I play it over and again. It is partly that this is, at four weeks, her first conversation. And it is partly that the communication is utterly divorced from the noise in our world being made by Trump, Covid-19 and Brexit. So here, in honour of the moment, is a poem by the Orkney poet George Mackay Brown, written for the daughter of a friend.[79]

A New Child.  11 June 1993

*i*

Wait a while, small voyager

    On the shore, with seapinks and shells.


The boat

    Will take a few summers to build

That you must make your voyage in.


*ii*

You will learn the names.

That golden light is 'sun' – 'moon'

    The silver light

That grows and dwindles.


And the beautiful small splinters

    That wet stones, 'rain'.


*iii*

There is a voyage to make,

    A chart to read,

But not yet, not yet.

    'Daisies' spill from your fingers.

    The night daisies are 'stars'.


*iv*

The keel is laid, the strakes

Will be set, in time.

A tree is growing

    That will be a tall mast


All about you, meantime

The music of humanity,

    The dance of creation

Scored on the chart of the voyage.


*v*

The stories, legends, poems

Will be woven to make your sail.


You may hear the beautiful tale of Magnus

    Who took salt on his lip.

Your good angel

    Will be with you on that shore.


*vi*

Soon, the voyage of EMMA

    To Tir-Nan-Og and beyond.


*vii*

Star of the Sea, shine on her voyage.[80]

**Monday, 5 October 2020.  Red Cross.**

Whatever may be said against it, the worldwide web has kept me usefully occupied during the lockdown.  In pursuit of my current research, I wish to read the rare text, *A Collection of Very Valuable and Scarce Pieces Relating to the Last Plague in the Year 1665*, published in 1721.  Once this would have meant a trip to the British Library.  Now, thanks to the Internet Archive and the recent extension of fibre broadband to my riverside village, I have it instantly on my desk.  The collection, which formed the basis of Defoe's *Journal* the following year, outlined the approach taken to the epidemic.  Prevailing medical opinion discounted the role of 'insects' and instead explained that 'the Pest's Invasion … is unanimously agreed on to be by Contagion, viz,.  When venenate [poisonous] Expirations are transmitted from infectious Bodies to others working a like Change and Alteration in them.'[81]  It was the wrong explanation, but rendered the event distinctly modern.

Then as now the authorities concentrated on identifying the infected and keeping them apart from the healthy.

Those with symptoms were locked in their houses, together with the rest of their household.  The dead were to be buried between sundown and sunrise, 'and … no Neighbours nor Friends be suffered to accompany the Corpse to Church, or to enter the House visited, upon pain of having his House shut up, or be imprisoned  and this is the quarantine.'[82]

If 'Hackney-Coachmen', the Uber drivers of their day, had carried 'infected Persons to the *Pest-House*, and other Places' they could not ply for passengers 'till their Coaches be well aired, and have stood unemployed by the space of five or six Days after such Service.'[83]

The entertainment industry was shut down: 'all Plays, Bear-baiting, Games, singing of Ballads, Buckler-play, or such like Causes of Assemblies of People, be utterly prohibited, and the Parties offending, severely punished by every Alderman in his Ward.' As in recent weeks, early closing was imposed on drinking: 'no Company or Person be suffered to remain or come into any Tavern, Ale-house, or Coffee-house to drink after nine of the Clock in the Evening.'[84]

If the playbook for dealing with a pandemic was written three and a half centuries ago, how is it that we continue to lurch from crisis to crisis in responding to the coronavirus? Today the government is trying to explain how 15,000 infections were not recorded, causing a failure to track nearly 50,000 contacts.

Amongst the many answers, two may be mentioned.

In 1665, the rules for responding to the plague in the capital were not the responsibility of the vestigial early modern state, nor, of course, private companies such as Deloitte (founded 1845) or Serco (1987). They were drawn up and enforced by the Aldermen of London who knew the progress of the plague from parish to parish, knew their community, knew their powers and were prepared to enforce them.

Together with the structure of elected officials below them, they were in permanent session throughout the crisis:

> It is ordered and enjoined that the Aldermen, Deputies, and Common Council-men shall meet together weekly, once, twice, thrice, or oftner, (as cause shall require) at some one general Place accustomed in their respective Wards (being clear from Infection of the Plague) to consult how the said Orders may be duly put in execution.[85]

And the Aldermen understood the communication technology of their time. The present crisis over recording test results appears to be the consequence of a failure to grasp the limitations of Excel spreadsheets. In 1665, they had a simpler but brutally effective device for identifying infected households:

> THAT every House visited, be marked with a red Cross of a Foot long, in the middle of the Door, evident to be seen; and with these usual printed Words, that is to say, Lord have Mercy upon us, to be set close over the same Cross, there to continue until lawful opening of the same House.[86]

**Friday, 9 October 2020. Noli me Tangere.**

An obvious victim of the quarantine measures imposed since March is touch. Parents cannot hug children and grandchildren living elsewhere.

Relatives of the sick or dying cannot give physical reassurance. The bereaved cannot ease their pain by embracing each other.

It is timely, therefore, that this week Radio 4 is broadcasting a set of programmes on the topic.

They are made by Claudia Hammond, a rare presenter capable of moving between academic research and popular communication through her regular BBC series 'All in the Mind.' In conjunction with the Wellcome Collection and front-line academics she has conducted global surveys on loneliness (to which I contributed), rest and relaxation, and now touch. Nearly 40,000 respondents from 112 countries answered a series of questions about attitudes and practices.

The subject was chosen as a means of measuring the impact of increased virtual contact through the use of social media, and of growing sensitivity to the need for consent, particularly by women, in physical encounters. The interviews were conducted in the first three months of 2020, and only glimpsed the impact of the pandemic at the very end of the project. In presenting the results, however, Claudia Hammond talked to researchers who are currently focussing on the consequences of current forms of lockdown.

This is the beginning rather than the end of a discussion of this feature of the pandemic, but some truths begin to be visible. In this realm, as in so many others, coronavirus struck populations already struggling with needs and aspirations. Amongst the sample, nearly three quarters thought touch important, and over a half stated they did not have enough in their lives. A mere three per cent believed they had too much. The shortfall was attributed to a lack of social interaction more generally, and a change in attitudes about consensual physical contact. Those with a positive attitude towards touch reported greater wellbeing and lower levels of loneliness.

Michael Banissy, the London University professor in charge of the research, referred to a persistent longing for touch rather than a widespread crisis. The patchwork of further research since the lockdowns began suggests that this longing has grown. An American survey found a shortfall not so much in the levels of contact as in the quality. It is where it is most needed, in care homes, in hospitals, at funerals, that the lack is most acutely felt. There is an interesting suggestion that amidst the social dislocation, the baseline for an acceptable level of physical embrace has risen. As memories of the warmth of touch are re-visited, the enforced restrictions become more painful.

What to do as prohibitions on physical contact are re-imposed? Virtual hugging apparently has some effect. The American survey found that long walks in the open air buffered the consequences of diminished touching. And then there is the sharp rise on both sides of the Atlantic in the purchase of soft, huggable, pets.

The tortoise I once owned (see Diary April 28) won't do at all.

**Monday, 19 October 2020.  Pandemics and Plots.**

Covid-19, and earlier outbreaks of bubonic plague and influenza, are undoubted facts.  They are material events that cause death, suffering and widespread dislocation of ways of living.

Yet the two most influential and widely-read accounts of pandemics in the west are works of fiction.

Daniel Defoe's *Journal of the Plague Year* features an invented document written by an imagined individual about an event which took place when the author was a child.  Albert Camus's *La Peste*, or *The Plague*, which uses a line from Defoe as its epigraph, is a novel about an outbreak that never occurred at all.  Yet if you were to introduce a new reader to all the complexities and truths of living through an epidemic, these remain the key texts.

There are of course good histories of the major outbreaks.  Paul Slack's *Plague.  A Very Short Introduction* (Oxford, 2010) is a particularly useful introduction to the field.  But none of these works, nor the scholarship which they build upon, lodge in the memory in same way as the classic fictional accounts.

The conventional form of the novel, which Defoe had a hand in creating, allows the writer to focus on the central question of the relation of individual to collective experience.  However much evidence the historian accumulates about deaths and behaviours, the moral dilemma of how to subsume personal interest to general wellbeing remains difficult to bring into focus. A pandemic presents choices which define the possibilities of human action in the face of suffering. Novelists find it easier to move between the registers of conduct and to draw larger conclusions from them.

Freed from the tyranny of footnotes, such writers can deploy their imaginations to illuminate the complexities of emotion and calculation. They both depend upon and transcend even the best histories. We see this process at work in Hilary Mantel's successful *Wolf Hall* trilogy. She fully respects the framework of historical fact, earning the respect, amongst others, of the foremost historian of Thomas Cromwell, Diarmaid MacCulloch. But she clothes that scaffolding with explorations of motive, belief and behaviour at a convincing level of detail only attainable by an outstanding writer who has spent decades refining her craft.

Further, novelists readily work with plots. Whilst pandemics have effects which last decades for polities, economies and societies, and for some part of a subsequent lifetime for individual survivors, they are for the most part framed events. Other great threats of our age, such as poverty, racial injustice, climate change, have no clear beginnings and no timetable for their completion. Covid-19, like the bubonic plague and the Spanish flu, arrived at a certain moment, and will depart, at least for the time being (as it already appears to have done in China). What is happening now is that all the players, from Trump upwards, are seeking to narrate plots whose final chapter keeps retreating before them. When, as was reported in the press yesterday, politicians demand 'an exit strategy' from the renewed lockdown restrictions, they are just trying to organise the event into a manageable narrative, which like the novels of Defoe and Camus, reaches an end in the closing pages.

And like the best works of imagination, there is always room for a sequel. These are the last lines of *The Plague:*

> Indeed, as he listened to the cries of joy that rose above the town, Rieux recalled that this joy was always under threat. He knew that this happy crowd was unaware of something that one can read in books, which is that the plague bacillus never dies or vanishes entirely, that it can remain dormant for dozens of years in furniture or clothing, that it waits patiently in bedrooms, cellars, trunks, handkerchiefs and old papers, and perhaps the day will come when, for the instruction or misfortune of mankind, the plague will rouse its rats and send them to die in some well-contented city.[87]

In that regard, there was an outbreak of bubonic plague around the River Orwell in Suffolk early in the twentieth century. Public health officials were still testing rats in the area for *Yersinia pestis* as late as the 1970s.

Vigilance cannot be relaxed.

**Friday, 23 October 2020. Time Passes.**

Time is becoming an independent factor in the experience of coronavirus.

In the early weeks, the reaction against a total lockdown was conditioned by the expectation that summer would witness a return to something like a normal life. For a while that seemed to be the case as restrictions were lifted, the daily death rate fell to low double figures, and offices and schools opened.

Now the ending is disappearing over the horizon. There seems little prospect of any of the Government's semi-privatised schemes ever working, nor is it likely that a vaccine will get on top of the pandemic until well into the New Year. As Christmas is imperilled, prolonged anxiety and unending isolation are wearing away at the spirits.

Nowhere is this more apparent than in the prisons, which, as I have argued in earlier posts, have been exposed to destructive solitude on a scale not seen anywhere in civilian life. Time has been the currency of the penal system in Britain since it began to move away from physical punishment in the early nineteenth century. The gravity of a crime is measured in the years that must be served.

It was apparent from the beginning that locking prisoners up for twenty-three hours a day to protect them from infection was likely to cause serious harm to inmates who were rarely in good psychological condition at the outset.

Peter Clarke, the Chief Inspector of Prisons, has just published his final report before retirement. He draws attention to the consequences of the lockdown in prisons:

> Given the obvious linkage between excessive time locked in cells and mental health issues, self-harm and drug abuse, it was concerning to find that the amount of time for which prisoners were unlocked for time out of cell was often unacceptably poor. Nineteen per cent of adult male prisoners told us that they were out of their cells for less than two hours on weekdays, including 32% in men's local prisons. Is it any surprise that self-harm in prisons has been running at historically high levels during the past year?[88]

As the months passed, with no early release of prisoners to reduce pressure within the system (unlike in France, where the prison population was swiftly reduced by 10,000), the effect worsened:

> All social visits had been suspended in March, and by the end of June this was beginning to cause frustration among prisoners... Time out of cell was still extremely restricted for nearly all prisoners, and with the almost complete lack of work, training or education, frustrations were beginning to build.[89]

In subsequent interviews he challenged the prospect of such a regime continuing without prospect of amelioration:

> The question is: it is intended to keep people locked up for 23 days ad infinitum? Or until the virus is eliminated? That simply cannot be right.[90]

Caught between an obdurate Prison Officers Association and an obtuse Ministry of Justice, it looks indeed as if the regime will continue until it explodes or causes irreparable damage to inmates.

Daniel Defoe's *Due Preparations for the Plague* covered the question of what to do with prisoners in such an outbreak. His solution was straightforward:

> Seventhly. — That all criminals, felons, and murderers should be forthwith tried, and such as are not sentenced to die, should be immediately transported or let out on condition of going forty miles from the city, not to return on pain of death.[91]

You can argue with his prescription, but at least he recognised that drastic action needed to be taken.

**Saturday, 24 October 2020.  Plague-free communication.**

Much has been written, and will continue to be written, about the merits and demerits of the digital phone.  The early excitement of a device that could free the user from all structures of power has been overtaken by a growing pessimism.  It exposes the owner to commercial and state surveillance, abolishes privacy, erodes face-to-face contact, destroys conversation, locks the individual into a private bubble of fantasy and disinformation.

What was not apparent until the present pandemic was the virtue of the digital phone as the cleanest possible form of making contact between people.  It can of course carry germs on its crevice-free surface (for which there are a range of cleaning liquids on the market), but unless you are very careless, they will be your germs, not someone else's.

In an earlier entry ('Smoking the Mail', September 10), I cited the description by Defoe of the London merchant who went to ever more elaborate lengths to avoid getting the disease from his post, before abandoning letters altogether. In Camus's fictional account of an outbreak in Oran, 'a new decree forbade the exchange of any correspondence, to prevent letters from transmitting the infection.'[92]

Letters remain under suspicion.  In my household we place incoming mail in quarantine for a couple of days, except on the rare occasion, such as the recent envelope of drawings from two grandchildren, when we choose to open and sanitise, rather than put on one side.

By the time Camus was writing, the corded, landline telephone had been in use for more than half a century. But in the 1940s, it was still only to be found in businesses and middle-class households. It was intrinsically a shared device. One instrument was accessible to all members of a household. In an office anyone could pick up a handset lying on a desk and insert their finger in the dial. This came to be recognised as a health hazard, and until lately there were firms offering services to clean regularly all the phones in a building. Multiple cordless handsets in the home allowed calls to be made in greater privacy, but the equipment was still available to different possible sources of infection. The digital mobile, by contrast, is essentially a personal possession, protected by increasingly sophisticated security devices which ensure that it is only capable of being used by its owner.

More basic forms of communication are viewed with still greater suspicion. Uttered speech transmits droplets of virus. Hence the two-metre distancing and the face masks which curtail but do not wholly abolish risk. Public houses are shut early, because the later the time and the less restrained the drinkers, the greater the danger of raised voices and increased transmission. The still more fundamental mode of making contact, physical touch, is generally forbidden except between intimate couples.

The i-phone rescues us from silence and isolation. Had Steve Jobs been as far-sighted as he is seen to be, he would have held up the first device in 2007 and simply said,

*'Behold, here is what we have been looking for since Biblical times, the world's first plague-free mode of communication.'*


**Monday, 26 October 2020.  Happy Highways.**


My county has its own poet laureate.  A. E. Housman's *A Shropshire Lad* was first published in 1896.  Its theme of the transience of male youth found a wide readership in the First World War and it has remained one of the landmarks of British poetry.

The collection of verses is a taste I have never acquired.  Housman was a Cambridge classics don, who never lived in Shropshire nor even visited it very often.  He projected upon a rural way of life a set of preoccupations which were narrow in their range and melancholy in their outlook.  His poems are not observations of a particular landscape but incantations:

> Clunton and Clunbury,
> Clungunford and Clun,
> Are the quietest places
> Under the sun.

A pleasing alliteration, but Clun, on the Welsh border some thirty miles south of where I live, is in fact a bustling market town, as it must have been in Housman's time, complete with its own castle.  He could, however, fashion a memorable line, a number of which have entered the national consciousness. Dennis Potter borrowed the title of one of Housman's poems for a famous television series in the 1970s:

> Into my heart an air that kills
> From yon far country blows:
> What are those blue remembered hills,
> What spires, what farms are those?
>
> That is the land of lost content,
> I see it shining plain,
> The happy highways where I went
> And cannot come again.

The final two lines come to mind as I contemplate the countryside beyond the Severn below our garden. Wales, unlike England, is now in national lockdown. The happy highways that take us to our favourite walks, to the nursery that stocks our garden, to Powys Castle for a day out, to the seaside at Harlech, are closed (except for work and exceptional needs).

The border that runs down the Welsh Marches has always seemed more of an historical relic than a practical fact. It is only marked on the larger thoroughfares. Driving west along country roads, the only sign that you have crossed into another country is the appearance of a single word painted on the tarmac: ARAF. It means slow, at once a warning, and a description of the entire transport system in Wales.

The appearance of a hard border within the United Kingdom has been a threat since the pandemic began (See my entry for 14 April: 'Borders'). It feels like one of the many emergency constraints that could be difficult fully to remove once the crisis is over. In this particular case, however, there may be some gain in the determination of Welsh politicians to find their own solution.

During the recent row between Manchester and the Government, television journalists kept filming a large, badly-painted graffiti on the side of a building: 'The north is not a petri dish.' You could see the point. On the other hand, a petri dish is a perfectly useful piece of laboratory kit, crucial, so the story has it, for the discovery of penicillin. The total lockdown over the border can be seen as a timely experiment. Conservatives and Labour are arguing about whether a short-term 'circuit breaker' is the right way forward.

Thanks to the Welsh Government, we should soon have an answer to that question.

**Thursday, 29 October 2020. Morale in the time of Covid-19.**

Here's a puzzle.

Not since 1945, has there been so dramatic a year. Daily headlines report the imposition, lifting and re-imposition of unprecedented peacetime controls over personal behaviour, steep rises in infection and death rates, dropping to a plateau in the summer and now sharply increasing again, and an unending drama of failed personal protection equipment and malfunctioning test and trace systems.

Since late March, social scientists have been striving to measure the impact of the crisis on what in the second world war was called 'morale'. I have discussed some of their findings in earlier posts. The most recent data in the UCL and ONS surveys are broadly similar, and oddly counter-intuitive. Whereas the drivers of material change represent a fairground roller coaster during an event which is far from reaching its conclusion, the dominant shape of the graphs of emotion over the period is a gentle countryside, a landscape of gradual inclines and declivities. Why this should be so is difficult to understand.

Take, for instance, the basic category of what the ONS terms 'life satisfaction' (see also diary entries for 30 June and 24 July), where 10 is 'completely satisfied with your life nowadays' and 0 is 'not at all.' On their index, it stood at 7.2 when the first lockdown was imposed at the end of March, fell to 6.8 at the peak of infections and deaths at the end of April, and since then has oscillated between these figures, only falling a little below 6.8 at the beginning of October.[93]

The baseline for those 'very or somewhat worried about the effect of COVID-19 on their life right now' is higher, but nothing like as volatile as the surrounding events. It runs at the low 80s during the first crisis of infections and deaths, falls to the upper 60s by the end of May where it remains until the end of September when it climbs just above 70. The last recorded figure, for 14-18 October, is 76.

Similarly, the 'percentage of adults that say their wellbeing is being affected by COVID-19' falls from 53 to the low 40s by the beginning of May, stands at 39 in mid-September, and is back up to 49 in the last return. The 'percentage of adults with high levels of anxiety' falls from 50 to the low 30s by the beginning of May and is still at 33 in mid-October.[94] There are discernible changes tracking the surges in the pandemic, but nowhere near on the same scale. And the base level of emotional wellbeing is far less disastrous than might be supposed in this most tragic year. Most of us would settle for a life satisfaction of around seven at any time in our lives.

Why this should be is far from clear. It is partly a consequence of averaging experience. Those who have encountered the loss of health, loved ones or employment, will report widely different scores. Nonetheless the relative stability of the graphs over the whole period is a striking fact.

We appear to be a more phlegmatic society than we might suppose, as was also the conclusion of the wartime studies of 'morale'.

**Tuesday, 3 November 2020. Open Learn.**

Following my previous post about the varying topography of the responses to Covid-19, here is a sudden ascent. As the first lockdown began at the end of March, traffic on the Open University's *OpenLearn* site jumped fivefold, reaching a peak in the final week of April.

*OpenLearn* was established in 2006, as the University began to move its commitment to be 'open to people, places, methods and ideas' into the digital age.

From its foundation, the OU had deployed the leading communications technology of the time to reach an audience far beyond its student body. Programmes supporting its courses were broadcast on the BBC late at night, attracting an audience not just of paid-up students, but large numbers of insomniac self-improvers. The university has continued to maintain a relationship with the BBC, sponsoring a wide range of television and radio programmes.

By the beginning of the twenty-first century, however, it was becoming evident that there were new channels for reaching an audience for higher education. I obtained an award of $10m from the Hewlett Foundation to enable the OU to develop a platform that would make freely available its quality-assured learning materials to a global audience. Structured extracts from a wide range of programmes were posted online.

The object was both outward facing, in that it would allow anyone in the world to engage with university-level learning materials, and inward facing in that it would be a means of attracting students to the OU who could make a preliminary trial of particular subjects to establish whether they wanted to commit themselves to a full-length course (one in eight of University's students now enter the institution by this route).

According to its newly-published Annual Report,[95] *OpenLearn* had an audience of 13.5 million visitors over the last twelve months. Just over half the users were from the UK, the rest from around the world. Set against the followers of digital influencers, this may be small change [Kim Kardashian, I note with bemusement, has 189 million followers on Instagram and 30 million on Facebook]. But in the context of the deeply constricted higher education system, the numbers are astronomical.

A typical Russell Group University will employ world-class researchers to teach classes of perhaps fifteen or twenty students at a time (or devolve the task to post-docs). Oxford and Cambridge were still offering one-to-one teaching in parts of their curriculum before the crisis. Faced with the lockdown, these institutions are struggling to film their lectures and seminars for viewing in their rooms by students who are paying over £9,000 a year plus accommodation costs for the privilege.

*OpenLearn* was ready and waiting for the sudden upsurge in demand for digital learning. It responded to those with time on their hands who wished to explore new fields of knowledge. The university rapidly devised units to enable people to acquire recreational skills, and to provide support for those experiencing mental-health difficulties. It provided materials for sixth-form students whose teaching and exams had been disrupted. Its pedagogic capacities were made available to the many educational institutions which were having to pivot towards online learning at great speed. Those whose occupations had suddenly ceased to exist were set on the road to re-training.

*OpenLearn* was devised for less stressful times. But this is its moment.

**Wednesday, 4 November 2020.  Waggons, Carts and Lear Jets.**

It is the historian's business to show that everything changes. 'The past is a foreign country;' wrote L. P. Hartley, 'they do things differently there.'

Well mostly.

In some cases, the only change is the technology.  Take, for instance, the rich fleeing a pandemic lockdown whilst the rest of the population remain trapped in their neighbourhoods.

Early in his *Journal of the Plague Year* Defoe reported on the flight out of London by those who could afford the transport:

... and the richer sort of People, especially the Nobility and Gentry, from the West-part of the City throng'd out of Town, with their Families and Servants in an unusual Manner; and this was more particularly seen in *White-Chapel*; that is to say, the Broad-street where I liv'd: Indeed nothing was to be seen but Waggons and Carts, with Goods, Women, Servants, Children &c. Coaches fill'd with People of the better Sort, and Horsemen attending them, and all hurrying away.[96]

Now it's Lear Jets. There was a rise in bookings before the first lockdown in March. Companies were marketing 'evacuation flights' out of countries hit by the virus. Whilst commercial airlines have almost ceased operating, private planes, which avoid crowded terminals and aircraft cabins, have continued to do good business.

Travelling to a second home, or for a holiday, is specifically banned under the second lockdown restrictions which come into force in England tomorrow. There are, however, ways around the prohibition. It is reported that this week there is a renewed rise in business for alternative means of escape:

According to the *Guardian*:

Wealthy people in England are booking private jets to escape the lockdown set to be introduced on Thursday, according to jet brokers. Air Partner, one of the biggest aircraft charter firms, said there had been a 'sharp rise' in private jet bookings out of the country before Thursday. The company, which supplies planes to Premier League footballers, celebrities, the royal family and six of the eight governments in the G8, said it had been overwhelmed with inquiries.[97]

If you are tempted to follow suit, you may wish to know that the cost of a private jet to Tenerife for five people is about £24,000, one way.

Should you worry about this?   There is the moral issue.   Also the ecological.   Private jets apparently emit about 20 times more carbon dioxide per passenger mile than commercial flights.

**Monday, 9 November 2020.   Lord Sumption and civil liberties.**

Let us join with Lord Sumption in considering Lord Sumption.

The first practising barrister to be appointed to the British Supreme Court, distinguished historian of the Hundred Years' War, Reith Lecturer, and now leading opponent of the lockdown strategy.   A wearer of power braces, a man with a high regard for both his principles and his intellect.

In his Cambridge Freshfields Lecture of October 27, he denounced the entire political response to the pandemic, which he described as 'the most significant interference with personal freedom in the history of our country.'

The most famous definition of the freedom of the citizen in the modern world was made by John Stuart Mill in *On Liberty* of 1859:

'The only purpose for which power can be rightfully exercised over any member of a civilized community, against his will, is to prevent harm to others.'

The notion of 'harm to others' has since been much debated, but in 2020, it has a clear and unassailable meaning: the transmission of an infectious disease that will result in the serious illness or death of many thousands of people. Although they lacked the language of political rights, this was why medieval Venice put incoming travellers into quarantine and why mid-seventeenth London locked plague victims in their own houses. It is not an attack on personal freedom, rather a necessary restriction on the harm caused by its unlicensed practice. As a distinguished former vice chancellor of my acquaintance would say, 'it's not even a question'.

The debate that now needs to take place is not about liberty as an absolute principle, but the conditions which should surround its suspension.

The first condition is trust in the decision-making process. It has been argued by Peter Hennessy amongst others that the final fortnight in May, when Johnson failed to make any effort to take the devolved nations with him, then failed to sack Cummings over the non-apology for the flight to Durham, represented a loss of confidence that has never been regained. Now we are all critical statisticians, interrogating every expert pronouncement, most recently the claim that Britain was on course for 4,000 deaths a day, a figure since reduced to 1,000. Johnson's Brexit history of seeking to curtail or suspend Parliamentary scrutiny of his actions does not help here, and it is passing strange that now his fiercest House of Commons critics are those who cheered him on when he illegally prorogued Parliament last year.

The second condition is tacit consent by the population. Most legislation affecting significant areas of social behaviour follows rather than creates changes in attitude. Johnson's administration waited, perhaps fatally, until it was persuaded that the public was ready for a lockdown before imposing one in late March, and the same applied to the delayed re-introduction.

Sumption says that the government's actions mean that 'in a crisis the police were entitled to do whatever they thought fit, without being unduly concerned about their legal powers. This is my definition of a police state.' His ignorance of what a police state actually looks like in the twentieth and twenty-first centuries suggests he should confine his historical studies to the medieval period. In practice the police have neither wanted nor needed to enforce their powers except in extreme circumstances, nor could they if popular sentiment rejected the edicts (see USA *passim*).

The third condition is equality of treatment. As noted in my previous post, 'Waggons, Carts and Lear Jets', there is a long history of the wealthy fleeing a pandemic and leaving the government to impose controls on the poor and dispossessed who have been left behind. The issue is compounded by the wider tendency of a pandemic to expose and exacerbate the effects of personal and household poverty. There is a constituency for protest on this matter; who better to lead it than an old Etonian famous for his seven-figure income when practising the law.

The final and perhaps most important condition is the termination of the controls. After the Second World War, the last time when there was a widespread suspension of civil liberties in the interests of defeating a yet greater danger, most of the restrictions were lifted in 1945, although food rationing, and with it identity cards, remained in place for a further nine years. Conversely a more recent threat to public safety, the 9/11 attack, resulted in a permanent extension of the security state, some of it in plain sight, some not made public until the Snowden revelations in 2013. The question to be answered in relation to all the current regulations, whether debated by Parliament or not, is whether they will continue beyond the pandemic.

That's when Lord Sumption will need to ride out and save us

**Wednesday, 11 November 2020.  Consensus thinking.**

The problem with patrician mavericks like Lord Sumption is that they give intellectual cover for much less fastidious figures.

A week after his Cambridge Freshfields Lecture, Nigel Farage and Richard Tice crawled out of the decaying wreckage of the Brexit Party and announced the creation of 'Reform UK' dedicated to the libertarian rejection of the Government's lockdown policy.

They wrote in the *Daily Telegraph* that 'It's time to end the political consensus that there is no alternative to shutting people up in their homes.  The institutions and polices that require change are formidable, and once again we will have to take on powerful vested interests… We are showing the courage needed to take on consensus thinking and vested interests.'[98]

As with Sumption and the Great Barrington Declaration that they support, there is a wholesale rejection of the authority of political and medical elites.

In terms of the lockdown, this may no longer be important.  With this week's announcement of an effective vaccine, the focus of the argument is shifting to the issue of take-up.  Already the anti-vaxxers are attacking the alleged consensus thinking – that the medical establishment is united in regarding the Pfizer results as a major breakthrough even though regulatory approval has not yet been given – and the 'vested interests' behind it - particularly big pharma and Bill Gates.[99]

A succession of studies during the pandemic have described the scale of the anti-vax movement and the strength of its online presence (see also posts on 7 July, 15 July, 11 August). *Politico* reports a Eurobarometer survey stating that nearly half of Europeans believe that vaccines are a danger to health.[100] Last month *The Lancet* carried a story based on a study made by the Centre for Countering Digital Hate. It found that one in six British people were unlikely to agree to being vaccinated, and a similar proportion were undecided. Traffic on social media was growing. Globally, 31 million people followed anti-vaccine groups on Facebook and 17 million were subscribing to similar accounts on YouTube.[101] A more parochial investigation of Totness published this week in the *Guardian*, found a thriving Facebook community opposed to face masks, lockdown, and vaccination.[102]

It might be argued that such surveys do not matter. Despite the Pfizer breakthrough, there is no vaccine available today, no real-life decision to make. Opinion is bound to change once there is a call from the GP surgery. The question is what the take-up will then be, given that the online anti-vax movement is evidently capable to responding negatively to any claimed medical advance. It needs to be somewhere near 95% fully to eradicate the virus.

The issue constitutes an interesting case history for the capacity of digital communication to shape private behaviour. There is a tendency in the critical literature to assume that networked messages have a direct effect on the actions of those who receive them. That is what power means. The fertility of the conspiracies, the scale of the readership and of the investment in them by advertisers, lead to the expectation that consumers will do things they otherwise would not do if they relied solely on more traditional forms of communication.

In this instance the online-messaging will compete with conventional newspaper, radio and television outlets which at least in Britain are united in their support of the scientific breakthrough, even though some opponents are finding their way onto chat shows. For all the damage caused to the standing of politicians and administrators during the pandemic, medical researchers retain authority. The roll-out of the vaccine will start with care-home residents, who are unlikely to be spending their enclosed days following Facebook conspiracy theories, and with eighty-year-olds in the community who will not share the online-habits of eighteen-year-olds. Then there are the opinions of close friends and relatives whose views you respect and whose respect you do not want to lose.

I dare not contemplate the response were I to tell my children that I have decided to let nature take its course.

**Thursday, 19 November 2020.  Shopping.**

I am reading at nights Herodotus in the new translation by Tom Holland.  In section 94 of Book One, *The Histories* describe the practices of the Lydians:

'Their habit of sending their daughters out to work as prostitutes excepted, the Lydians live their lives in a way not dissimilar to the Greeks.  So far as we know, they were the first people ever to strike gold and silver coins, and to use them: the result was the invention of shopping.'

Future historians may come to see the Covid-19 pandemic as the beginning of the end of this practice.

Consider this.  With the second lockdown, I have bowed to the inevitable and embarked on a  redecoration of the inside of my house.  This is partly for want of a better occupation, partly to make long overdue improvements, and partly as a pact with the Gods.  If I make all the rooms as smart as may be, perhaps after all they will be occupied by my children and their families at Christmas.

Just before the lockdown began, I bought the necessary materials, but as was bound to happen, close encounters with neglected walls and woodwork caused me to run out of some essentials.  I was left with the choice of living with decommissioned rooms until the lockdown ended, or going online.

Thus it was that yesterday a van drove through the narrow roads to my village, up the unadopted lane that leads to my house, and a delivery man walked along my drive carrying a package containing a litre pot of Polyfilla.

This is an insane way to run a consumer economy. There is a real danger that after Covid-19 we will build back worse, incorporating habits that were only justified by the extreme circumstances of the lockdown.

I am not unduly sentimental about B&Q where I would otherwise have shopped. Over the last decade it has systemically put out of business every other DIY warehouse in the area, as well as all but two of the neighbourhood ironmongers in Shrewsbury, including Birch's opposite the river, where an elderly lady of irreproachable gentility in her manners and clothes, would emerge from her little office in the back of the shop and sell you a tin of polish or a dozen screws in a brown paper bag.

Nonetheless there is an economy of scale in making one trip to the shops every so often to acquire a range of essential and non-essential items. With all due respect to Herodotus, shopping as we now know it was the invention of the nineteenth century, when rising living standards intersected with innovations in the manufacture of all kinds of products. In this world, personal delivery was widely practised. Servants from middle- and upper-class households would leave orders at shops which would later be brought to the door by toiling delivery boys. Horses and carts passed by selling or delivering fresh food and larger goods.

During the twentieth century the bustling streets gradually emptied, and consumers became accustomed to travelling to the centres of towns and cities to make purchases.

Now the temporary closure of shops may become permanent as they fail to win back business from the online retailers. The robot-driven Amazon barns will multiply van journeys at just the moment when the necessity of reducing road transport is becoming apparent to all but a fringe of climate-change deniers. The solution to this problem is far from obvious, other than taxing online retailers to make good the loss of urban business rates and legislating to prevent the on-line sale of any single item below, let us say, £100. The exception would be food, where supermarkets should be encouraged to maintain or reintroduce minimum orders.

This morning, Royal Mail delivered a parcel from John Lewis containing three small picture frames to go on a redecorated wall. All were smashed, the box full of shards of glass.

**Thursday, 26 November 2020. Consider these panels**.

I have just painted them. Together with more than fifty other panels in several rooms in my house.

They stand for virtue postponed. It is a decade or so since last I carried out interior decoration on any scale. After the beginning of the first lockdown their neglect has been a continuing reproach. The pandemic, if ever, is the time to set about such a task. But the months have passed without activity, only partly excused by the need to attend to the garden as spring gave way to summer and what has been a long-flowering autumn. Finally, as Christmas approaches, I have run out of excuses not to clear the rooms, buy supplies of sail white emulsion and assemble my collection of brushes and rollers.

They stand for absorbed attention. All of us locked in our houses have been seeking occupations that will take our minds away from looming dangers and postponed pleasures. Hobbies and handicrafts have been embraced not so much for the outcome as for the distraction of their practice.

One of the consequences of living in one end of a cruck-framed medieval hall-house is that routine maintenance demands serious concentration. Over time, the oak moves one way with variations in heat and moisture, and the plaster in another. Minor cracks open up which have to be meticulously repaired (hence the pollyfilla delivery in my last entry) and then the edges of each panel have to be slowly painted, keeping clean the surrounding oak beams. There is no particular skill, just great care and patience as the brush is drawn down the edge of the plaster. The hours pass, amounting to almost a week for our bedroom alone and its thirty-odd rectangles. Radio 4 reminds me how often its programmes are repeated.

They stand for the domestic climate-heating disaster. The exterior panels consist of a single layer of brick, plastered on either side. Heat passes readily through them. Only some new panels in the gable wall are filled with a modern take on an ancient practice - chopped French hemp, a light, warm equivalent of wattle and daub. Most of the current housing stock is of course better constructed, but almost none of it has been designed to be carbon neutral. Johnson's new green strategy will fall at this hurdle. It is just too late and too expensive seriously to reduce the energy footprint of every residence from the latest Barratt estate box to the remnants of fifteenth century domestic accommodation.

And they stand for hope deferred. I set out on the task in order somehow to increase the prospect of a family Christmas. What, after all, is the point of such an effort if it is only to be enjoyed by the two of us? But as I put back the furniture and tidy away my paints, the lockdown rules for the festive season are announced. It would be possible for my children and grandchildren to join the Gadarene rush out of London two days before Christmas and back three days later, but the balance of risk is against travel, whatever the regulations. Rates of infection and death show no sign of declining. School ends too late, the parents cannot fully self-isolate. Our age-group is just as vulnerable as it was, and with the vaccines coming in the New Year, there seems no case for letting our guard drop.

So on Christmas Day we shall be inscribing our joys on the blank spaces of clean panels.

**Tuesday, 1 December 2020. A Covid-19 encyclical.**

A literary question: Who is the author of this concluding passage of a book published today?

> By making the integration of the poor and the care for our environment central to society's goals, we can generate work while humanizing our surroundings. By providing a universal basic income, we can free and enable people to work for the community in a dignified way. By adopting more intensive permaculture methods for growing food, we can regenerate the natural world, create work and biodiversity, and live better.... By making the restoration of our people's dignity the central objective of the post-Covid world, we make everyone's dignity the key to our actions. To guarantee a world where dignity is valued and respected through concrete actions is not just a dream but a path to a better future.

You might search amongst the leading ideologues on the left in Britain and the US, but the answer is Argentina via Rome. They are the words of Francis, 266th Pope of the Catholic Church, in *Let Us Dream. The Path to a Better Future*.[103]

I would not expect to find myself reading such a text amidst the widespread commentary on the pandemic. I was raised a methodist and have no sympathy for religious hierarchies and rituals.

More broadly, organised Christianity has been notably quiet in this crisis. There are accounts of individual clergy playing active roles in the plenitude of community support groups that have sprung up around the country. But as institutions, the churches have been marginalised. Their guidance is not sought, their views are rarely cited. The drama of illness and death, of caring and curing, has been largely secular. There have been polite protests by bishops at the controls placed on church services, and occasional acts of publicity-seeking disobedience by evangelical congregations, but little contribution to the main public discourse or programmes of action. It is a disjuncture that separates this plague from all that preceded it.

In England, the Catholic Church has been further distracted by the continuing fall-out of sexual abuse scandals. Most shockingly, the leading Catholic boarding school, Ampleforth, where Cardinal Basil Hume was a pupil and later Abbot, has just been forbidden by the Department for Education to admit any new pupils following a series of damning reports on its performance and management by the Independent Inquiry into Child Sexual Abuse, Ofsted and the Independent Schools Inspectorate. The school is appealing the decision but is fortunate that an over-full news agenda has not given the event more publicity.

The Pope admits in his book to a collective responsibility: 'As I will not tire of saying with sorrow and shame, these abuses were also committed by some members of the Church.'[104] Further he is aware of his many conservative critics who by arguing that 'there is too much 'confusion' in the Church, and that only this or that group of purists or traditionalists can be trusted, sow division in the Body.'[105] Nonetheless he is determined to use the pandemic to reassert his long-matured views on social and economic reform.

The engagement with the detail of Covid-19 is slight. There are no statistics of infection or investigations of particular experiences. Rather it is viewed as a revelation of the true fraternity of mankind and 'a moment to dream big, to rethink our priorities – what we value, what we want, what we seek – and to commit to act in our daily life on what we have dreamed of.'[106] Sundry biblical texts are cited in support of his case but so also, for instance, are the views of the economist Mariana Mazzucato in her recent *The Value of Everything*.

*Let us Dream* belongs on one side of the divide between those who believe the pandemic will be followed by a return to normal, with all its minor comforts and major inequalities, and those who see it as a once-in-a-generation opportunity to address the agenda for radical change.

'Today' it argues, 'we have to avoid falling back into the individual and institutional patterns that have led to Covid-19 and the various crises that surround it: the hyperinflation of the individual combined with weak institutions and the despotic control of the economy by a very few.'[107]

**Sunday, 20 December 2020. Last Writes.**

In my final post of the year, I want to return to the topic that has occupied most of my working hours over the last three years, culminating in the publication of a book in the midst of the crisis.

Solitude and its shadow, loneliness, have remained central matters of concern as unprecedented controls are imposed and re-imposed on who we may associate with. I noted in earlier entries how, in spite of the continuing drama of rising, falling and once more rising infection and death rates, the indices of emotional wellbeing have remained remarkably stable. As Christmas looms, I have looked again at the most reliable measurement, the 'social impacts' data published by the Office for National Statistics (ONS).

Solitude is not counted. Now, as in the past, the experience is too diffuse to be readily reduced to numbers, and there is no political imperative to generate tables that will justify or measure the consequences of government intervention.

Loneliness, on the other hand, is constantly quantified. The core category is 'often / always' lonely. This is where the serious psychological or physiological suffering takes place, creating an urgent need for formal or informal support. The score at the beginning of the pandemic was 6%, much the same as it was in the quieter waters of 2019. The latest score, for December 10-13, is just a point higher at 7%. For those over seventy it is 5%.[108]

ONS also publishes a time series for the larger group of 'often, always, or some of the time' lonely. There are 35 observation points between 20-23 March and 10-13 December. At the first point, 24% of the population fall into this category. At the last, again just a point higher at 25%. In between there are minor fluctuations between a high of 27, and a low, in late July, of 20.[109]

This stasis, which contrasts so sharply with the switchback ride of government regulation, generates conclusions which may hold more broadly for the pandemic.

The first is that managing solitude and loneliness has a long history (my book is available in all good outlets and can shortly be read in Korean, Japanese, Russian, Chinese and Spanish). Modern societies have developed a raft of techniques for exploiting the benefits of living alone and avoiding the worst of the pitfalls. In this regard as in so many others, Covid-19 struck a population full of resources built up amidst the consumer and communications revolutions in the modern era.

The second is that faced with a crisis for which no country was adequately prepared, individuals and social groups have proved far more adaptable than the arthritic structures of government. Community groups have come into being focusing on the needs of those suffering from the absence of company. Neighbours have looked out for neighbours with increased vigilance. And those most vulnerable have acquired new skills. As with so many of my generation I have gained a new mastery of Zoom and its rivals, without which my isolation from children and grandchildren would have been far more profound.

The third is that we live in time. Any experience, negative or otherwise, is conditioned by its duration. 'One definition of loneliness' I wrote in my book, 'is that it is solitude that has continued for longer than was intended or desired.'[110] If there is no ending that we can see or control, then it becomes unbearable. With yesterday's emergency Tier 4 lockdown, Christmas is going to be a trial for many separated families, despite the special dispensation to form a support bubble with others if 'you are the only adult in your household'. But we do know that the vaccine is coming.


**Tuesday, 5 January 2021. Time Divides.**


At first it was a calculation of infection scores. My son and his wife and four-month-old baby had found a loophole in the Tier 4 regulations and driven up to spend Christmas with us. As the year ended, it seemed prudent to delay the return to London.

In Shropshire, in common with other counties on the western fringe of England, the infection rate is still relatively low. In the last week of

2020, it stood at 150 per hundred thousand, half the national average. In Waltham Forest, my son's borough in East London, the rate was six times higher at 913. Safer to stay here, with the clean winds blowing in from the Welsh hills.

Then two further developments. A neighbour rings. A couple in a house at the bottom of our lane are in hospital with Covid-19. Both are in the middle years of life, but are seriously unwell, one is receiving oxygen. On the other side of the lane, a woman whose land abuts our garden is also stricken, though still at home. That's three cases in twenty nearby villagers, the equivalent of 15,000 per 100,000. So much for aggregate statistics.

Later in the day, Boris Johnson is back on our television. There is to be a complete lockdown in England and the vulnerable must once more shield themselves. No one should travel except for limited and necessary purposes. No end date is given. My granddaughter and her parents who came for a fortnight will be here until Spring.

Thus time divides. At one level, it crawls to a standstill. It has always been difficult to detect the diurnal pulse in January and February, and now there will be nothing to separate one day from the next, one week from another. In sympathy with the state's prohibitions, even the weather is at a halt, the thermometer travelling between minus and plus two from a late dawn to an early dusk.

In my post-employment life, I have no deadlines to structure my labours; even zoom-world seems asleep. There is no timetable to manage or anticipate. My wife and I are in the fourth category of vaccination. To reach us by mid-February according to Johnson's vague 'given a fair wind' strategy, 13.2 million procedures will have to be carried out at a rate of two million a week. History, it has to be said, offers no comfort.

At another level time is changing almost minute by minute. When she finally goes home, our granddaughter will have spent around half her life with us. We visited and were visited by our other London-based grandchildren and took immense interest and pleasure in their company, but such encounters amounted to little more than snapshots of their growth. Not since our own children were born have we had a ringside view of the minute but fundamental developments that continually take place. And on this occasion we don't have to deal with nappies or lose acres of unrecoverable sleep.

So, for instance, I watch her hands, waving about almost uncontrollably when she arrived, now increasingly precise instruments for manipulating objects. Toys, which on Christmas day were beyond her reach and comprehension, are now being incorporated into her daily activities.

Keep her safe, keep us all safe, and the next months are going to be nothing but a drama.

**January 7.  One Flag or Two?**

In Zoomworld, we have all become conscious of the backgrounds behind our heads as we talk.

Bookcases are the default for those whose business is words, but then which spines should be in view (not my Elmore Leonard collection, safely out of sight in a bedroom), and for regular dialogists, should there be occasional changes on the shelves to indicate that they are more than wallpaper?

You may be certain that serious thought has been given to the sets in front of which we are addressed by our political masters.

Boris Johnson's handlers long ago determined that a rather dull, bookless room in Number 10 should be enlivened by two union jacks, identically furled so that the bright red of the cross of St. George is prominent.  Apart from the panelling in the room and a slogan tacked to the podium, there is nothing else to inform the eye. The clearly brand-new flags convey the principal message.  Never mind that Johnson and his Government, through Brexit and the clumsy handling of Covid negotiations with the nations have done what may be irreparable damage to the Union.  Shame was surgically removed from Johnson's psyche long before he became a public figure.

Thus, on Monday the third lockdown is announced from Downing Street with the two flags just to the left of his podium as the Prime Minister looks at the camera. At a subsequent news conference, they are placed on either side.

We live in a democracy. Johnson's broadcast is followed a day later by a response from the Leader of the Opposition. Here again the set has been carefully designed. Behind Keir Starmer's head and shoulders is a dark screen to minimise any distraction. The only other object on view is, again, a union jack, also on his left side. It looks exactly like Johnson's, freestanding on its pole, once more furled to foreground the cross of St. George. It is clearly unused, very definitely not a banner that a trade union once marched behind, or that had been waved on a barricade, shot through with bullets by the forces of reaction.

So, what does Starmer's flag mean?

Most obviously that the Party is desperate to escape the label of unpatriotic that was hung around Corbyn's neck, most notoriously when he failed to blame the Russians for the Salisbury novichok poisoning.

More generally that Starmer sees his role in the midst of the pandemic as a loyal echo of the official message. In a five-minute address he makes only the most generalised criticism of the Conservatives. 'There are serious questions for the Government to answer', he says, furrowing his brow, mentioning the wasted £22 billion on testing, and the recurrent delays in announcing actions. But, he concludes, 'whatever our quarrels with the government and the prime minister, the country now needs us to come together'. Most of the speech repeats Johnson's vaguely uplifting call for a national endeavour. It ends by appropriating the Queen: 'We will recover. We'll rebuild. We'll see each other again.'

There is a recognisable short-term strategy at work, and without question the country needs a collective effort, as Johnson and/or Starmer puts it, to win the race between the vaccine and the virus.

But it will not do. If we are to end this crisis with any sense of forward propulsion, Starmer has to ride two horses, wave two different flags. The delays reflect the incompetence of a government recruited from Brexit loyalists and led by a serial liar. The maladministration, from PPE shortages to testing scandals, to the likely failure of the vaccination timetable, is a product of a semi-corrupt faith in the private sector and the hollowing out of local democracy. The immense variations in every aspect of the pandemic experience, from infection and death rates to coping with school closures, are a consequence of decades of growing inequality which have urgently to be reversed. If the union jack is waved, there must be some sense of how the loyalty of the Scots in particular can be regained by a party whose representation north of the border has been all but wiped out.

In the midst of the Second World War, Churchill viewed any attempt to plan for peacetime as a distraction from the fight with Hitler. But in 1942, when victory was far from certain, Beveridge wrote his plan and Labour won the 1945 landslide because the Tories were, rightly, not trusted to implement it.

We need to come out of this national struggle with a vision for the future already conceived and articulated.

## Friday, 8 January 2021. Baroness Barran and the Epidemic of Loneliness

The *Guardian* runs a piece on loneliness over Christmas:

'A volunteer phone call service for older and vulnerable social housing residents and a homemade Christmas food delivery service are among a number of initiatives being singled out for praise as the government announces a £7.5m fund to tackle the epidemic of loneliness in England.'[111]

It's the kind of story that makes you want to give up as a writer altogether.

Last Spring, I published a book whose penultimate chapter sought to outlaw forever the phrase 'epidemic of loneliness' which was then in widespread use and fuelling what Fay Bound Alberti described as a 'moral panic'. I reiterated my arguments in sundry interviews and blogs.

At the time it seemed as if history was on my side. The casual use of a medical term as a metaphor for a social condition surely could not survive the arrival of a real epidemic. In reality, severe loneliness was nowhere near as prevalent as was claimed, and it was in no sense an infectious disease. There could be no vaccine against it (though, as discussed in the 7 August entry, there are continuing reports of attempts to find a pill to reduce loneliness).

But here, eight months on, with Covid-19 running rampant, the phrase leads a story in a reputable newspaper with no attempt at authorial distancing. Ed Davey, leader of the Liberal Democrats, never the brightest candle on the parliamentary Christmas cake, is elsewhere quoted as saying that the pandemic has 'created a silent epidemic of loneliness',[112] forgetting that such an 'epidemic' originally preceded the pandemic. As has been the case throughout, the Office for National Statistics scores for 'often/always' lonely have barely moved. The latest figure, released today, covering the Christmas period of 22 December to 3 January, is unchanged at 6%.[113]

In part it is just lazy journalism by the *Guardian*, copying across the language of press releases.

More broadly it is a legacy of the Government's initial loneliness strategy published in 2018,[114] and the concomitant appointment of the world's first 'loneliness minister', now Baroness Diana Barran, who is lodged in the Department for Digital, Culture, Media & Sport [Who she? Good works on domestic abuse, but perhaps most notable for her father, no less than Count Cosmo Diodono de Bosdari – straight out of *The Leopard*]. Then as now, there is a vast mismatch between ambition and investment. In 2018, £20m was to be spread round various projects to achieve a reconnection of British society. In the new initiative, pocket money is to be spent 'bringing society and communities together' in the midst of a crisis where the standard currency for state intervention is counted in billions.

The founding strategy was reviewed in January 2020. The Department was still working on measuring the problem, stated to be 'somewhere between 6% and 18% of the population,' [115] a gap of merely eight million lonely people. It reported on various small-scale ventures designed to 'celebrate and better support organisations who work tirelessly to help people build stronger connections and develop their sense of belonging.' Looking forward, just as Covid-19 reached our shores, the review promised that 'The Minister for Civil Society will continue to lead this work and to chair the cross-government Ministerial Group on Tackling Loneliness, ensuring government commitments are delivered and built on so that far fewer people feel alone and disconnected over the next decade.'

There is a certain charm in the survival of this kind of misty goodwill at a time when everything is more desperate and much, much, more expensive.

It is also simply a distraction. The main causes of searing loneliness are systemic failures in mental health care, inadequate access to GPs and hospitals especially by those with disabilities, declining community services, both professional and voluntary, and material deprivation including housing. The only short-term counter to these pressures during the pandemic has been greater neighbourhood engagement with the lives of those separated from each other by lockdown and shielding, and increasingly sophisticated use of the connecting technologies of communication.

In the short term, the balance sheet has yet to be drawn up. Beyond the pandemic, the solutions will only be found in large-scale structural reforms.

**Tuesday, 12 January 2021. Stoats and Weasels.**

Badger, Rat, Mole, and Toad would be deeply concerned. As a result of the enforced absence of humans from the National Trust property of Plas yn Rhiw on the Lleyn Peninsular, it is reported this week that stoats and weasels have moved out of the wild wood and have been seen in the gardens around the house.

The effect of successive lockdowns on the natural world have been complex. In broad terms, the story is one of an initial impact followed by a slow return to the prevailing crisis. There are many accounts of the sudden pleasures afforded by the cessation of noise and pollution. Here, for instance, Tobias Jones writes of Northern Italy in mid-April, at the time a global hotspot of the virus:

> I live in Parma, but despite the profound anguish here in Italy, it also feels, paradoxically, as if the world has come right in some way. With our despoiling suddenly stopped, wildlife is returning with innocent ebullience. Bottlenose dolphins have been playfully leaping in the waters around Venice. The canals are so crystalline that swans, and shoals of fish, have returned. Hares graze undisturbed in parks in Milan. Deer have been strolling the golf courses of Sardinia and paddling along sandy beaches. Mallards are bathing in Piazza di Spagna and birds have been nesting in the crooks of closed-up, disused wing-mirrors... In some ways it's like a blissed-out stoner's dream of what the world might be. The 'Pianura Padana', the flat plain of the Po valley, usually has some of the worst air pollution in the world. The air is now perfumed by spring. You can see the mountains. Two weeks ago we were singing Rino Gaetano's The Sky Is Evermore Blue from our balconies.[116]

Professional naturalists like Helen MacDonald sniff that such wildlife had always been around, but no-one noticed it. Nonetheless the glimpse of what could be a new normal was at once a relief from the pandemic and a promise of what might in the future be possible.

The true measure of the pandemic year comes in the newly-released figures for the global temperature in 2020. It might be expected that with an overall fall of 7% in fossil fuel burning there would be at least a temporary decline. Instead, the year registered the joint highest temperature on record, shared with 2016. All that has been avoided as a consequence of the pandemic is a new highest figure in its own right.

In the short term, there are few positive signs. Road traffic has returned to or exceeded 2019 volumes as soon as restrictions have been lifted. London and other cities have not rediscovered the birdsong-rich silence of the beginning of the first lockdown. Plane travel is set to resume at pre-pandemic levels whilst trains and buses are unlikely to recover for the foreseeable future. As factories recommenced production after the first lockdown, pollution in China rapidly reappeared. In developed countries, long-nurtured reforms were postponed whilst governments grappled with larger problems. In Britain the introduction of Clear Air Zones was halted in Manchester, Birmingham, Leeds, Bath and other cities. There was a general reprioritising of government activity away from the green agenda to more pressing, and more expensive, responses to the medical emergency. In the developing world, the collapse of eco-tourism defunded programmes for protecting wildlife.

Where there are grounds for hope over the last few months it is mostly in changes which have little or nothing to do with the health crisis, particularly the continuing sharp falls in the cost of renewable energy and the rapid adoption of electric vehicles.

The specific impact has to be measured not in figures but in states of mind. All over the developed world people in cities as well as the countryside have been afforded a real-time preview how nature could look and sound if human populations exercised better control of their activities.

And after a Trump-led decline in confidence in the potential of global co-operation, the borderless engagement with the virus, including the scientific endeavour of vaccine development, has renewed optimism about the potential of human collaboration to respond to the climate crisis. The pandemic itself will not generate change. It will require ambitious planning over the long term.

'… the Badger settled himself into an arm-chair, and said, "Well, we've got our work cut out for to-night and it will probably be pretty late before we're quite through with it."'

**Thursday, 14 January 2021.  Home Entertainment.**

'UK lockdowns fuel record year for home entertainment spending' runs a headline.[117]

A total of £9bn was spent during 2020 on digital home entertainment services in the UK.  The biggest winners were video channels such as Netflix, Amazon Prime and Disney+ whose sales 'surged by 38% year on year.'

That these companies and their share price have had a good pandemic comes as no surprise. 2020 constituted the perfect conditions for their market. For three quarters of the year their main rival, the cinema, was either subject to distancing regulations or closed altogether. Other entertainments outside the home were similarly constrained.

In such circumstances it must be questioned whether 'surged' is too strong a verb. When the UK Covid-19 death rate grows from 2 on 7 September 2020 to 1564 yesterday, that's a surge. The performance of the home entertainment industry looks by contrast to have been comparatively modest.

The pandemic struck a market that was already growing rapidly. During 2019, the number of UK subscribers to Netflix grew by 13% to over 11 million. That the rate of acquisition of new customers was three time higher the following year is the least that might be expected given the temporary destruction of its main area of competition.

There are perhaps two explanations for this limited expansion.

The first is that like so much of domestic consumer spending, the main patterns of behaviour were in place before the pandemic struck. The media analysist Omdia concludes that the performance of Netflix had 'exaggerated already existing and underlying trends',[118] which is probably true across the piece. My household had already acquired an internet-connected television and decided what it wanted to subscribe to. The only addition during the year were the art-house channels of Mubi and Curzon cinema, which we only occasionally watch (though we have discovered the strange and wonderful films of Roy Anderson). As with so many digital services, the graph of growth must flatten as penetration of the market nears saturation.

The second is that we all responded to successive lockdowns with greater effort and ingenuity than might have been expected. We did not just slump in front of the box with a drink in our hand. We took walks, we worked in the garden while the light lasted, and we addressed projects around the house. Amongst the recently published financial reports is one from Kingfisher, the leading DIY supplier through brands such as B&Q and Screwfix. The newspaper headline in this case is 'Lockdown DIY Craze.'[119] Over the two months between 1 November to 9 January, sales were 16.9% up over the same period the previous year. Again the report is subject to journalistic over-excitement. An increase of a sixth is no 'craze', but it does indicate a desire finally to undertake long-standing home improvements [see my post 'Two Panels', 26 November 2020].

We also have some information about what we chose to watch on our television sets during 2020. The most popular video, boxed or downloaded, was *Frozen II*, with sales of 973,000. This suggests a market driven by children, or by parents driven to distraction finding them something to do. I have yet to encounter this film, so have no explanation for its success. Instead, I ask my oldest granddaughter, now eight years old, to compare the sequel to the original. She writes:

> yes I have watched it and I do think that it is a little bit better than the first one because it has quite a lot more to it and so it is a bit more exciting. There is also a little bit of a mystery in it because they have to find out what happened to their parents and how they met. There are also lots of different elements to the story, more people and more adventures and more mysteries!

Better get a copy!

**Friday, 15 January 2021.   The Knightsbridge Circle.**

The Government has taken, or has had forced upon it, a decision of principle. The Covid-19 vaccines are not on the market. The rich cannot buy immunity.

There is a sense, indeed, in which the vaccine programme offers a temporary reversal of the pattern throughout the pandemic of the poor suffering more than the prosperous. Many of the staff in the NHS and care homes who are now at the head of the queue are amongst the relatively low paid who have been most at risk in recent months.

Initially it looked as if the wealthy were to be punished for their self-indulgence, as holiday-makers skiing in northern Italy came back to

Britain with the virus. But as it became embedded across the population, the most vulnerable were those who could not afford to work at home, or who lacked adequate domestic space, or who had acquired underlying health conditions through decades of poor diet and inadequate health care.

Now all were to be equal in the programme. However, the Government reckoned without the culture of the rich. The *Daily Telegraph* - where else - has just reported on the offer being made by the private concierge service, Knightsbridge Circle, which charges a basic £25,000 a year for membership. It looks to be worth every penny. 'A carefully curated membership', says its website, 'ensures that clients receive unparalleled access to the very best of everything that life has to offer.'

This includes jumping the vaccination queue.

The founder of Knightsbridge Circle, one Stuart McNeil, explained to the *Daily Telegraph* the recent addition to his service:

> the inoculations are already well underway, with members based both in the UK and abroad flying out for vaccination holidays, many on private jets. 'It's like we're the pioneers of this new luxury travel vaccine programme. You go for a few weeks to a villa in the sunshine, get your jabs and your certificate and you're ready to go,' says McNeill, who assumes that many such members have flown out under the

business/education trip exemption. 'Lots of our clients have business meetings in the UAE.'[120]

The cost for a curated member is certainly manageable: 'While the potential upper end cost of such a trip is mammoth, McNeill approximates a cost of around £40,000 for a month-long trip to Dubai with first class Emirates flights, meet and greet, accommodation in a sea view Jumeirah Beach apartment, vaccination and membership for two.

But, dear reader, you ask, is this not illegal?

Well yes, but then again no, but then again it depends on whether Priti Patel wants to enforce her own laws.

It is certainly illegal to take flights for pleasure. The wording of the new lockdown is clear enough: 'You must not leave or be outside of your home except where you have a "reasonable excuse". This is the law.' However, a 'reasonable excuse' includes 'work, where you cannot reasonably work from home.' As it is well known that the super-rich live in hovels without desk space or internet connections, it is of course necessary for them to go out to earn their weekly pittance. As for distance, the rules also say, 'if you need to travel you should stay local – meaning avoiding travelling outside of your village, town or the part of the city where you live.' The UAE, as we know, is just next door to the City of London, particularly when you have a private jet. No problem.

What is so heart-warming about Stuart McNeil is that he has not lost his moral compass in supplying this service. According to the article, he 'is keen to note that Knightsbridge Circle has not vaccinated anybody under the age of 65… We still have a moral responsibility to make sure that people that really need it get it, and that's what we've been focusing on.'

Yes, you read that last sentence correctly. McNeill's only regret is that the Government has yet to make the vaccine available to his private clinic in Harley Street: 'I'm really keeping my fingers crossed that Boris allows us to do this.'

It can only be a matter of time.

**Monday, 18 January 2021. Lord Sumption wrong again.**

It's getting nearer. Last week a ninety-three-year-old friend and neighbour was vaccinated. Today it is announced that my cohort, the seventy-plus and clinically vulnerable, are to receive invitation letters (in fact this morning's post brings only a bank statement and the latest edition of the *Journal of Cultural and Social History,* ojoy).

Despite earlier fears, this is a party which most of us want to attend. The latest survey conducted by the Office for National Statistics (ONS) reveals that 86% of the population said they were 'very or fairly' likely to accept a vaccination in the period 7-10 January, up from 82% in before Christmas. Most of the remainder were either uncertain or had already had it. Only 3% responded that they were 'very unlikely' to take one, the same figure as those who by then had been vaccinated.[121]

Given the inescapable presence of hard-core conspiracy theorists in any population, this is as near to a general acceptance in principle as might be achieved at this stage in the process. I argued in an earlier post ('Anti-Vax', July 7) that the numbers unloading to pollsters their grievances against the state, research-based science, big pharma, transmission masts, were likely to shrink once the hypothesis became a reality, and this appears to be happening.

According to the official timetable, the priority groups are to be vaccinated by mid-February, with the whole of the population gaining protection by September. There remains a question of whether this is the most sensible strategy.

We don't need to endorse the view of our old friend Lord Sumption, who is in more trouble this week for mis-construing the obvious and mis-describing the reality. He argued in a current affairs programme yesterday that the elderly were 'less valuable' than the young, elevating the simple arithmetical fact that they have fewer years to live into a profoundly unacceptable dismissal of their lives. And as with others opposing the lockdown regime, he was factually plain wrong in claiming that the restrictions on socialising do not reduce infection across the population.[122]

The more interesting question is whether the young should be left to last. The 70-plus cohort is not the most infected section of the population, and therefore not the most likely to infect others. We received last week a communication from Shropshire Council indicating that the rate for the elderly in the county is half that of the 20-29 age group. Nationally the ONS finds a similar distribution, using slightly different age-bands. On January 2nd, 3.16% of the 15-24 age group tested positive, with a steady decline across the cohorts to 1.06% for the 70 and over.[123]

At face, these disparities are not surprising. The retired do not need to go out to work, and are less likely to be found in shopping precincts, bars and all-night raves. My frail elderly neighbour who has now received his vaccination has been wholly locked down since the end of March, irrespective of the fluctuations in the official rules and advice. He is absolutely no threat to anyone else. The same is pretty much true of my household. Where they have gone out of doors, the 70-plus were found by the ONS to be more likely than the 16-29 cohort to answer positively to the question 'have you avoided physical contact with others when outside the home?'

Furthermore, the young appear to be suffering psychologically more than the old. The current ONS 'overall, how satisfied are you with your life nowadays' score rises steadily from 5.9% for the 16-29 cohort to

7.3% for those now due to receive their vaccination invitations. There is an even sharper disparity in the loneliness measure, ranging from 13% to 5% for the same groups.[124]

So, the young are having a tougher time and are more likely to catch and transmit the virus. Why not vaccinate them first?

The short and irrefutable answer, *pace* Lord Sumption, lies in the age-specific rates for hospitalisation and death, together with the obvious need to keep fit those caring for the ill and the elderly, and to prevent the NHS from being overwhelmed to the cost not only of Covid-19 sufferers but those with any other serious illness. But there is a price to be paid for this strategy. Assuming the vaccination roll-out continues as promised, the mortality rates will fall much faster than those for infection.

It really will be the autumn and not the spring before it will begin to be safe to resume anything like our normal lives.

**Wednesday, 20 January 2021. On Death and Dying.**

Last Sunday, my friend and colleague John Naughton, in his endlessly wise and informative daily blog, Memex1.1, appropriated the Kübler-Ross five stages of dying model in order to frame a coruscating attack on the political mismanagement of the pandemic both here and in the United States.

He addressed Denial, Anger, Bargaining and Depression, concluding with Acceptance:

> We're nowhere near that yet. People still haven't grasped that there's no going back to the way we were. That past is indeed a different country. It's also a country that was heading straight for climate catastrophe. So every time someone talks about a 'return to growth' you know that the reality of what lies ahead hasn't yet been appreciated. The only kind of growth worth having post-pandemic is a greener, carbon-neutral one. And the only question worth asking is: could we create such a future?

The piece caused me to take down from my shelves the original, enormously influential book, *On Death and Dying*. Since its publication over half a century ago, the notion and labelling of the five stages has been the subject of widespread debate. The hospice movement, which Kübler-Ross did so much to inspire, no longer uses them. But re-reading the text highlighted some basic truths about dying in the pandemic.

Kübler-Ross's opening premise was that 'dying nowadays is more gruesome in many ways, namely, more lonely, mechanical and dehumanized.'[125] Despite the major improvements in palliative care since 1969, the technologies of medical intervention have become still more impersonal, the patient yet more subordinated to the authority of doctors and the routines of hospitals.

Her insistence that fear of death can only be effectively countered if the issue is explicitly considered by those not yet dying, remains entirely valid. 'It might be helpful' she writes, 'if more people would talk about death and dying as an intrinsic part of life just as they do not hesitate to mention when someone is expecting a new baby.'[126] A beneficial outcome of the pandemic tragedies may be a new era of public engagement with what in most social settings remains an unvisited land.

However debatable the particular issue of 'stages', there can be no questioning Kübler-Ross's central premise that it is the responsibility of all those working with the dying to be informed, caring listeners and that the reactions of those enduring a terminal illness are in their different ways rational and comprehensible.

The departure from the present crisis lies in the context of how this listening takes place. The book begins by listing the changes that separate modern medicine from the past, including significant therapeutic interventions, increasing life expectancy, and the absence of pandemics. The return of mass infection and death has fundamentally altered a basic assumption of the text. 'If a patient has had enough time', Kübler-Ross writes, '(i.e., not a sudden, unexpected death) and has been given some help in working through the previously described stages, he will reach a stage during which he is neither depressed nor angry about his "fate."'[127]

The whole enterprise assumes the resources of a well-found (American) hospital, with teams of professionals including not only doctors and nurses but psychiatrists, social workers and chaplains, ready and able to spend long periods communicating with the patients as their disease takes its course over months or years.

The essence of dying with Covid-19 is that neither patients, nor their families, nor the staff of hospitals or hospices have remotely enough time to work through any sequence of emotional expression or support. The common experience of those who are infected is for little to happen for the first few days, and then for the unlucky minority there is a sudden descent into breathlessness and other symptoms which leads rapidly to an intensive care unit. Even if they ultimately survive the mechanical ventilators, they will have been unconscious throughout that part of their treatment. Hospital staff are overwhelmed by the sheer pressure of numbers, radically reducing staff/patient ratios whilst at the same time trying to stand in for the presence of next of kin excluded by quarantine regulations.

It is the absence of time for death and dying which, more than the pathogens and the remedies, most connects the Covid-19 pandemic with the flu and plague outbreaks that preceded it down the centuries.

Those on the front line have not given up on the challenge. In the collection of radio podcasts, *Letters from Lockdown* (broadcast by the BBC PM programme), there is a particularly fine piece by a doctor which focuses on the multiple uses of her mobile phone. It gets employed to keep in touch at speed with staff around the hospital, to take pictures of the property bags of deceased patients, to relieve stress by playing music when in bed after an exhausting shift, and to provide at least a small window of communication to dying patients:

> my phone has been placed next to an old lady's ear, on her pillow as she drifts into unconsciousness, breathing with shallow, irregular gasps, with hopes and promises from her daughter, hoping that her mum will be able to hear her final words of love, even though she can't be there to say them.[128]

**Sunday. 24 January 2021. Otherwise.**

This is in response to Anne's vivid account of heat and drought in Australia. It is otherwise on the other side of the world.

The picture was taken from the bottom of my garden as the snow fell this morning.[129] In the background, grey beneath the heavy clouds, is the River Severn in flood. Heavy rainfall in the Welsh hills has sent it over its banks for the second time in a month.

Nothing changes as a consequence. The land below us constitutes a run-off for excess water, reducing flooding downstream in Shrewsbury. To keep its cattle safe, the farm opposite us has erected a fence across the field just above the highest level which the river normally reaches. In a week or so it will have dropped ten feet, back within its course.

In normal times, a snowfall would create a temporary lockdown in the village, until the farmer who holds the contract from the Council starts up his tractor and clears the lanes. But we are already locked down; no plans to go anywhere. It might as well snow until Spring.

All we can do is enjoy the view.

**Wednesday, 27 January 2021. Computing the Sorrow.**

Boris Johnson says it is 'hard to compute the sorrow' after the official Covid-19 death rate passes 100,000 in the UK.

In fact there is a perfectly simple calculation that can be made. Grief professionals work on the basis of at least five bereaved people for every death.[130] On current figures that gives us a population of half a million in the UK facing a lonely future. If we take the more accurate figure of those dying with Covid-19 on their death certificates, the number is already 600,000. Globally there are now 2.2 million deaths generating a population of over 11 million coming to terms with traumatic loss.

Estimating the length of the sorrow is a more difficult task. There seems to be an inverse ratio at work: the more rapid the event of dying, the more extended the process of grieving.

The struggle to come to terms with a loss begins more uncertainly and is likely to proceed more slowly than is the case for non-pandemic bereavements. In this sense Johnson was for once correct in his account. It will be a long time before we can take a measure of the suffering generated by a death rate that is the fifth highest in the world, and the second highest as a proportion of the population.

A recent review of the first tranche of academic papers on Covid-19 bereavement summarises the difficulties facing the relatives of victims:

> There is sometimes little chance to say farewell in accustomed ways, or to observe cultural or religious mourning practices; there may be regrets or anger about the possible preventability of the death. A persisting difficulty has been noted: social isolation has brought with it the lack of physical support from family and friends or physically-present spiritual support, reflecting sometimes severe societal disruptions in general. Such distancing can intensify feelings of loneliness that is part of any bereavement experience, even without isolation orders in place.

'In the face of such difficulties,' the paper concludes, 'one might speculate that letting go, finding a place for the deceased in ongoing life, relinquishing the old ties/bonds and moving on may not be tasks that can yet be dealt with.'[131]

The established rituals of bereavement, whatever they may be, work on the basis of manageable numbers. Defoe's account of the 1665 plague stands for every pandemic: 'It is here, however, to be observ'd, that after the Funerals became so many, that People could not Toll the Bell, Mourn, or Weep, or wear Black for one another, as they did before, no, nor so much as make Coffins for those that died.'[132] In our own event the pressures are compounded by regulations designed to prevent the spread of infection. No more than 30 socially distanced mourners can attend an English funeral, and only six can gather at the wake (but none in Wales and Scotland).

Every manual on bereavement stresses the importance of listening to those who are left alone, which becomes more difficult as physical encounters are limited. The comfort of touch is frequently out of reach. The small pleasures that can provide escape from the intensity of grief become unobtainable. Those whose lives have been shattered have difficulty occupying the centre of their own dramas when all around them are competing narratives of loss. The novelist and counsellor Rebecca Abrams, in a training seminar for Cruse, the leading bereavement charity, stresses how the young in particular, accustomed to talking through their crises with networks of friends, find it difficult to commence their mourning.[133]

There are compensating resources.  There was already in existence a range of organisations, including Marie Curie, Cruse, Sudden, The Loss Foundation, The Good Grief Trust, the Samaritans, Supportive Friends, with established bereavement methodologies and networks of volunteers, although most of their work has had to become virtual.  Social networking more generally has never been as important, especially amongst the young who are already accustomed to working through their problems online.

Medical researchers are drawing attention to a bodily 'long covid', where a range of often serious conditions persist after the initial symptoms have been overcome.  Amongst those who have lost people close to them, as well as health workers exposed to post-traumatic stress disorders, there is also going to be a long covid of the mind, which may in turn have further physical outcomes.

The army of the bereaved will be living amongst us for years to come, patching together their recovery as best they can.

**Friday, 29 January 2021.  The doctor will not see you now.**

I cannot remember the last time I had a face-to-face conversation with my doctor.  Probably in 2019, perhaps earlier.  To know how he and his profession are managing in the pandemic I turn to the new account by an Edinburgh GP, Gavin Francis.

Francis and his publisher, together with the Wellcome Collection, deserve praise for getting the book out while the crisis is still in full flood. Inevitably there is a cost in coverage. The narrative ends in the autumn of 2020, before the third surge in infections and deaths.

Throughout *Intensive Care*, Francis is concerned with the consequence of talking with patients only by phone or through masked faces:

> As GPs we're taught to value the subtleties of human communication – to glean as much from what the patient doesn't say as from what they do say. As trainees we have to submit videos of our consultations to demonstrate how carefully we attend to body language, to silences, to the way patients hold or evade eye contact.[134]

My surgery is located in a nearby large village. In common presumably with all practices, its switchboard has been greeting callers with a recorded message explaining that only telephone appointments can be made; the doctor will then decide whether it is necessary to see a patient in the surgery or at home. If you stay online, you then get a recorded message purchased from some third-rate utility: 'Your call is very important to us. Please wait for the next available agent.' This week, however, there is an additional message which I encounter when I ring to renew a prescription:

> Our phone lines are very busy due to the volume of calls we are receiving about the Covid-19 vaccine. The NHS is prioritising

vaccinating those people who experts have agreed would benefit from it the most. We will let you know when it is your turn to book you a vaccination. If you would like more information about the vaccine, please visit http://www.nhs.uk/covid/vaccination. If your query was about the covid vaccine, please hang up now.

So not even a someone to talk to on the other end of the phone. Rather implied censure for making the call in the first place. Clearly this is a surgery under stress. But it is possible to suggest another response which acknowledges that:

• receiving the vaccine is for vulnerable groups by a distance the single most important event, medical or otherwise, that they are facing;

• at this moment, potential recipients are being treated differently in different regions and you well may know of people in similar circumstances who have already been vaccinated;

• in so large a project there must always be an apprehension that as an individual you may fall through some bureaucratic crack;

• over your lifetime you have been used to treating your GP surgery as your portal for all health enquiries, and that being re-directed to an impersonal website offers little comfort.

In the concluding discussion of his book, Gavin Francis is preoccupied with the defects of non-face-to-face medicine, necessary though it may be in the crisis:

> As time goes on, and if telemedicine prevails, those relationships forged in person will become more remote, and the medicine GPs practise will become more perfunctory, based on the avoidance of being sued rather than on what's best for the patient. Those conversations would be not 'consultations,' but triage, fire-fighting, damage limitation. It's difficult enough to engage with the unique complexity of another human being's suffering in ten or twelve minutes when sharing the same space, but on the telephone it's near impossible.[135]

With doctors, as with so much else, the meaning of this pandemic will not just depend on the temporary expedients that are adopted. Rather the question is which emergency devices are rescinded the moment the crisis is over, and which are allowed to persist, whether out of inertia or institutional self-interest.

**Tuesday, 2 February 2021.  Monuments**.

'History', writes the Guardian columnist Jonathan Freedland, 'suggests we may forget the pandemic sooner than we think.'[136]

He is commenting on the milestone of 100,000 Covid-19 deaths in the UK.

Freedman begins with the point I made in my Computing the Sorrow post last week: 'So far, the act of remembering has been deferred or even forbidden. Second only to the deaths themselves, perhaps the greatest pain the coronavirus has inflicted has been its denial of the right to say goodbye.' But his subsequent argument that thereafter there may be no collective memory seems at best premature and in most respects open to question.

He repeats Laura Spinney's observation that there are no public memorials to the 1918-20 Spanish flu epidemic which killed probably between fifty and a hundred million people, in contrast to the current Covid global death toll of 2.2 million in a much larger population.[137] This is to confuse monuments with memory. London erected a column in honour of the Great Fire, not the Plague a year earlier, but two generations later Defoe wrote his Journal of the Plague Year for a readership still traumatised by the epidemic.

He states that the 'facts' of pandemics can 'take years to emerge', noting that initial estimates of the 1918-20 outbreak were decades later revised sharply upwards. But thanks in particular to the Center for Systems Science and Engineering at Johns Hopkins University, this has been a minutely calibrated disaster. There remain some variations in how Covid19 deaths are measured in different countries, but there is not going to be some subsequent recount which adds tens of millions to the death toll.

More broadly he draws a contrast between military and medical narratives. 'Wars offer a compelling, linear story', he argues. 'There are causes and consequences, battles, surrenders and treaties, all taking place in a defined space and time. Pandemics are not like that.' As I argued in an earlier post,[138] set against the other great misfortunes of our time, particularly inequality and climate change, the pandemic does have a plot, with a beginning, middle, and a now somewhat delayed ending. This is why the most influential accounts of such events, those of Defoe and Camus, have taken the form of conventional novels. The dynamics of inequality, as Thomas Piketty has shown, can be traced at least as far back as the late eighteenth century and have no resolution in sight. Equally the destruction of nature commences with the industrial revolution and to take the most optimistic view, will not be overcome for decades.

Freedland's final point is more fundamental. A viral infection is unlike a world war. 'Crucially,' he writes 'a pandemic lacks the essential ingredients of a story: clear heroes and villains with intent and motive.' There is an obvious truth in this. The ultimate cause is bats, not people (unless the Wuhan lab leak theory turns out to be true). Covid-19 infections occur by chance, carelessness or neglect, and for all the errors of a Trump or a Johnson, the event as a whole cannot be blamed, except by conspiracy theorists, on individual or collective malevolence.

And yet, as in the stories of Defoe and Camus, the accounts emerging from the pandemic are full of personal courage and achievement as well as individual and institutional shortcomings. In the midst of the struggle, it is fruitless to determine how countries will revise their national narratives in the aftermath of so seismic an interruption to their affairs. It will in the end be a matter of choice rather than historical inevitability.

We can remember and then act, or we can forget and then repeat the failings of human agency in this pandemic. We can keep in front of our minds the lessons learned about collective endeavour in the national health service, in science laboratories, and in communities up and down the country. Or we can allow the incompetence and self-interest of politicians and the private sector to be buried with the victims.

**Thursday, 4 February 2021. Truth Telling**.

There is published today a new book by the journalist Peter Oborne: *The Assault on Truth: Boris Johnson, Donald Trump and the Emergence of a New Moral Barbarism*.[139]

'I have been a political reporter for almost three decades,' he writes. 'I have never encountered a senior British politician who lies and fabricates so regularly, so shamelessly and so systematically as Boris Johnson.'

The standard response to this kind of exposé, however well conducted, is that lying is priced into the Johnson brand, and here he is, world king with an eighty-seat majority and his party still ahead of Labour in the opinion polls.

Covid-19 has, however, created a new and more urgent response to Johnson's mendacity.

Also just published is a report from the front line, *Breath taking. Inside the NHS in a time of pandemic*, by Rachel Clarke.[140] It describes the experiences of a doctor during the early months of the outbreak. Clarke was a television journalist before retraining as a doctor specialising in palliative care. When the crisis broke, like many others from different medical disciplines, she volunteered to an intensive care unit in a nearby hospital.

A theme throughout her book is the enhanced importance of truth in communicating with seriously ill patients:

> When drugs run dry, when cure is no longer an option, I deal in words like my patients' lives depend on it. Words build trust, allay fears, dispel myths, inspire hope. They clarify, challenge, encourage and console. Words leap beyond the constraints of masks and gloves and gowns. Titrated carefully, dosed just right, words can take a dying patient all the way from the depths of despair to a place of hope and even serenity… It follows that doctors have a duty to use our words with exceptional care. We

are nothing if our patients cannot trust us. Above all, our words must be our bond.[141]

Other accounts emerging from intensive care units stress the urgency of what may be final words.

An anaesthetist writes of his experience preparing a patient for a ventilator:

> 'I need to phone my family,' she gasps. I nod and say OK, almost shouting to be heard over the noise of the alarms. The patient tries to talk to her family on FaceTime. She is extremely breathless and looks like she is dry drowning in thin air. Tears pour down her face. I hear someone on the phone crying and saying 'I love you' ... While we are pre-oxygenating her, I take off her CPAP hood and lean closer. 'We're here to look after you. Everything will be OK.' I stop talking because I think I might cry. I worry she is dying. I hold her hand. She squeezes it and I squeeze hers back.[142]

Every word, however brief and obscured by machinery, masks or bad phone reception, is freighted with a lifetime's meaning.

An individual or institutional crisis places an additional premium on truth. Stressed and exhausted by her days on the ward, Rachel Clarke was enraged by the casual, self-regarding misrepresentations in Boris Johnson's daily press conferences. She knew just what was happening in the hospitals, how much worse matters really were for both patients and staff.

'I never wanted Red Arrows, medals or minutes of silence' she writes at the end of her book: 'Like my colleagues, my needs were more prosaic. Really, I just wanted honesty from those who rule us...'[143]

**Saturday, 6 February 2021. Ludlow Races.**

On Tuesday evening we drove down to Ludlow Racecourse for our Covid-19 vaccination. No horses, no riders, no vets, just teams of volunteers in a couple of marquees, remarkably cheerful towards the end of what I was told had been a twelve-hour day checking identities and administering jabs.

We waited in lines of spaced seating. None of us in our first youth, and all of us, it now strikes me, white. This was rural Shropshire and should come as no surprise. A county which voted decisively for Brexit immigration controls has in fact very few immigrants.

But with the new finding that white over-eighties are twice as likely to have been vaccinated as black, there is a fresh concern that the BAME community is not participating in the vaccination programme.[144] There are similar worries about medical staff who have been offered the vaccine. The *Health Service Journal* reports that at the Guy's and St Thomas' Foundation Trust in London there has been 'substantially lower covid vaccine uptake among its black African, black Caribbean and Filipino staff so far.'[145] Challenged about these discrepancies, the minister in charge, Nadhim Zahawi, took a glass 85%-full line, stressing the large numbers who had taken the vaccine, and admitting that the Government was not fully recording those who had not done so.

Since the pandemic began there has been opinion-poll evidence from many countries about the scale of what are now politely described as 'vaccine hesitants.' The latest survey finds that nearly 40% of the French and 23% of Germans say they will definitely or probably refuse a vaccination.[146] I have always been cautious about these reports. No one ever died of giving a negative response to a pollster. It's easy enough to unload grievances against politicians, health services, big pharma, when, as is still the case in Germany and France, the issue is largely hypothetical.

One positive consequence of these widely-reported figures is that they have provoked governments, health providers, community leaders and celebrities into launching educational programmes to counter on-line anti-vax propaganda. The British government has set aside £23m for this purpose. Unfortunately, according the Centre for Countering Digital Hate, anti-vax social media in the UK have also redoubled their efforts now that the choice has become real.[147]

It comes down to a question of speed.

There is a large body of literature on the centuries-old anti-vaccination movements, and on the pervasive presence of malign channels of communication. But we do not have the time to continue debating the excessive individualism of the modern world. The current higher BAME mortality rate is going to increase dramatically if we have to wait for generations of folk remedies to be challenged, or for the community's mistrust of the NHS and agencies of authority such as the police to be overcome. Equally it is a fantasy to suppose that the main digital platforms are going to deny themselves the advertising revenue generated by alternative Covid-19 cures any time soon.

This is why the most effective response to the present dilemma may be that adopted by doctors in Liverpool. They are treating vaccine resistance by BAME groups as an immediate practical matter. It's no good, they argue, depending solely on large-scale venues which, like Ludlow Racecourse, can be a long way from where people live (though to be fair the racecourse had organised a special bus service). Instead, they have started pop-up vaccination centres in local neighbourhoods. Rather than waging war against social media in general, they have engaged with channels of communication up and down particular streets. And if specific groups do not trust representatives of white society, alternatives have been sought.

According to a newspaper report,

> Dr Cait Taylor, a GP who is joint clinical director of the Central
> Liverpool primary care network, decided she and other white

medics would not be giving the inoculations. Instead, they put a call out for medical students from BAME backgrounds, offering £10.21 an hour for Urdu and Arabic speakers. 'We wanted to inspire confidence' she said. 'People felt more comfortable there than at a GP surgery where you might be met with a white receptionist, or a white vaccinator, or a doctor who doesn't explain things to you properly, or doesn't know your language.'[148]

Cait Taylor concludes, 'the message we've got loud and clear from local communities is: come to us and we'd love to take the vaccine, thank you very much.' As should have been the case from the outset with the test and trace system, as much of the delivery as possible should be left in the hands of health professionals who know and are known by the neighbourhoods they are seeking to assist.

**Tuesday, 9 February 2021. Hitler, Shipman, Satan and Mengele**.

The sense of optimism as the vaccines are rolled out is colliding with the battle weariness of medical staff.

As noted in the 4 February post, Rachel Clarke published the first book-length account from inside an intensive care unit.[149] Its anger with the government and anguish at the bleak and lonely deaths suffered by Covid-19 victims was balanced by a joyful account of the sense of community that the pandemic had created. Writing about the first wave last Spring she discovered something new:

> Not once in my lifetime have I seen anything like this grassroots eruption of improvised altruism. Communities coming together, the young and healthy offering to shop for those shielding, restaurants delivering mountains of takeaways to overworked hospital staff, everywhere the desire to be useful, to do something, to make it better, to help out. It startles and thrills me. There *is*, it turns out, such thing as society. We *do* have more in common than that which divides us.[150]

Nine months later she has written a newspaper article, clearly exhausted by her continuing labours on wards that are still operating at peak capacity and overwhelmed by the hostility of covid deniers and anti-vax campaigners. 'I've been called Hitler, Shipman, Satan and Mengele for insisting on Twitter that our hospitals aren't empty,' she writes. Inside the hospital, all is joint endeavour:

> Outside, on the other hand, the virus has once again carved up the country into simmering, resentful, aggrieved little units. It's too old, too cold to be doing this again. One way or another, lockdown hurts us all. But instead of unity, community and a shared sense of purpose – that extraordinary eruption of philanthropy last springtime – we seethe like rats in a sack, fractious, divided… In short, we have reached the point in the pandemic where what feels like armies of trolls do their

snarling, misogynistic utmost to silence NHS staff who try to convey what it's like on the inside. Worse even than the hatred they whip up against NHS staff, the deniers have started turning up in crowds to chant 'Covid is a hoax' outside hospitals full of patients who are sick and dying. Imagine being forced to push your way through that, 13 hours after you began your ICU shift. Some individuals have broken into Covid wards and attempted physically to remove critically ill patients, despite doctors warning that doing so will kill them.[151]

So what now of the new sense of togetherness and joint endeavour? There are two destructive factors at work. The first is simply extreme tiredness, both physical and emotional, and explains why the NHS and the Government have been so desperate to bring down the levels of hospitalisation in the second phase. In Clarke's book, which ended in April last year, the long hours were compensated for by excitement at the drama which she had volunteered to join, and by her justified pride at the way in which the entrenched procedures of hospital medicine had been revolutionized in the face of the crisis. But now it has just gone on too long.

The second is a product of the incivility of contemporary protests, which draw their language from un-moderated social network sites. A community is not a thing, but a set of relationships embodied in discourse. There is a need to interrogate official statistics, up to and including the current debate about vaccine effectiveness. There are quiet reasons for vaccine hesitancy, from inherited folk beliefs to fear of needles. What so demoralizes overstretched medical staff are the ease and frequency with which dissent becomes face-to-face aggression. Those working in emergency medicine have always had to deal with ungrateful, shouting drunks. I was once in an A and E unit with a slightly injured child late on a Friday evening where there were more police than nurses in the waiting room.

But now the pubs are closed. The verbal violence is coming from those who respect nothing except their own views and accept no constraints on their expression. It is not to be borne.

**Wednesday, 10 February 2021. Zuckerberg Repents**.

I wrote in my post of February 6 ('Going to the Races'), that 'it is a fantasy to suppose that the main digital platforms are going to deny themselves the advertising revenue generated by alternative covid cures any time soon.' Evidently Zuckerberg read my words and was shamed. Today he announced that:

> we are expanding our efforts to remove false claims on Facebook and Instagram about COVID-19 vaccines and vaccines in general during the pandemic. Since December, we've removed false claims about COVID-19 vaccines that have been debunked by public health experts. Today, following consultations with leading health organizations, including the World Health Organization (WHO), we are expanding the list

of false claims we will remove to include additional debunked claims about the coronavirus and vaccines. This includes claims such as:

• COVID-19 is man-made or manufactured
• Vaccines are not effective at preventing the disease they are meant to protect against
• It's safer to get the disease than to get the vaccine
• Vaccines are toxic, dangerous or cause autism[152]

That Facebook and Instagram were still publishing such claims a year after the pandemic began, gives pause for thought.

**Thursday, 11 February 2021.  Pray Devoutly and  Incessantly.**

Almighty God uses thunder, lightning and other blows which issue from his throne to scourge the sons whom he wishes to redeem. Accordingly, since a catastrophic pestilence from the East has arrived in a neighbouring kingdom, it is very much to be feared that, unless we pray devoutly and incessantly, a similar pestilence will stretch its poisonous branches into this realm, and strike down and consume the inhabitants.[153]

Thus Bishop Ralph of Shrewsbury wrote to the archdeacons of his diocese on 17 August 1348.

Unfortunately, the prayers and the processions that he ordered failed to prevent the Black Death crossing the Channel from France. A year later the Prior of Canterbury asked the bishops in the southern province to take action:

> Terrible is God towards the sons of men, and by his command all things are subdued to the rule of his will. Those whom he loves he censures and chastises; that is, he punishes their shameful deeds in various ways during this mortal life so that they might not be condemned eternally. He often allows plagues, miserable famines, conflicts, wars and other forms of suffering to arise, and uses them to terrify and torment men and so drive out their sins.[154]

The populations suffering the devastating pandemics of the fourteenth century were at once powerless and active agents in their own destiny. All were exposed to the wrath of a vengeful God, but through prayers, penitential processions and reformed morals it might be possible to hasten the end of a plague and delay its recurrence.

Over the succeeding centuries, the practical task of managing populations and devising cures in a pandemic has gradually transferred to governments and scientists. The moral drama of sin, retribution and repentance, has, however, continued in a new form.

Successive outbreaks of respiratory diseases in this century have been blamed on man's increasing exposure to infected wildlife. SARS

(Severe Acute Respiratory Syndrome) in 2003, MERS (Middle East Respiratory Syndrome) in 2012, and now Covid-19 have crossed the species barrier, probably from bats which carry a wide range of pathogens. An increasing body of literature, together with organizations such as the Coalition for Epidemic Preparedness Innovations, have warned that, like the Black Death in the fourteenth century, one pandemic is almost certain to be followed by another in a matter of years.

Animals may be the proximate cause, but the fundamental problem is the behaviour of people. Land is cleared for population growth, exploitation of raw materials, and for dairy and meat farming, and as a consequence there are lethal encounters with hitherto isolated reservoirs of viruses. The risks are compounded by the rapid increase in international travel and commerce. The pandemics thus become a metonym for the ecological crisis more generally. As the Professor of the History of Medicine at Oxford writes, '"emerging diseases", as they are often termed, have been seen as Nature's retribution for environmental degradation.'[155]

Mankind has misbehaved, is being punished, and, with increasing urgency, is seeking effective forms of repentance.

The Christian churches, pushed to the side-lines by the secular response to disease, are seeking to reclaim the leadership of what they see as a new moral crusade. 'I think the future we are called to build', writes Pope Francis in response to Covid-19, 'has to begin with an integral ecology, an ecology that takes seriously the cultural and ethical deterioration that goes hand in hand with our ecological crisis.'[156] The Archbishop of Canterbury wrote in 1375, that, 'in our modern times, alas, we are mired in monstrous sin and the lack of devotion among the people provokes the anger of the great king to whom we should devote our prayers. As a result we are assailed by plagues or epidemics'.[157] In a pale echo, we have the words of the 105th incumbent: 'Around the world, climate change is affecting food security, creating social vulnerability, and disrupting peace and security. There is no doubt we need to act.'[158]

This time, praying will not be enough.

**Monday, 15 February 2021. UK: Concentrating the Mind.**

When the awards are handed out at the end of this pandemic, a gold medal must surely go to the Office for National Statistics (ONS).

From the beginning it has been the source of sober, relevant and trustworthy data not just on the progress of the disease but on a wide range of associated behaviours and attitudes. It has published reliable answers to the right questions, including attitudes to vaccination now that the programme has gained real momentum.

It has just issued data relating to the end of January. With vaccinations being offered to the top four categories it found that 99% of those aged

70 and over had accepted or would accept a vaccine.[159] Last autumn, when it was being reported that a sixth of the UK population would certainly refuse an offer, and a similar number might do so, I wrote that 'the question constitutes an interesting case history for the capacity of digital communication to shape private behaviour.'[160] Since then the anti-vax campaign has increased its efforts as the vaccines were given approval, and Facebook continued until the last minute to carry its messages.

The ONS survey suggests that orthodox medicine has won a decisive victory. When the invitations were sent out, the conspiracy theories evaporated. Even amongst those still hesitating, the ONS found that most of the doubts had little or nothing to do with stories in the social media. The lead concerns were anxiety about side and long-term effects, then waiting to see if the vaccines actually worked. Only a small proportion of negative respondents declared an outright opposition to vaccines in general.

The most obvious reason for the outcome, which is critical to the defeat of the coronavirus, is the difference between a hypothetical and a practical choice. The conspiracy theories promoted by the internet should be divided into two categories.

There are those which reflect a state of mind that need never be tested in the real world, and those which sooner or later will have to be. Views about race, sex and religion, about the unreality of climate change and the reality of extra-terrestrial beings, may coalesce into active protest, but there is no requirement, no point at which a behaviour has to occur. Like a flu virus they may just mutate over time. Whereas other beliefs, such as the misbehaviour of elected governments, or the evils of vaccination, will at some juncture become a formal choice, when the polling cards or the medical invitations arrive. In those circumstances, interim interrogation of attitudes are contributions to a debate, not predictions of an outcome.

Also this week it is reported that the Conservatives have opened up a five point gap over Labour. No-one mistakes this for an accurate description of an election that is still four years away. It just has an impact on current political debate. Similarly the anti-vax findings last year stimulated on-line counter-propaganda by orthodox medicine, which may have helped in the final result.

The choice itself foregrounds practical concerns. Since the early weeks of the pandemic, we have been told by the ONS and many other authorities, that the elderly and those with pre-existing conditions stand a far greater chance of becoming seriously ill or dying from Covid-19. To paraphrase Samuel Johnson, 'Depend upon it, sir, when a man knows he is likely to end up in an intensive care unit, it concentrates his mind wonderfully.'

It is not surprising, therefore, that the ONS returns for those under 70 currently display a greater resistance to vaccination, though the difference is not large. Of the 3% of 50-69 year-olds who currently are not fully committed, two thirds are just saying they are not certain yet.

Amongst 30-49 year-olds, where 89% respond positively, the next largest group is 6% don't know / won't say. Except for younger medical workers (where there are worrying accounts of BAME resistance) and a few clinically vulnerable, most of these age groups are still discussing only the possibility of vaccination.

There is also the effect of the group. In my network, the over 70s and the clinically extremely vulnerable, emails and blog posts have been buzzing since the New Year with descriptions of what it was like, accounts of after-effects (usually very minor), and complaints from those who had to attend inconvenient centres or had yet to receive their invitation. It was a party everyone was joining and from which no-one wanted to be excluded. The minority of the young, invited because of their role in health or social care, had less of a sense of what in a related area is termed a herd behaviour.

Alongside the vaccine data, the ONS has also updated its measure of the mood of the nation: 'Following a decline in well-being in early January 2021, this week well-being scores for life satisfaction (6.4), happiness (6.4) and feeling that things done in life are worthwhile (7.1) remained at some of the lowest levels recorded since the survey began in March 2020.'[161]

This reflects my own view. I have been surprised by how small the lift in spirits has been since I drove down to Ludlow Racecourse to get my jab at the beginning of the month.

Euphoric is not a term I would use. At best mildly relieved, and aware of the road yet to be followed.

**Wednesday, 24 February 2021. Sadly**.

We have become accustomed to the ritual announcement of Covid-19 data.

The Government is producing daily figures on the progress of the pandemic. It falls to the newsreaders on the main television channels to deliver these at the head of the bulletin. There are scores for infections, hospital admissions, deaths within 28 days of a Covid-19 diagnosis, and recently, vaccinations.

When it gets to the deaths, always the same feeling is inserted. 'Sadly' XXX deaths were reported in the last twenty-four hours. The point of this extra descriptor is presumably to indicate that the broadcasters comprehend the tragedy that is unfolding day by day. They are not just reading from a teleprompter, but somehow engaging with their own emotions. When they can remember, politicians will also furrow their brows and put the word in front of the deaths they are discussing.

'Sadly', when repeated night after night, is an oddly featureless term. I might use it to describe the recent demise of several roses in the arctic winds that blew through my garden last week or the failure of an online order to arrive. I would not think it adequate to encompass the pain I might feel if I were being connected to a ventilator or if a close relative had died.

There is, after all, a thesaurus of terms commentators could use: 'tragic', 'devastating', 'infuriating', 'unnecessary'. Instead, repetition turns 'sadly' into a cliché, expressing little more than indifference. This week it means, 'who cares as long as the figures are coming down.'

Finding a public language to describe the constellation of grief that Covid-19 causes is far from easy. Attention has lately been drawn to an American study which recalculates the bereavement multiplier, the number of individuals left suffering after a death.[162] The research increases what has been the conventional ratio of five (see my post 'Computing the Sorrow', January 22) to just under nine. In the UK context, the current death toll of 121,000 would generate a little over a million bereaved people; globally the figure would be twenty-two million.[163]

As is often the case, however, sophisticated mathematical tools are being applied to very coarse data. The American study focuses on the nuclear family network of grandparent, parent, sibling, spouse, or child, and asks, given the age-specific Covid-19 mortality and US demographic patterns, how many people would be affected by a death. It is essentially a connections survey. No attention is paid to wider networks of relatives, friends and neighbours, nor are there any questions about the nature of the loss, which presumably can range from shattering grief to passing regret. In the end it is just another version of 'sadly', a generalised description of an event which in the States has now accounted for 500,000 lives, or, by this multiplier, 4.5 million bereavements.

More useful research is beginning to appear on the quality of the experience.

Deborah Carr and colleagues (good to see the old stars still working) identify two kinds of death: 'Good deaths ...are distinguished by physical comfort, emotional and spiritual well-being, preparation on the part of patient and family, being surrounded by loved ones in a peaceful environment, being treated with respect and dignity, and receiving treatments concordant with one's wishes.'

Whereas: 'bad deaths ... are distinguished by physical discomfort, difficulty in breathing, social isolation, psychological distress, and care that may be discordant with the patient's preferences.' For the bereaved they are characterised by 'the erosion of coping resources like social support, contemporaneous stressors including social isolation, financial precarity, uncertainty about the future, lack of routine, and the loss of face-to-face mourning rituals that provide a sense of community and uplift.'[164]

Yesterday evening's newsreaders should have said: 'in the last twenty-four hours there have been 548 bad deaths.'

**Friday, 26 February 2021.  One's Jab.**

To lifelong republicans, the Queen is a continuing disappointment.

Not only is she still protecting us from the unpalatable prospect of Charles III, she remains capable of embodying essential truths amidst a national crisis.

As the vaccination programme spreads out across the population, voices are being raised about potential discrimination against those who decline the offer. The people in question are not those who for medical reasons should not be vaccinated, such as pregnant women. Nor those who have somehow fallen through the cracks in the official bureaucracy and are not on the radar of the NHS.

We are discussing those who have been invited, could have accepted, and have refused. As I have written in earlier posts, when attitude becomes choice, the numbers of those declining seem to be much smaller than was at first feared. Nonetheless they do exist and may multiply as the programme reaches younger cohorts who do not feel much threatened by a death on a ventilator.

It is argued that they could suffer discrimination if vaccine passports are issued, denying them access to pubs, restaurants and other organised pleasures, or, in the form of some yet to be agreed documentation, travel to the beaches of Europe. Or they could face actions by employers who will only recruit those who can prove they are unlikely to infect fellow workers or customers of the enterprise. This is seen to be unjust in the case of those who have comprehensible long-term issues with secular authority, including the NHS.

I assume that the Monarch was at the head of the queue when the vaccination programme started, if only because of her age. But today she has made a public statement about her experience:

> Once you've had the vaccine, you have a feeling of, you know, you're protected, which is I think very important. I think the other thing is, that it is obviously difficult for people if they've never had a vaccine … but they ought to think about other people rather than themselves.

The morality is not complex, but it is fundamental to the struggle against Covid-19 since the first lockdown eleven months ago. In all parts of the country, in all walks of life, people have taken actions which cause private harm in the interests of public good. And give or take the odd illegal rave and concealed wedding, mostly they are still doing so.

The current debate about the non-vaccinated threatens to reverse that calculation. The harm that is discussed focusses wholly on the individual, their right to make up their own mind on the risks of illness, their right to oppose any kind of injection, their right to uphold long-held religious objections, their right to dwell in the playground of conspiracy theorists, their right to earn a living irrespective of the health of the larger workforce.

Someone has to point out that they are just making a wrong decision.

The Queen has done so. And she has said why.

**Wednesday, 3 March 2021. The Two Queens**.

The last post featured Britain's Queen. This time it is America's, Dolly Parton, singing as she was vaccinated, to the tune of 'Jolene':

> Vaccine, vaccine, vaccine, vaccine, I'm begging of you, please don't hesitate.
> Vaccine, vaccine, vaccine, vaccine, because once you're dead, then that's a bit too late.

I have just read the latest of the doctors' diaries of the early months of the pandemic. Jim Down is a consultant anaesthetist at University College Hospital London. His account nicely balances a self-deprecating perspective with a clear-eyed account of the scale of the difficulties he and his colleagues faced in the Intensive Care Unit.

There is plenty of detail on the medical processes involved. If you want to know exactly how a doctor intubates a patient, what the techniques are, what are the risks of failure, this is the place to go. At the end there is a useful glossary for the scientifically challenged.

Two features of the experience stand out, beyond the mounting exhaustion experienced by all the staff in the crisis months of late March and April. The first is the constant uncertainty about what to do. We are used to politicians and epidemiologists working through their doubts in news conferences. On the wards, large teams of professionals were debating day in and day out the correct procedures in the absence of any reliable data about how to manage the disease.

The second is the pervasive low-level apprehension that they might themselves become victims  or take the virus home to their families. When their own colleagues began to be admitted to the Intensive Care Unit, the anxiety increased. 'I was stressed and I was fearful' writes Down. 'I am not claiming that Covid didn't frighten me. Like almost everyone I was waiting to get it, expecting at any moment to develop a fever and a cough, and take to my bed.'[165]

Nearly a year later, we have the means of addressing those fears. At the same time, as discussed in my previous post, there is evidence of a deliberate refusal of the vaccine by some medical staff.

The issue was addressed in an opinion piece in yesterday's *Guardian*. It went through all the reasons for hesitancy, including the factors of race and class. But it came to a conclusion which both Queens would endorse:

> Compulsory vaccinations for all NHS and care staff are surely
> a valid last resort. Concerns about protecting individual liberties

are reasonable, but vaccines for healthcare workers cannot be spun as a matter of personal choice. Your freedom does not include the right to potentially harm others. Besides, if the pandemic has taught us anything, it is that we each have a collective responsibility to protect one another – something that is never more true than for those who have signed up to do so as a professional duty.

These are complex ethical and practical questions to address, but there are lives at stake. For the past year, high-risk people have had to fear every interaction with another person. It is unfathomable that they will be expected to see potentially infected nurses and care workers at a time when they are already at their most vulnerable – not least when the vaccine now offers such an easy solution.[166]

Difficult to sing that though.

**Thursday, 4 March 2021.  Dead Horses**.

I respect but find it difficult to share David Maughan Brown's reaction to the mistreatment of a dead race-horse.

Although, unlike my wife, I have never ridden a horse, I am pleased enough by their company. When they are in the field adjacent to our garden, I feed them windfall apples over the fence, carefully halved (under instruction) to prevent choking.

What my sojourn in the countryside has taught me, however, is how unsentimental farmers can be about their livestock. The field next to us was owned by one of the last representatives of the age-old tradition of working the land with horses, a culture celebrated in the books of the oral historian George Ewart Evans.

Tractors were introduced before the First World War but did not become commonplace in agriculture until the 1950s. Jim had started work on a farm at Clun, deep in the Welsh Marches, where there was minimal machinery. As a lad he learned how to plough behind a pair of horses. His employer was also a dealer and one of Jim's tasks was to break in new animals which could then be sold. The technique was to harness an experienced with an untrained horse, which over time would learn the discipline of drawing a plough. Jim was a short man and these horses were the size of small buses. It was, he said, a dangerous occupation. But as he told me with pride, in a good year he could, plough ninety acres.

In his retirement he kept the seven-acre field next to us, which was the fiefdom of his stallion, a mix of carthorse and hunter. Jim never bothered to name him, at best calling out 'Jim-boy' amidst a stream of guttural curses and injunctions. A mare would keep 'Jim-boy' company through the year, producing a foal in early summer. So casual was the care of this mare that one June day it was noticed that she had given birth yet there was no sign of a foal. Various theories about predators were rehearsed before a search was organised, assisted by my wife and a couple of neighbours, and eventually it was found, unharmed if unfed, hiding in a copse on the edge of the field.

Other retired horses were put out to graze in the field. In the middle of an afternoon, I saw that one of them was lying motionless on the grass. On investigation it evidently had died. Jim was told and came over to inspect it. A heart attack he thought. The next morning a borrowed excavator appeared, and a hole was dug where the horse lay.

This was entirely at variance with veterinary regulations, but for Jim as with many of his colleagues, the law was always a distant obligation. So far as I recall he did not employ the horse as a seat whilst he used a phone, if only because, then in his late eighties, he did not possess such a device. Otherwise, the event was conducted with an absolute minimum of respect and feeling.

When Jim himself died a few summers later, his son took over the field. He is a contract farmer, driving large machines to plant and harvest potatoes for crisp manufacturers. 'Jim-boy' was sold to a farm in South Wales, where, we were told, he was to have the company of five mares.

We hope he is content.

**Wednesday, 24 March 2021. Developing a Conscience**.

Most days we have a delivery to our house. Apart from one pre-breakfast raid on B&Q in the moment of relative freedom last summer, neither of us have been inside a shop for almost twelve months.

Instead we depend on vans and drivers, for whom we are the most troublesome customers. The final leg of a delivery is up an un-made, un-named, hundred-yard-long lane, too narrow for a large vehicle to turn round in. Most drop-offs end with a reverse through puddles lately filled by a series of storms.

There are occasional peaks of business. This week it has been my wife's birthday. The family has been active on the websites, piles of empty cardboard boxes have accumulated. So when my wife met the same, middle-aged driver coming to the door on consecutive days, in the wind and rain, she apologised for the trouble we had caused him.

'We can't have you developing a conscience about it, madam', he replied, with a smile, and returned to his van.

Difficult not to though. Delivery firms normally pay by piece rate, up to £1 an item on completion. If there is no-one at home and nowhere to leave a parcel, no fee. If the house is in a distant village where only the postman can find his way around a series of randomly numbered addresses, the fee is the same. Small wonder a recent driver left a parcel at our gate, claiming on the company website that he was deterred by a dog. We have no dog.

The weekly food deliveries pay by the hour – £10 50p in the case of Sainsbury's – but expect so much more than simply unloading boxes:

> Being a Sainsbury's Driver isn't just about delivering goods on time and in great condition. It's about being yourself, offering a friendly approach and a service that will really wow our customers. We'll expect you to make every delivery a great experience, always doing the right thing for our customers and keeping them aware of any delays, so they ask us to drop their shopping off again and again.

In the case of Waitrose (this is an actual job advert for the shop that supplies us):

> This is a really important 'front line' role. You represent us with every single customer you meet, and their impression of Waitrose is down to you. So, as well as having a flexible approach and the ability to use your initiative to deal with unexpected situations, you should be passionate about providing the very highest levels of customer service.

The whole pandemic has been conducted on the basis of an extended class system. Lockdown, particularly for the two million 'extremely vulnerable', has been totally dependent on this rapidly expanded proletariat. Their labours lack the frontline drama of nurses and doctors, but in their way have been just as crucial and not without risk to health.

I am currently reading a collection of Mass Observation diaries covering the early weeks of the crisis. Until the online-delivery systems of the major supermarkets caught up with the sudden surge in demand and developed a working algorithm for prioritising the vulnerable, there was widespread apprehension about whether, where, and how it would be possible to obtain basic supplies, let alone the myriad of other goods a household needs to keep itself going over time.

Millions of people have avoided infection and run something like normal lives at the expense of men (just occasionally women) driving from home to home at all hours and in all weathers. It's not just our material wellbeing. This is Sunday, and there has been a Waitrose delivery to feed us (cheerful, if not passionate), and two other deliveries bringing Mother's Day presents, uniting us with our children still separated by lockdown.

When this is over, there will be no national pay award of any kind, just redundancies as the shops open.

**Friday, 9 April 2021. The technology of bereavement.**

'Always go to other people's funerals,' advised Yogi Berra, 'otherwise they won't come to yours'.

The list of other people's funerals I have not attended is growing. Early in March my godfather died at 94 in London. A fortnight later a contemporary died in Scotland, six weeks after the death of his wife. Neither of these fatalities, as it happens, were directly from Covid19. Pneumonia, cancer, falls in old age, have not taken vacations during the pandemic.

We are particularly diminished by the sudden loss of our friends in Scotland. We began our careers and our families together, living and working alongside each other for three decades, and then regularly exchanging visits as our paths diverged. In John Donne's terms, a full promontory has been washed away from our lives.

In each case, the lockdown has prevented us from attending the final ceremony. In Scotland the current rules permit a congregation of no more than twenty. They must not sing, for fear of infection, although by arrangement a bagpiper is allowed. What science has determined that the coronavirus will be safely contained within a bagpipe I know not. In any case our friend, from a professional Edinburgh family, a world-class Russian linguist in his working life, had, like many Scots, no sympathy at all for kilts, tartans, bagpipes, and, at least until Brexit, the nationalist movement.

Instead we depend on Obitus, which describes itself as 'a leading UK provider of bereavement technology services.' The firm was apparently founded a decade ago, an indication that virtual mourning was not invented by Covid-19. It has expanded in the last year, working with funeral directors to connect the congregations unable to attend. We sit at home, three hundred miles away, equipped with a login and a password, and five minutes before the ceremony is due to begin, an empty, unnamed, funeral chapel appears on our screen.

It is easy to criticise the proceedings. There is one fixed camera at the rear of the chapel, transmitting an unchanging view of the backs of twenty mourners. The sound quality is indifferent, the visual effects non-existent. After half an hour the congregation leaves separately, unable to attend a wake larger than six people, and we close the lid on the laptop. In a week's time we will repeat the process for my godfather.

Obitus fully occupies the digital universe, with all its perils. The small print of the contract specifies that,

> in particular, we will not be liable for any damage or loss caused by a distributed denial-of-service attack, any viruses, trojans, worms, logic bombs, keystroke loggers, spyware, adware or other material which is malicious or technologically harmful that may infect your computer, peripheral computer equipment, computer programs, data or other proprietary material as a result

of your use of the Website or you downloading any material posted or sold on the Website or from any website linked to it.

Not problems faced by a clergyman with his prayer book.

But as in so many Covid-19 contexts, the technology is better, much better, than nothing at all. Whilst the long-standing debate about the threat posed to privacy by digital communication becomes ever more urgent, in the pandemic, computer screens have in all kinds of ways helped to keep families and networks of friends together. And they need not be the final means of bidding farewell. In the case of our Scottish friends, a more relaxed memorial is planned for when physical gatherings are once more possible.*

That is what we must do when the pandemic is over. We will spend our days celebrating the lives of those we have lost.

*The memorial took place in Edinburgh on 18 March 2023.

# References

[1] James Lockhart', 'Autobiography', *Quarterly Review,* XXXV (28 December 1826): 149.

[2] Rebecca Solnit, *Wanderlust. A History of Walking* (London: Verso, 2001), 264-5.

[3] Chris Husbands, 'Universities face meltdown without a proper rescue package', *The Times*, 27 April 2020.

[4] [Daniel Defoe], *Serious Reflections during the Life and Surprising Adventures of Robinson Crusoe: with his Vision of the Angelick World. Written by Himself,* edited by G. A. Starr (1720; London: Pickering & Chatto, 2008), 66.

[5] Toby Helm, Robin McKie and Lin Jenkins, 'Fearful Britons remain strongly opposed to lifting coronavirus lockdown', *Guardian*, 3 May 2020.

[6] Vikram Dodd, 'UK police receive 194,000 calls from lockdown "snitches"', *Guardian*, 30 April 2020.

[7] *Wakefield Express*, 17 April 2020.

[8] Aitor Hernández-Morales, 'Corona-snitches thrive in lockdown Europe', *Politico*, 3 April 2020.

[9] David Vincent, *Poor Citizens*, (London: Longman, 1991), 86.

[10] Now on the cover of this book.

[11] Rebecca Solnit, '"The way we get through this is together": the rise of mutual aid under coronavirus', *Guardian*, 14 May 2020.

[12] In their tedious instinct to overthrow a good story, historians have now suggested that the exchange was a translation error. Zhou Enlai,

speaking in 1972, may have thought the question was about the French Days of May of 1968. More likely, less fun.

[13] Office for National Statistics (hereafter ONS), 'One in eight British households has no garden' (14 May 2020).

[14] Cited in Magnus Linklater, 'Coronavirus in Scotland: No evidence for shielding, expert warns ministers', *The Times*, 16 May 2020.

[15] *UCL COVID-19 Social Study. Results Release 39*, 13 May 2020.

[16] *UCL COVID-19 Social Study. Results Release*, 6 April 2020, 6 May 2020, 13 May 2020, 20 May 2020.

[17] Jack Malvern, 'The cure for loneliness? Try waiting until you're older', *The Times*, 28 May 2020.

[18] Devi Sridhar and Yasmin Rafiei, 'The problem with "shielding" people from coronavirus? It's almost impossible', *Guardian*, 29 May 2020.

[19] *Guardian*, 28 May 2020.

[20] UK Statistics Authority, 'Sir David Norgrove response to Matt Hancock regarding the Government's COVID-19 testing data', 2 June 2020.

[21] Letter, UK Statistics Authority.

[22] Harriet Sherwood, 'Bishops turn on Boris Johnson for defending Dominic Cummings', *Guardian*, 25 May 2020.

[23] Dennis Campbell, 'UK coronavirus victims have lain undetected at home for two weeks. Doctors say there have been dozens of cases and warn of "epidemic of loneliness"', *Guardian*, 8 June 2020.

[24] ONS, 'Coronavirus and loneliness, Great Britain: 3 April to 3 May 2020' (8 June 2020).

[25] Ian Lovett, Dan Frosch and Paul Overberg, 'Covid-19 Stalks Large Families in Rural America', *Wall Street Journal*, 7 June 2022.

[26] Charles Dickens, *Little Dorrit* (1857; London: Penguin, 1967), 67-8.

[27] *Report on short scrutiny visits to Prisons holding women by HM Chief Inspector of Prisons* (19 May 2020).

[28] To be broadcast on July 6.

[29] John Bunyan, *The Pilgrim's Progress* (1678, London: Penguin, 2008), 20-23.

[30] In February of this year, naturalists claimed that after all they had found thirty near relatives. Too late for George.

[31] *UCL COVID-19 Social Study. Results Release 1-14.*

[32] Nicola Davis, 'UK's mental health has deteriorated during lockdown, says Mind', *Guardian,* 30 June 2020.

[33] Food Standards Agency, *Covid-19 Consumer Tracker* (July 2020). 6-8.

[34] Charles Mackay, *Memoirs of Extraordinary Popular Delusions*, 3 vols. (London: Richard Bentley, 1841), vol. 1, 336.

[35] A propos my last post on cherries, I discover that V-Bombs were colloquially known in German as 'kirschkern' – cherry stones. I don't know why.

[36] Jennifer Rigby, 'Up to one third of people in UK may refuse coronavirus vaccine, new poll finds', *Daily Telegraph*, 7 July 2020.

[37] David Masci, 'For Darwin Day, 6 facts about the evolution debate' (Pew Research, 11 February 2019).

[38] https://www.historyofvaccines.org/content/articles/history-anti-vaccination-movements.

[39] BMA, *Secret Remedies* (1909), vii.

[40] Ministry of Justice, *Official Statistics, Prison population figures: 2020* (3 July 2020).

[41] Cited in House of Commons Justice Committee, *Prison population 2022: planning for the future* (19 March 2019).

[42] Jonathan Metzer, 'Are "squalid" prison conditions and the response to the Covid-19 pandemic breaching human rights?' (UK Human Rights Blog, 6 July 2020).

[43] Matt Hancock, 'By acting collectively to test and trace, we will keep Covid cornered', *Daily Telegraph*, 12 July 2020.

[44] Debbie Andalo, 'Can mental health services cope with the devastating effects of Covid-19?', *Guardian*, 15 July 2020.

[45] Rhys Blakely, Tom Whipple, Robert Miller, 'Coronavirus vaccine hopes raised by success of early trials', *The Times*, 16 July 2020.

[46] Anne Borden King, 'I Have Cancer. Now My Facebook Feed Is Full of "Alternative Care" Ads', *New York Times*, 10 July 2020.

[47] https://www.gov.uk/government/publications/understanding-disabilities-and-impairments-user-profiles/saleem-profoundly-deaf-user.

[48] *Charles Booth's Notebooks. Poverty Map and Police Notebooks* (1898-99). Booth/B/346, 99-101.

[49] *Charles Booth's London Poverty Maps* (London: Thames and Hudson, 2019), £49 95.

[50] Booth/B/349, 33.

[51] Booth/B/349, 247.

[52] David Vincent, *A History of Solitude* (Cambridge: Polity Press, 2020), 252.

[53] Simon Kuper, 'Don't touch me I'm British', *Financial Times,* 4 March 2011.

[54] George Orwell, *England Your England* (1941, London: Penguin, 2017), 7. Here published separately, this was the first part of *The Lion and the Unicorn* (1941).

[55] Ferdynand Zweig, *The British Worker* (Harmondsworth: Penguin, 1952), 149-53.

[56] Katherine Purvis, 'Beyond sourdough: the hobbies that helped readers cope with lockdown', *Guardian*, 21 July 2020.

[57] Tamsin Calidas, *I Am An Island* (London: Doubleday, 2020).

[58] Sara Maitland, *How to be Alone* (London: Macmillan, 2014).

[59] Alex Petridis, 'Don Black: "the Pele of lyricists" on Bond themes, Broadway and Born Free', *Guardian*, 30 July 2020.

[60] https://www.museumoflondon.org.uk/discover/recording-london-soundscapes-past-present.

[61] The modern London recordings were made on behalf of the Museum by Will Cohen of 'String and Tins.'

[62] See, for instance, OpenSAFELY Collaborative, 'factors associated with COVID-19-related hospital death in the linked electronic health records of 17 million adult NHS patients' (7 May 2020), 11.

[63] *The Culture of Secrecy* (Oxford: Oxford University Press, 1998).

[64] Cited in, Ian Sample, 'Secrecy has harmed UK government's response to Covid-19 crisis, says top scientist', *Guardian*, 2 August 2020.

[65] Victor Bailey, *The Rise and Fall of the Rehabilitative Ideal, 1895-1970* (London: Routledge, 2019).

[66] Ofcom, *Media Nations 2020* (5 August 2020).

[67] Laurie Taylor and Bob Mullan, *Uninvited Guests* (London: Coronet, 1987), 184.

[68] Abby Carney, 'Can loneliness be cured with a pill? Scientists are now asking the question,' *Guardian,* 6 August 2020.

[69] You can read the full thesis at: https://qmro.qmul.ac.uk/xmlui/handle/123456789/1495.

[70] Daniel Defoe, *A Journal of the Plague Year* (1722; London: Penguin, 2003), 48.

[71] Daniel Defoe, *Due Preparations for the Plague,* (1722). 63.

[72] Defoe, *Journal of the Plague Year*, 219-20.

[73] *UCL COVID-19 Social Study. Results Release* 19, 26 August 2020, 44-50.

[74] Lars Mytting, *Norwegian Wood. Chopping, Stacking and Drying Wood the Scandinavian Way* (London: MacLehose Press, 2015), 113.

[75] Michael Safi, Helen Davidson, Angela Giuffrida, Aamna Mohdin, Matilda Boseley, Caio Barretto Briso and Noa Yachot, 'One million coronavirus deaths: how did we get here?', *Guardian,* 29 September 2020.

[76] ONS, 'Coronavirus and the social impacts on disabled people in Great Britain. Opinions and Lifestyle Survey (Covid-19 module), 14 May to 24 May 2020' (May 2020).

[77] Archie Bland, '"Like the English civil war": Covid crisis inflames neighbour disputes', *Guardian*, 28 September 2020.

[78] Defoe, *Journal of the Plague Year,* 18

[79] *The Collected Poems of George Mackay* Brown, ed. Archie Bevan and Brian Murray (London: John Murray, 2006), 328-9.

[80] The story of St Magnus is told in the Orkneyinga Saga. He gives his name to the cathedral in Kirkness, Orkney, founded in 1137. George Mackay Brown wrote a novel about his life, and later an opera was composed by Peter Maxwell Davies. Emma is the child addressed in the poem. Tir Nan Og is the Land of the Young in Irish Mythology.

[81] *A Collection of Very Valuable and Scarce Pieces Relating to the Last Plague in the Year 1665* (London: J. Roberts, 1721), 16-17.

[82] *A Collection of Very Valuable and Scarce Pieces*, 6.

[83] *A Collection of Very Valuable and Scarce Pieces*, 6.

[84] *A Collection of Very Valuable and Scarce Pieces,* 11.

[85] *A Collection of Very Valuable and Scarce Pieces,* 12.

[86] *A Collection of Very Valuable and Scarce Pieces*, 8

[87] Albert Camus, *The Plague* (1947; London: Penguin, 2013), 237-8.

[88] HM Chief Inspector of Prisons for England and Wales, *Annual Report 2019–20* (20 October 2020), 15.

[89] HM Chief Inspector of Prisons for England and Wales, *Annual Report 2019–20* (20 October 2020), 18.

[90] Jamie Grierson, 'Covid: prisoner mental health at risk of irreparable damage'", *Guardian,* 20 October 2020.

[91] Daniel Defoe, *Due Preparations for the Plague, as well for Souls as Body. Being some seasonable Thoughts upon the visible approach of the present dreadful Contagion in France; the properest measures to prevent it, and the great work of submitting to it* (1722; New York: Harvard University Press, 1903), 17.

[92] Camus, *The Plague*, 54.

[93] ONS, *Coronavirus and the social impacts on Great Britain* (23 October 2020).

[94] ONS, *Coronavirus and the social impacts on Great Britain. Opinions and Lifestyle Survey (COVID-19 module), 7 to 11 October* (16 October 2020).

[95] https://openuniv.sharepoint.com/sites/intranet-learner-discovery-services/SharedDocuments/OpenLearn2019-20AnnualReport.pdf

[96] Defoe, *Journal of the Plague Year*, 9.

[97] Rupert Neate, 'Private jet bookings soar as wealthy flee second England lockdown', *Guardian*, 3 November 2020.

[98] Nigel Farage and Richard Tice, 'We're relaunching the Brexit Party to fight this cruel and unnecessary lockdown', *Daily Telegraph*, 1 November 2020.

[99] Haroon Siddique, 'Coronavirus: anti-vaxxers seek to discredit Pfizer's vaccine', *Guardian,* 10 November 2020.

[100] Jonathan Kennedy, 'How populists spread vaccine fear', *Politico*, 7 May 2019.

[101] Talha Burki, 'The online anti-vaccine movement in the age of COVID-19', *The Lancet Digital Health* (October 2020).

[102] Sarah Marsh, 'Covid: Totnes concerns reflect UK-wide rise in conspiracy theories', *Guardian,* 11 November 2020.

[103] Pope Francis, in conversation with Austen Ivereigh, *Let Us Dream. The Path to a Better Future* (London: Simon and Schuster, 2020), 132-3.

[104] Pope Francis, *Let Us Dream*, 25.

[105] Pope Francis, *Let Us Dream*, 71.

[106] Pope Francis, *Let Us Dream*, 6.

[107] Pope Francis, *Let Us Dream*, 45-6.

[108] ONS, 'Coronavirus and the social impacts on Great Britain: 18 December 2020, Opinions and Lifestyle Survey (COVID-19 module), 10 to 13 December', Table 13.

[109] *Ibid*, Table 1, Trends on Headline Indicators.

[110] Vincent, *A History of Solitude*, 241.

[111] Utteeyo Dasgupta, 'History tells how people act in pandemics – selfishly, but also with surprising altruism', *Guardian*, 20 December 2020.

[112] Michael Savage, 'Poll reveals scale of "home alone" Christmas in the UK this year', *Guardian*, 5 December 2020.

[113] ONS, *Coronavirus and the social impacts on Great Britain* (8 January 2021).

[114] Department for Digital, Culture, Media and Sport, *A connected society A strategy for tackling loneliness – laying the foundations for change* (October 2018).

[115] Department for Digital, Culture, Media and Sport, *Loneliness Annual Report: the first year* (20 January 2020), 3.

[116] Tobias Jones, 'After coronavirus, the penny has dropped that wellbeing isn't individual but social', *Guardian*, 12 April 2020.

[117] Mark Sweney, 'UK lockdowns fuel record year for home entertainment spending', *Guardian*, 8 January 2021.

[118] Hannah Boland, '12 million more Britons sign up to streaming in lockdown', *Daily Telegraph*, 26 December 2020.

[119] Joanna Partridge, 'B&Q owner says lockdown DIY craze boosted festive sales', *Guardian*, 12 January 2021.

[120] Eilidh Hargreaves, 'Private members club vaccinating clients abroad is "proud" to offer the service', *Daily Telegraph*, 12 January 2021.

[121] ONS, 'Coronavirus and the social impacts on Great Britain. Opinions and Lifestyle Survey (COVID-19 module, 7 to 10 January 2021' (15 January 2021).

[122] Clea Skopeliti, 'Lord Sumption tells stage 4 cancer patient her life is "less valuable"', *Guardian*, 17 January 2021.

[123] ONS, 'Coronavirus (COVID-19) Infection Survey, UK' (8 January 2021).

[124] ONS, 'Coronavirus and the social impacts on Great Britain. Opinions and Lifestyle Survey (COVID-19 module), 7 to 10 January 2021' (15 January 2021).

[125] Elisabeth Kübler-Ross, *On Death and Dying* (1969: New York: Touchstone, 1997), 21.

[126] Kübler-Ross, *On Death and Dying*, 150.

[127] Kübler-Ross, *On Death and Dying*, 123.

[128] Dr. Lisa Linpower, 'Through My Phone', *Letters from Lockdown* (London, Chatto and Windus, 2020), 171.

[129] See cover.

[130] Julia Samuel, *Grief Works. Stories of Life, Death and Surviving* (London: Penguin Life, 2017), xii.

[131] Margaret Stroebe and Henk Schut, 'Bereavement in Times of COVID-19: A Review and Theoretical Framework', *OMEGA— Journal of Death and Dying*, 82, 3 (2021): 500–522, 501.

[132] Defoe, *Journal of the Plague Year*, 164.

[133] Rebecca Abrams and Cruse Clinical Director, Andy Langford, recorded as a webinar on 5 May 2020. https://www.cruse.org.uk/training/covid-19-different-kind-grief.

[134] Gavin Francis, *Intensive Care. A GP, A Community & Covid-19* (London: Profile Books and Wellcome Collection, 2021), 56.

[135] Francis, *Intensive Care*, 191.

[136] Jonathan Freedland, 'History suggests we may forget the pandemic sooner than we think', *Guardian*, 29 January 2021.

[137] Laura Spinney, *Pale Rider* (London: Penguin, 2017), 291.

[138] 'Pandemics and Plots', 19 October 2020.

[139] London: Simon and Schuster 2021.

[140] London: Little, Brown, 2021.

[141] Clarke, *Breath taking*, 212.

[142] 'I'm an NHS consultant anaesthetist. I see the terror in my Covid patients' eyes', *Guardian,* 31 January 2021.

[143] Clarke, *Breath taking*, 215-16.

[144] Nazia Parveen and Caelainn Barr, 'Black over-80s in England half as likely as white people to have had Covid jab', *Guardian*, 4 February 2021.

[145] Ben Clover, 'Exclusive: Fewer black and Filipino NHS staff vaccinated amid "hesitancy" concern', *HSJ*, 28 January 2021.

[146] Jon Henley, 'A quarter of people in France, Germany and the US may refuse Covid vaccine', *Guardian*, 4 February 2021.

[147] Seren Boyd, 'Pushing back – tackling the anti-vax movement', *BMA News and Opinion*, 11 January 2021.

[148] Helen Pidd, 'Inspiring confidence: Liverpool GPs tackle the vaccine race gap', *Guardian*, 4 February 2021.

[149] Clarke, *Breath taking.*

[150] Clarke, *Breath-taking,* 159-60.

[151] Rachel Clarke, "'I've been called Satan": Dr Rachel Clarke on facing abuse in the Covid crisis', *Guardian,* 6 February 2021.

[152] An Update on Our Work to Keep People Informed and Limit Misinformation About COVID-19 – About Facebook (fb.com).

[153] *Register of Bishop Ralph of Shrewsbury, Somerset Record Society* X (1896), 555-6, cited in Rosemary Horrox, trans. and ed., *The Black Death* (Manchester: Manchester University Press, 1994), 112. Despite his title, Ralph, formerly Chancellor of the University of Oxford, was Bishop of Bath and Wells, where he was described by the Dictionary of National Biography as 'a wise and industrious bishop, learned and extremely liberal.'

[154] David Wilkins, *Concilia Magnae Britanniae et Hiberniae* (1739), vol. II, 738, cited in Horrox, *Black Death,* 113

[155] Mark Harrison, *Disease and the Modern World. 1500 to the Present Day* (Cambridge: Polity, 2004), 189. See also, Mark Honigsbaum, *The Pandemic Century. A History of Global Contagion from the Spanish Flu to Covid-19* (Penguin: London, 2020), xiv-xv, 280.

[156] Pope Francis, *Let Us Dream,* 35.

[157] Wilkins, *Concilia,* III, 100-1, cited in cited in Horrox, *Black Death,* 120.

[158] https://www.churchofengland.org/about/policy-and-thinking/our-views/environment-and-climatechange/why-you-should-act.

[159] ONS, 'Coronavirus (COVID-19) weekly insights: latest health indicators in England' (5 February 2021).

[160] 11 November 2020.

[161] ONS, 'Coronavirus (COVID-19) weekly insights: latest health indicators in England' (5 February 2021).

[162] Mona Chalabi, 'Covid in US has left 4 million family members grieving, study finds', *Guardian*, 22 February 2022.

[163] Ashton M. Verdery, Emily Smith-Greenaway, Rachel Margolis, Jonathan Daw, 'Tracking the reach of COVID-19 kin loss with a bereavement multiplier applied to the United States,' *Proceedings of the National Academy of Sciences of the United States*, 117, 30 (28 July 2020), 17695-17701.

[164] Deborah Carr, Kathrin Boerner, Sara Moorman, 'Bereavement in the Time of Coronavirus: Unprecedented Challenges Demand Novel Interventions', *Journal of Aging & Social Policy*, 32, 4-5 (2020): 425-431.

[165] Jim Down, *Life Support. Diary of an ICU Doctor on the Frontline of the Covid Crisis* (London: Penguin, 2021), 111.

[166] Frances Ryan, 'Healthcare professionals in the UK have a moral duty to get the Covid jab', *Guardian*, 2 March 2021.

Printed in Great Britain
by Amazon